Dedication

This book is dedicated to my parents,
Gerry Murphy Jensen and William Jensen.
Throughout my life they have inspired and believed in me.

– Mary Murphy Jensen

GANGS

STRAIGHT TALK, STRAIGHT UP

A Practical Guide for Teachers,
Parents, and the Community

Dr. Mary M. Jensen
Western Illinois University
Lt. Phillip C. Yerington
Davenport, Iowa Police Department

Edited by Jami McCormick
Text layout and design by Sherri Rowe
Cover design by Eye for Design
Box Icon Illustrations by Brian K. McCrae

ISBN #1-57035-053-1

Printed in the United States of America

Published and Distributed by:

Sopris West

1140 Boston Avenue ▪ Longmont, CO 80501 ▪ (303) 651-2829
http://www.sopriswest.com

Acknowledgments

The production of this book would not have been possible without the support and assistance of a number of people along the way. We would like to thank Dr. Bill Jenson for giving us the confidence to approach a publisher with the idea for a book on gangs. We are most appreciative for Dr. Jenson's suggestion that we submit a proposal of the gang book idea to Sopris West.

We are very appreciative of the unfailing support and optimism from the staff at Sopris West. Many thanks to Dr. Stuart Horsfall and Dr. Duane Webb who gave us the chance to produce this text that we think is critically important for all adults who work in any capacity with youth. Thanks to Karen Jardine for the outstanding marketing plans. Thank you to Sherri Rowe for her expertise in desktop design. Her technical and creative skills are much appreciated. Jami McCormick is a master editor. We will be eternally grateful for her support, her suggestions (maybe even her red pen), and perpetual optimism about the book. Jami continually went over and above an editor's typical responsibilities in helping to make this book complete. Her genius with editing is what gave our ideas a professional polish.

We are blessed with family who supported and encouraged this project. An extra-special thank you goes to Bryan and Bart. They patiently put up with all of the long hours and were always happy to see Mary finally get home, even when she was very late.

Phillip Yerington would like to thank his buddy Kyle; his daughter Brandi; and his parents, Donna and Charles Yerington, for their encouragement.

Dr. Jensen also wishes to thank the very helpful and efficient Cheryl Sappington for her assistance in typing (and retyping) this manuscript, and for researching and tracking down critical details.

A huge thank you goes out to the law enforcement personnel all over the country who have graciously shared their expertise about gang characteristics and gang activities with us. They provided a font of invaluable information during the researching, writing, and editing phases of this book.

Dr. Jensen would personally like to thank Lt. David Chong of the New York City Police Department for his generosity and willingness to provide expert consultation on Chinese and other Asian gangs. Many thanks to Sgt. Wes McBride of the Los Angeles County Sheriff's Department for taking Dr. Jensen on so many ride alongs, and for being incredibly patient in answering a million questions. These officers have the difficult and often very dangerous job of dealing with serious gang crime on a daily basis. They deserve to be commended for their dedication to the law enforcement profession. This book would not have been possible without their willingness to collaborate. Thank you!

About the Authors

Photo Credit: Larry Dean, Visual Productions, Western Illinois University

Dr. Mary M. Jensen is a professor in the Department of Special Education at Western Illinois University (WIU). She teaches classes in the area of behavioral disorders and behavior management. Dr. Jensen was the 1994 recipient of the Outstanding Teacher of the Year Award for the College of Education at WIU, and of 1995 and 1996 Faculty Excellence Awards. Her main area of research interest and expertise is in positive strategies for students who are aggressive and noncompliant, and in youth gangs.

Prior to teaching at the university level, Dr. Jensen taught students with learning and behavioral disorders for ten years in the public schools and in residential treatment programs. She has often been heard to remark that she " . . . still misses her wild kids." In order to compensate for that feeling, Dr. Jensen actively collaborates on practical research projects with classroom teachers. Her interest in youth gangs and management strategies for them developed as educators and parents voiced a need for practical management strategies to apply at school, in the community, and at home. Dr. Jenson makes frequent presentations for school districts and at conferences on practical and positive behavior management strategies for students who show hostile, aggressive, and other antisocial behaviors.

Research for practical information on youth gangs to be used in her classes at the university led to the initial meeting with **Lt. Phillip**

Yerington. He volunteered to be a guest speaker and turned out to be not only an excellent lecturer but also had a wealth of direct experience in managing the youth gang problem on the streets.

Lt. Yerington has a Criminal Justice degree from St. Ambrose College and 23 years of law enforcement experience in a number of areas including patrol, accident investigation, personnel administration, and the Special Operations Unit of the Davenport, Iowa Police Department. He has a research interest in youth gang crime, and is considered to be an authority on gang activity in the Quad City area.

In 1992, Lt. Yerington formed the Special Operations Unit on Street Gang Crime. He then served as commander for this specially trained group of officers who were charged with the responsibility of identifying active gang members and suppressing criminal gang activity in Davenport. In June of 1994, he was assigned to the Criminal Investigation Division specializing in gang intelligence work for the Department. Lt. Yerington presently serves as commander of the Patrol Division, afternoon shift.

Additionally, Lt. Yerington is a member of the Midwest Gang Investigators Association (MGIA) which was established to combine intelligence and enforcement tactics in an effort to identify members of street gangs and to discourage their criminal activity. Lt. Yerington is recognized as an expert witness for legal testimony in the area of youth gang crime.

Dr. Jensen and Lt. Yerington team up to make a variety of presentations at conferences, school inservices, and workshops on youth gangs. One popular component of these presentations are the actual gang-related items that Lt. Yerington quips have been "graciously donated" by youth gang members. The collection includes clothing with gang signs and symbols; graffiti examples; weapons, both commercially produced and home made; and illegal narcotics including marijuana and crack/cocaine. Actually seeing these items firsthand helps educators and parents to recognize them in the school or home environment. The combination of "the teacher and the cop" provides a solid foundation of both research and real-life practical experience in dealing with hostile and aggressive gang-oriented youth in the classroom, and home, and on the street.

Preface

This book is written about youth gangs with the aim of educating teachers and administrators, parents, law enforcement personnel, and all others who work with youth. The major emphasis is on gang identifiers in addition to positive behavior management strategies and crisis intervention techniques that will help to make both school and home more positive and rewarding environments. The main goal is for these kids to receive the necessary support and encouragement to remain in school, to become involved in family and community activities, and to stay off the streets. Adults will have to take the lead—to demonstrate their interest in and to provide the time and the support kids need.

Within the confusion and turmoil in the lives of many youth today, there is also hope for a better tomorrow. It is critically important to remember that these youth need the support and encouragement of committed adults in order to achieve their goals. They need strong and dedicated leaders and role models. Reach out a hand; they are worth it. A previous gang member who is now attempting to turn his life around explains it this way:

> *I, a person of this generation, know what most of my generation are thinking about. Most of us dwell on short-term goals which shorten our lives. It seems to them [gang-involved youth] that gangs . . . are more convincing than the right way to live. You the people must be more convincing to this generation to do the right thing.*

> – LaMark Combs
> February, 1993

Table of Contents

Case Studies 269

Conclusion 295

Appendix: Gang Prevention/Intervention Resources 297

Other Sopris West Publications of Interest

SECTION 5

Introduction

Male Gang Member Facts
90% are arrested by age 18
75% are arrested twice by age 18
95% do not finish high school
60% are dead or in prison by age 20
The average life expectancy of an active gang member is 20 years, 5 months
(**Source**: Texas Youth Commission, Office of Delinquency Prevention, 1993)

These are incredibly alarming statistics compiled by law enforcement agencies. Although they have not been gathered in a scientific manner because they relate to gang members who have been either arrested or killed, they present a bleak future for youth involved in gang activity. They document the fact that gang members lead exceptionally violent lives.

A Gallup poll (1994) surveyed 1,326 adults over the age of 18 during May and June 1994 to determine their thoughts on public schools. Fighting, violence, and gangs were perceived as the major problems facing public schools. Growth of youth gangs was cited by 72% of respondents as a major problem in schools. Another survey was completed by the Council of the Great City Schools (1994) to determine the major concerns about their schools of superintendents and school board members from large urban districts. Violence and gang-related activities were the number one concern of 82.7% of the respondents.

Teachers and parents are required to cope with youth gang members without the benefit of formal training. In contrast, police officers deal with the same individuals on the street equipped with specialized qualifications and weapons to protect themselves. Gangs create problems in communities of all sizes across the country. They are not simply a law enforcement problem nor just a school problem. Gangs are a national challenge. Systematic approaches incorporating comprehensive and collaborative services must be employed for prevention, intervention, and elimination of street gangs.

This book was written in an effort to provide factual but also practical and useful information to individuals who are charged with the responsibility of teaching, raising, or otherwise interacting with children who are at risk for or already involved in gang activity. When we first began searching for basic written information on gangs, we found any number of the shocking, "war story" type accounts of gang violence. However, we didn't find much of anything practical. Gangs have received a great deal of negative media attention because of their violent impact. Some media reports are accurate, but many are sensationalized resulting in misinformation to the public. The result of this misleading and inaccurate information is

the perpetuation of the conception that a generation of American youth has "gone bad."

We don't believe this is entirely true. Many students do demonstrate problems, and the violent activity of juveniles does seem to be steadily increasing. (Nationwide data on the number of juveniles involved in gang activity is lacking.) However, the consensus among both regular and special education teachers seems to be that yes, kids today do have problems, but many react very positively to firm and consistently fair and respectful teacher guidance. We challenge you to see beyond the problems, the dangerous reputations, and the poor attitudes these kids present to the public, and to realize the potential they have. That potential can be developed when an adult discovers the right way to teach these kids and is able to get through the exterior armor to reach the children inside.

On the street, the slang term "straight talk," or "straight up" indicates that one is telling the complete, honest, and unvarnished truth. *Gangs—Straight Talk, Straight Up* peels away the layers of mystery from the gang culture by providing easy-to-read and very practical information for anyone who is interested in learning more about youth gangs. Strategies to identify and effectively manage the behavior of school-age children involved in gang activity comprises the foundation of the book.

The issue of race as associated with the gang mentality must be addressed in an honest and forthright manner. Within this book, when gang members are identified as being of some specific race or nationality, the reference is to a criminal subgroup of that race. Beginning with the Irish gangs in New York during the 1800s to the various criminal gangs of the 1990s, there is probably no ethnic group, race, or subset of American culture that has not contributed to the phenomena of today's gangs. Ethnic and racial labels are used in this book simply to communicate factual information. To reiterate, stating that a gang is composed of a certain ethnic or racial group is by no means meant to be a slur on any of these groups' rich cultural heritage.

Color

It shouldn't matter what color I am; I'm human.

I have a heart and a life to live just like you do.

I may be black and you may be white, but we are brothers and sisters.

We're just two different colors.

God created man to love and to work with one another not fight nor call names.

If you help me, I will help you and together we can work as one.

– Lakeisha Williams, 13 years old
Edison Junior High School
Rock Island, Illinois

Gangs have traditionally been organized around racial or ethnic boundaries (e.g., Asian, African-American, Caucasian, Chinese, Hispanic, Irish, and Jamaican). Black and Hispanic gangs still predominate in sheer size. However, Asian gangs, South Pacific groups, white supremacist groups, and more mixing of ethnic groups within gangs is becoming more common than in the past. The National Institute of Justice (NIJ) reported on the ethnic composition of gangs in 1992. Data indicated that 48% of gang members are black, and 43% Hispanic. However the reported number of black gang members increased by 13% between 1990 and 1991, while the number of Hispanic gang members increased by 18% during the same period. Although significantly fewer in actual numbers, gang members identified as either Asian or white have been increasing in number at a significantly higher rate. From 1990 to 1991, the number of Asian gang members increased by 66% and the number of white gang members increased by 55%.

As educators, other concerned professionals, and as parents, the youth gang problem is worthy of our attention because it potentially involves all of our children, regardless of our race.

Goal of This Book

The goal of this book is to educate teachers, parents, and other adults about youth gangs. Knowledge about gang formation, characteristics, identifiers, and motivators for joining is the key to prevention and intervention tactics. There is no data base specifying how many school-age students across the country are involved in youth gang activity. What **is** known is that statistics show the occurrences of youth-oriented violence and crime in addition to family problems of divorce, abuse, and neglect are climbing steadily each year. There isn't a single family in any community that is potentially immune from the problem. Gang activity and its associated violence cross all socioeconomic and racial boundaries. Youth gang violence has been documented from inner city to rural areas across the nation.

The epidemic of youth gangs requires that every teacher have the practical knowledge and skills to handle the problems that accompany gang members into the classroom. This book is intended for teachers as well as parents, community members, and other professionals to provide basic information on identification of and effective management strategies for school-age children in youth gangs. The major focus is on very practical information and methods for dealing with youth gang members in a proactive manner.

Overview of This Book

This book is divided into five sections. Section 1, **Youth Gangs Past and Present**, provides the framework of information on which to build an awareness of gangs. Characteristics of youth gangs are provided, including early history, identifiers of gang activity in an area, and motivational factors detailing why youth and adolescents join gangs. An understanding of these components is essential to prevention and intervention efforts.

Section 2, **Identification of Youth Gang Involvement**, outlines "pre-gang" behaviors. These are specific behaviors that parents and teachers must be aware of in order to intervene early with gang "wannabes." In addition, the major youth gangs from across the country are described, including specific gang identifiers, colors, and graffiti.

Section 3, **Controlling Gang Activity at School: Prevention and Intervention**, provides information on preventive behavior management strategies. The strategies are appropriate for use with youth gang members as well as other students who are noncompliant or aggressive/violent. Proactive, positively-oriented strategies designed to boost students' self-esteem are emphasized. The goal is for teachers and parents to recognize and build upon the strengths of every individual student. Methods for designing proactive school policies, devising relevant behavior management plans, and suggestions for collaborating with parents are included.

Section 3 contains an outline of topics appropriate for a "Basic Gang Awareness" seminar which the reader could conduct for school staff and/or parents. The authors are also available for staff development training. Their training seminars have been very well-received by teachers, parents, law enforcement personnel, other professionals, and interested community members due to the practical, educational, and entertaining nature of the program.

In Section 4, **Developing Crisis Management Plans**, crisis intervention techniques are presented. There will be times when even the best classroom management systems will be ineffective. In the event that behavior problems become out of control and a crisis occurs, teachers and parents must know how to deal with the crisis competently and effectively. Establishing and rehearsing a crisis management plan is a crucial component of managing a crisis in a safe manner. Practical, step-by-step instructions for the development of such a plan are included. Both teacher and student safety are emphasized.

Section 5, **Case Studies**, is composed of a variety of situations teachers may encounter with gang members at school. Each case study involves some sort of student behavior problem, ranging from gang behaviors to noncompliance and hostile behavior, to weapons in the classroom to assaults on teachers and students. Questions for discussion and role play ideas are provided after each case study.

Sections 1-4 contain **Summary Boxes**. The Summary Boxes contain concise information that would be handy to photocopy and distribute to staff members and parents within a school. These boxes give concise summaries of important points of information from the text. **Real-Life Teacher Tales** document some experiences classroom teachers have had in dealing with gang-related, noncompliant, or aggressive behaviors at school. **Speaking Up!** boxes relate comments made by students who have had gang or delinquency problems.

Some of the **Speaking Up!** quotations are reprinted from a book entitled *Gangs and Schools* (Arthur & Erickson, 1992), which details an administrator's experiences with gang members in the school environment. The majority of the **Speaking Up!** comments come from conversations the authors and other law enforcement personnel have had with youth involved in gang activity.

The **References/Resources** found at the end of Sections 1-4 list annotated references and suggestions for additional reading.

References/Resources

Arthur, R. & Erickson, E. (1992). *Gangs and schools*. Holmes Beach, FL: Learning Publications.

This book details the experiences of an educator working with gang members as a teacher, principal, and neighborhood counselor. His extensive experience provides practical insights about school and community interventions.

Gangs and Schools (ISBN #1-55691-036-3) may be ordered from Learning Publications, 5351 Gulf Drive, P.O. Box 1338, Holmes Beach, FL 34218; Phone (941) 778-6651; FAX (941) 778-6818.

Council of the Great City Schools. (1994). *Critical educational trends: A poll of America's urban schools*. Washington, DC: Author.

This study indicates major concerns of school executives from large urban schools across the country.

Critical Educational Trends: A Poll of America's Urban Schools may be ordered from the Council of the Great City Schools, 1301 Pennsylvania Avenue NW, Suite 702, Washington, D.C. 20004; Phone (202) 393-2427.

Curry, G.D., Ball, R.A., & Fox, R.J. (1994, June). *National Institute of Justice research in brief: Gang crime and law enforcement recordkeeping* (NCJ 148345). Washington, D.C.: National Institute of Justice.

This paper describes various methods of data collection, record keeping, and statistics on gang crime across the nation.

Staff. (1994). *26th annual Gallup poll of the public's attitude toward the public schools*. Bloomington, IN: Gallup Organization and Phi Delta Kappa.

This survey polled adults regarding their opinions on problems related to public schools. Fighting, violence, and gangs tied with lack of discipline for the biggest problems in public school settings.

26th Annual Gallup Poll of the Public's Attitude Toward the Public Schools may be ordered from the Gallup Organization, Phone (609) 924-9600; Phi Delta Kappa, P.O. Box 789, Bloomington, IN 47402-0789; Phone (800) 766-1156.

Staff. (1993). *Catalog of programs and research.* Austin, TX: Texas Youth Commission, Office of Delinquency Prevention.

This publication is comprised of research-validated studies, outlines of material gathered by law enforcement personnel, summaries of community-based programs, and factual material created by the gang specialist unit of the St. Louis, Missouri Police Department for educators in the St. Louis area.

Catalog of Programs and Research may be ordered from the Office of Delinquency Prevention, Texas Youth Commission, 4900 North Lamar Boulevard., P.O. Box 4260, Austin, TX 78765; Phone (512) 483-5000; FAX (512) 483-5089; Email: prevention@tyc.state.tx.us.

Youth Gangs Past and Present

The purpose of Section 1 is to provide a history of the origins of and a current picture of today's youth gangs. Information about where the four major gang factions originated and how they were formed is presented. These gangs include the Folk and People Nations and the Bloods and the Crips. The discussion of the origination and formation of these gangs will give adults an idea of the manner in which they spread and just how powerful these gangs have become. Other background information, including gang membership hierarchy, initiations, and motivational factors for joining, will provide the reader with a basic foundation upon which to build a realistic preventive or intervention program for youth gang members.

Evolution of Youth Gangs

Gang activity is not a new or an isolated problem. Gangs have existed on the streets and in penal institutions for hundreds of years. Formation of gangs can be traced back to immigrant groups organized during the early 1800s. A publication by the Illinois State Police (1995) provides an explanation of the early gangs. A group of Irish-Americans calling themselves the Forty Thieves was the first documented gang in the United States. Beginning in 1820 they held meetings in the back room of a grocery store in the "Five Points" district of New York City. This gang formed for much the same reasons as present day gangs. The Forty Thieves were a group of young men rebelling against their low social status and the prejudice shown to Irish immigrants. There were few economic or employment opportunities through which they could improve their situation. At first they may have been seeking simple camaraderie based on a shared frustration about social and economic injustices. Ultimately, however, their resentment was demonstrated through criminal activity for profit including murder, robbery, arson, street muggings, and other assorted acts of violence. It is interesting to note that some younger Irish immigrants formed a "subgang" composed of juveniles, which was appropriately dubbed the Forty Little Thieves.

The Five Points district is also credited with the second recognized street gang. This gang was also composed of strictly Irish-Americans. They immigrated from County Kerry in Ireland and called themselves the Kerryonians. This gang strictly limited their membership to only those young men who could trace their ancestry back to County Kerry in Ireland.

The Irish gangs were soon followed by German, Italian, Chinese, Jewish, black, and Hispanic gangs in America. There is probably no race or ethnic group in America that has not contributed to the present day phenomenon of criminal street gangs. These groups evolved to provide a means of protection, recreation, and financial gain for members. At

that time, gang activity usually involved disagreements over "territory," or neighborhood boundaries which limited where these individuals could live and recreate. Unlike modern-day gangs, however, these disagreements between gangs were not always violent.

Over the years, a variety of societal and sociological factors contributed to street gangs becoming more criminally-oriented. Those factors included the decline of the economy, a growing population in the large cities, inadequate educational opportunities, and fierce competition for jobs. In the mid-1800s gang-related homicides began and drugs (such as morphine, laudanum "knock-out drops," and cocaine) first appeared on the gang scene. Gang apparel (having all members of an ethnic gang wearing the same type of clothing) also became popular during this time period.

GANG ACTIVITY INCREASE IN THE 1900S

Gang activity became widespread in this country in the late 1800s and early 1900s. Floods of immigrants poured into the United States from all over the world, and the gap between the rich and the poor increased dramatically. Poverty and hopelessness for a better way of life were the main reasons for the formation and growth of gangs.

During the 1960s and 1970s gangs became a significant influence in prisons.

(It was during this time period that the powerful west coast and midwest gangs originated. A detailed history of these gangs is provided later in this section.) Early release programs from prisons in the 1970s resulted in gang leaders returning to their neighborhoods. Consequently, the prison gang mentality and organized gang activity surfaced on the streets. Recruiting of younger members to carry out wishes of the adult gang members became widespread. Gangs also began to use brutal violence to gain control of the majority of illegal drug trafficking on the streets.

Although the mafia were also becoming extremely dangerous during this time period, mafia families and street gangs did not mix. Mafia can be described as white collar crime (such as money "laundering"). In contrast, street gangs are described as blue collar criminals committing blue collar crimes.

CRIMINAL ACTIVITY IN THE 1990s

The 1990s have brought a rampant epidemic of brutal street gang violence to communities of all types and sizes in this country. Most of the violent gang activity stems from the sale of illegal narcotics. Incredibly high profits from illegal drug sales, the easy availability of guns to kids, and societal problems of often ineffective education and unemployment compound the youth gang problem.

Over the past 200 years the basic motivation for individuals joining gangs has not changed much. Financial gain, personal protection, social opportunities, and recreation were and continue to be the most notable reasons for gang participation. As with the early immigrants, present day groups of unhappy adolescent males (and increasingly, females) continue to feel hopeless and to rebel against their perceived lack of opportunities and their fate in life. They viciously express their frustrations against their community as a whole. Many individuals see gangs and their violent lifestyle as a way out of a life previously filled with only poverty, mediocrity, and failure.

Summary Box 1.1 summarizes the evolution of street gangs.

Summary Box 1.1
Street Gang History

- Early **1800s**: Immigrant gangs organized in America to protect their territory.

- Late **1800s**: Gang murder, drug sales, and gang apparel became common.

- **1900s**: Gang activity became widespread in larger cities.

- **1960s**: Gangs became powerful influences in prisons.

(CONTINUED)

Summary Box 1.1 (CONTINUED)

- **1970s**: Early release prison programs put many gang leaders back on the streets

- **1990s**: Gang crime became brutally violent, primarily due to the sale of illegal narcotics and rival gang warfare.

DEFINITION OF A YOUTH GANG

Teachers and parents must understand the definition of a youth gang, as this knowledge will enable them to provide appropriate intervention and prevention services. There are a variety of definitions that illustrate the essence and spirit of a youth gang. Most contain a similar set of four to five characteristics. The following definition, adapted from Goldstein and Huff (1993, p. 4), provides a concise definition of the typical youth gang:

> *A youth gang consists primarily of male adolescents and young adults who: (1) routinely interact with one another; (2) are frequently and deliberately involved in illegal activities; (3) share a common group identity that is usually represented through a gang name; and (4) typically communicate their identity by adopting certain symbols, colors, mannerisms, and "turf."*

This definition provides basic identification information that adults need to be aware of in order to recognize youth at risk for gang involvement. Identification begins with understanding the three main types of gangs currently operating on the streets in communities in the United States today, which will be detailed following.

Types of Gangs

TRADITIONAL GANGS

There are three types of criminal street gangs. The first is called a "traditional" gang. Traditional gangs historically stem from the early 1960s when the Chicago and Los Angeles gangs were gaining power. These gangs are generational (that is, they include many family members such as parents, children, brothers/sisters, cousins, etc.), have a set membership hierarchy, and operate on the original creeds or manifestoes that were created during the formation period. Gang leaders, as well as high ranking members, developed and distributed literature that covers organizational objectives and the rules and regulations of the gang.

TERRITORIAL GANGS

The second type of gang is called a "territorial" or "transitional" gang. This group usually stays together for short periods of time (such as a year or less) due to the loose structure and lack of strong leadership. These gangs are unique to the neighborhood in which they are organized and active, and are generally not recognized by traditional, hard core gangs. Their criminal activity is generally less drug-oriented and more associated with assaults, intimidation, vandalism, and thefts. They are known to fight violently for their neighborhood territory and about being "disrespected." Over a period of time, the territorial gang is either absorbed into a traditional gang or fades out of existence. This may be due to a lack of conformity with a traditional gang, simply a result of the group passing through a phase, or because a stronger leader takes over.

FRANCHISE GANGS

The third main gang type is called a "franchise" gang. This group is composed of members of different and possibly rival gangs. Franchise gangs put aside their rivalries to collaborate on criminal actions that will result in financial gain. Like the territorial gang, a franchise gang is unique to the area in which they are criminally active. If this gang disbands, the members simply return to their original gang.

Summary Box 1.2 lists these three types of gangs.

Summary Box 1.2
Main Types of Gangs

- **Traditional Gangs**

  Stem from the Chicago and Los Angeles gangs; are heavily into drug sales for financial gain and ruthless violence

- **Territorial Gangs**

  Neighborhood gangs with a short history; criminal activity involves assaults, intimidation, vandalism, and theft

- **Franchise Gangs**

  Composed of members from different (often rival) gangs; purpose is to collaborate on high profit, illegal activities

Five Main Characteristics of Youth Gangs

No matter what type of gang a youth is involved with, adults should be able to observe certain common behavioral characteristics. Knowing and understanding the characteristics that define a street gang is the first step toward intervention. Adults often wish to deny that street gangs exist and operate in their community. This is a common feeling, as street gangs are a scary problem that most would rather not think about or address. Unfortunately, many adults who have the power to intervene in a gang problem early persist in denying the problem until a crisis erupts in their school or the community.

Often, only after panic sweeps through a school or community is a gang problem acknowledged. In order to avoid the denial/crisis/panic cycle commonly associated with youth gangs, adults should be aware and knowledgeable of the definition, identification, and behavioral characteristics of gang members. Following is a description of the five main characteristics of gangs.

THREE OR MORE INDIVIDUALS

First, gangs are groups of three or more individuals who choose a traditional gang (such as the Vice Lords or the Black Gangster Disciples) to identify with or to emulate. While traditional gangs often have hundreds, or even thousands of members, local territorial gangs may consist of just a few neighborhood kids or a group that mingles at school.

ASSOCIATING ON A CONTINUOUS BASIS

The second main characteristic of a youth gang is that the kids in a gang like to "hang around" together. Once the gang is formed, the members associate together on a continuous basis. They will often be seen together in the community and at school. Congregating may be for casual social purposes, for a demonstration of unity and gang allegiance, or for a mandatory meeting. Both formal and informal meetings are generally held to discuss gang business.

As a group, gang members use their numbers to intimidate others. At the same time, they rely on each other for protection not only from rival gangs but also to discourage anyone else who is not a part of their gang set from infiltrating. Parents, other family members, and teachers have been the target of gang intimidation and violence due to their efforts to extricate a child involved in a gang. Members stick together in good times and in bad, and a loyalty develops to the point where gang members are comfortable only with each other.

REPRESENTING UNITY WITH COLORS AND SYMBOLS

The third major characteristic of youth gangs relates to colors and symbols. A significant, observable characteristic of youth gangs is that they show their unity by wearing the same colors and styles of clothing in addition to using specific hand signs and symbols to identify themselves as a group. Each gang set (or subfaction of a gang formed by an individual with leadership ability and the motivation to carry out the mission of street gangs) uses symbols and colors that stem from those used by the traditional gang they either associate with or strive to imitate.

CLAIMING A TERRITORY

The fourth major characteristic is that gangs are territorial in nature. This means that they claim a "turf" or a territory that they control. Turf can be the neighborhood where they live or the area where they sell drugs. The territory is marked by graffiti. Graffiti is a special type of written language that is used to communicate the identity of the gang; some call it the "newspaper of the streets." Graffiti can also show disrespect to a rival gang if written in a certain way. (More specific information on graffiti will be provided later in this section.)

CRIMINAL ACTIVITY FOR FINANCIAL GAIN

Finally, gangs are organized for the primary purpose of engaging in criminal activities for profit. While illegal drug sales are the most prevalent source of financial gain for gangs, other crimes such as intimidation, extortion, thefts, and burglaries are carried out for the purpose of enhancing the gang's reputation for violence and retaliation.

Summary Box 1.3 describes the five main characteristics of a youth gang.

Summary Box 1.3

Five Main Characteristics of a Youth Gang

- A group of three or more individuals

- Associate together on a continuous basis

- Display their unity with colors, signs, and symbols

- Establish and defend a specific territory, or turf

- Carry out criminal activities for financial gain

Pack Behavior

For teenagers, being part of a group is considered ordinary, age-appropriate behavior. However, teenagers with violent tendencies carry the group association to an unacceptable extreme. Youth gangs are radically different from the social groups of teenagers who gather on weekend nights at a local video game arcade or pizza place. Many youth gang members demonstrate hostile and aggressive personalities through their vicious, almost sociopathic patterns of behavior. These violent teens usually congregate in groups that could also be described as "packs." Pack behavior is evident in street gang activities.

WELL-EQUIPPED ARMIES

Teenagers who currently "hang around" together in gangs can be compared to well-equipped armies. The members carry out orders from their leader without question in a disciplined fashion, and are equipped with various types of lethal weaponry. In fact, it has been suggested (Kantrowitz, 1993) that individuals being discharged from the new juvenile "boot camps" are highly recruited by gangs because they are already well-trained and disciplined to follow orders.

"Pack behavior" tends to diminish socially appropriate judgment, conscience, and behavior. Operating under this mentality, the gang is more active at night or under cover. They specifically choose victims who can be easily taken advantage of—an activity commonly referred to as "wilding." Innocent victims are often attacked because they are perceived as being weak or defenseless. Violent behavior is enhanced by this gang mentality. There is a synergistic effect; one particularly violent kid can persuade others to commit crimes they might not think of or ever consider performing on their own.

Speaking Up!

Don't ever underestimate the power of the gang. Never. As a group, they got power. All they need. They can control a neighborhood, a school, a city, you name it. Never underestimate them, man.

– Incarcerated gang member

PEER PRESSURE IN GANGS

Peer pressure is an incredibly influential motivator for most teenagers. It is often very difficult for an adolescent to be assertive and act as an individual in front of a peer group. This requires a great deal of will power and a strong sense of self-esteem. Thus many kids will choose to go along with the gang and even commit brutal crimes rather than choose not to be part of a gang.

Speaking Up!

I wanted to have friends. I wasn't smart enough to get good grades. I wasn't on any of the teams. When I tried out for cheerleading, I didn't make it. I started hanging out with guys who were Vice Lords. They liked me. They accepted me. To keep up with them I did a lot of bad things. I knew they were wrong. I lied, I stole, I sold drugs, and I hurt

(CONTINUED)

Speaking Up! (CONTINUED)

other people. I knew it was wrong but I did it anyway. I guess I'd do it again to be accepted—to belong to the group.

– Shannon, 14 years old

Hierarchy of Gang Membership

Youth gangs have an organized hierarchy of membership similar to a military organization. Rank is achieved through serving the gang by carrying out whatever activity is assigned. Rank or status level in gangs range from leaders, hard core members, "peewees," and "wannabes." The age range of gang members varies widely from children in early elementary grades through adults past middle age. Traditional, territorial, and franchise gangs all follow this basic organizational structure. The role that each member plays is described following.

TRADITIONAL GANG LEADERS

Traditional gang leaders have "worked their way up" through the gang. They are often older than lower ranking members, tend to be charismatic, and demonstrate leadership ability. Traditional gang leaders have earned their respect, reputation, and position in the gang

through the amount and severity of the violent criminal acts they have committed. In a traditional gang, most members respect the leader and would be quite hesitant to challenge his established authority. Vicious retaliation to the mutinous gang member would be the most likely result.

Leaders of traditional gangs often direct gang activities from inside prisons. These gang leaders are career criminals usually serving time for violent offenses such as murder and kidnapping. The leaders run the gang from prison by relaying their commands to street members through visitors going into and out of the prison. These "visitors" are usually high ranking gang members, and are trusted as messengers by both the incarcerated leaders and those gang members waiting for orders out on the street.

TERRITORIAL GANG LEADERS

Territorial gang leaders are the young males, predominately, who organize these local gangs and appear to know much about the traditional gangs, even though they may never have been a member of one. A territorial gang leader will be the kid who has natural leadership abilities and the charisma to attract peer followers. Or he may be the bully with the bad reputation who is feared the most by his peers. The territorial gang is organized by the leader gaining the confidence of a few close friends and initiating them into the gang way of life. He then requires the members to convince or intimidate others to join the gang. His leadership ability may be challenged at any time by the other members, and he may often have to fight to maintain his reputation and rank in the gang.

The leader of the territorial gang has a direct influence on all of the gang's business and actions. The criminal activity of the gang will be determined by what type of criminal the leader is himself. If he is a drug dealer, the gang will deal drugs. If he is a thief, the gang will commit robberies, burglaries, or thefts. Essentially, the leader plans the gang activity and then issues commands or directives to the hard core members who have the responsibility of enforcing the leader's orders.

Speaking Up!

When advised by a peer to " . . . be a leader, join the gang," this student replied, "Gang members aren't leaders, they're followers!"

– Nicki, 14 years old

HARD CORE MEMBERS

Hard core members can range from individuals in their pre-teens to their early twenties, with a few middle age and older members. They have been initiated into a gang and their lives revolve around gang activity. The gang is their

job. Due to their characteristic lack of education, most would not be able to obtain legal employment other than a minimum wage, no benefit, no future type of a job. Thus these individuals find that crime is much more lucrative. Once gang members get used to earning the high profits associated with illegal drug sales, it is most difficult, if not impossible, to persuade them to attempt to undertake any legitimate type of employment.

The hard core members may be called "lieutenants." High ranking hard core members will be required to carry out a wide range of criminal activities. These unlawful operations may range from recruiting new members for the gang; to setting up drug and weapon sales; to performing burglaries, extortions, and robberies. They also are responsible for implementing and enforcing the gang leader's discipline commands which are often brutal and violent. Consequently, hard core members are often in and out of jail on a regular basis. They tend to become very streetwise and knowledgeable about the legal system in general.

PEEWEES (FRINGE MEMBERS/ASSOCIATES)

Peewees are younger, initiated members of the gang. They are used to used to carry money, drugs, and weapons for the older members. Hard core gang members actively recruit children.

There are two main reasons for this. First, children are less likely to be stopped and searched. Second, if they are caught, children typically receive much less severe punishment from the justice system than would an adult carrying out the same illegal actions.

As they are replaced by newer young members, peewees are eventually accepted as hard core members after having served the gang for a period of time.

Speaking Up!

My dad left my mom and my brother and me when I was six. I didn't have anyone to look up to. The guys on the street paid attention to me. They paid me money to carry stuff, to deliver it for them. I was just a kid. They told me if I got caught I'd get off easy. I never got caught.

– Joey, 12 years old

WANNABES

Wannabes have not been initiated into the gang. They tend to drift in and out of the periphery of gang activity. Wannabes are typically youth who imitate the dress and the style of the initiated gang members. They usually have friends or family members in the gang, and tend to idolize the gang and its activities.

Wannabes are the group who have the potential to respond most successfully to gang prevention activities. At this stage, they have not been initiated into the gang, nor have they become entrenched in the gang mentality. But without consistent prevention/intervention services, "wannabes" are "gonnabes."

Summary Box 1.4 outlines the gang membership hierarchy.

Summary Box 1.4

Gang Membership Hierarchy

Gang Leader . .	Earns respect and position in the gang by demonstrating leadership ability and violence
Hard Core Members . .	Enforcers for the leader; they carry out orders, sell drugs and weapons; are very streetwise; various levels of rank within gangs
Peewees . . .	Younger, initiated gang members used to carry drugs, money, and weapons; will receive reduced legal

(CONTINUED)

---

                    punishment if
                    caught due to age

Wannabes . . Individuals **not**
                    initiated into the
                    gang; tend to
                    idolize gang
                    mentality; usually
                    have family

Ethnic Composition

Traditionally, youth gangs have been composed primarily of individuals from ethnic minorities.* In 1993, Goldstein and Huff reported that 55% of all gang members were African-American, while 33% were Hispanic. The remainder of gang members were whites, Asians, and others.

Historically, whites have joined gangs that focus on "white supremacy" and hate crimes against minority groups. However, in recent years the ethnic make-up of gangs has undergone quite a transformation. Law enforcement personnel report that white teenagers, both male and female, are joining gangs at a higher rate than minority youth. This trend is a result of large numbers of white (and Asian) individuals now being allowed to become members of gangs that previously had strict ethnic boundaries.

One way ethnic composition plays a role in gang participation is in the use of nicknames, or "street names." Black gang members tend to make up their own street names based upon what kind of reputation they would like to have. Names like "C Money," "Bang," "Big Mac," or "Crazy" are examples. Hispanic gang members generally are given their street names by fellow gang members, usually based upon physical appearance. Names such as "Porky," "Little Bean," "Fats," or "Greasy" are some examples. White gang members usually make up their own street names that are related to others' perceptions of their personality or physical characteristics. Examples include "Shy Girl, "Bull Dog," and "Green Eyes."

---

* Please note that ethnic labels used in this book are simply provided to convey the facts about gang participation. There is absolutely no intent to stereotype certain ethnic groups or provide sweeping generalizations of people from minority cultures. When terms such as "black gangs," "Hispanic gangs," or "white supremacist groups" are mentioned, they refer to a group of individuals who carry out criminal activities. There is no intent to tarnish the cultural heritage of any one race.

Violence Associated With Youth Gangs

Speaking Up!

When you live each day in hell, dyin' don't look so bad.

– Crip gang member

Recently, gang violence has received a great deal of media attention. The ruthless criminal influence of youth involved in gang activity has reverberated across the nation, from inner city to urban to rural areas. Gang violence has affected schools, neighborhoods, communities, and private citizens alike.

However, street gang history confirms that gang violence is not a new or an isolated problem. Gang violence is in part the result of long-term sociological problems including poverty, lack of education, lack of employment prospects, and lack of recreational and social opportunities.

Gang members reap their reward (i.e., income) from crime. So most members feel as though they have much more to gain than to lose from being a gang member. Their lives revolve around the gang, and thus, gang violence. Many gang members live in neighborhoods that are socially and economically deprived. In these neighborhoods violence is observed in daily life and becomes an accepted means of interaction with others. A violent death, either their own or someone else's, is an accepted fact of life for most gang members.

The frequency with which youth are involved in violent street gang crime has risen dramatically during the past two decades. Due to the lack of systematic, nationwide collection of gang demographics, accurate data on the actual number of individuals involved in street gang violence is difficult to quantify. However, what has been nationally documented is that violent crime (i.e., murder, rape, robbery, aggravated assault) increased 600% between 1953 and 1986 (Goldstein, 1992). Juvenile arrests for violent crimes (e.g., robbery) escalated 41% from 1982 to 1991. During that same time period, the number of juvenile arrests for murder climbed 93% and rose 72% for aggravated assaults (Walker, Colvin, & Ramsey, 1994). Much of this increase can be attributed to juveniles involved in gang activity.

Speaking Up!

These kids today, man, they don't care 'bout nothin'. Drive-bys, shootin' each other, it don't matter. It's gonna get worse before it gets better, I can tell you that.

– Ex-Crip gang member

The National League of Cities surveyed communities in urban, suburban, and rural areas nationwide in 1994. When asked about violence in classrooms, hallways, and playgrounds at school, 80% of respondents said violence is a serious problem. Forty percent of respondents reported that violence in schools had increased noticeably during the past five years. Twenty-five percent of all the schools reported that their students had died or suffered injuries requiring hospitalization as a result of violence. (The response to that question for big city schools only was 41%.) Forty percent of the suburban communities and non-metropolitan towns and cities said gangs were a factor in the violence in their schools.

Metropolitan Life Insurance Company polled teachers, students, and police officials in 1993. Results indicated that 23% of students and 11% of teachers had been victims of violence in and around schools. When asked about police officers in schools, 60% of teachers thought that the federal government should put more police officers on the street in high crime areas in which schools were located. In turn, 54% of the teachers thought there should be more security personnel in the schools to combat violence.

Law enforcement officials describe an absolute epidemic of youth violence during the past five years not only in the inner cities but in the suburbs and rural

areas of the country as well. The National School Safety Center (1994) estimated that approximately 100,000 students carry guns to school on a daily basis. Self-defense is the most frequently reported reason for needing a weapon; students say that school is a dangerous place.

Almost half of the robberies and more than one third of the assaults on urban youth take place in schools. The 1986 "National Crime Survey" estimated that three million thefts and violent crimes occur on school property each year. This is an average of approximately 16,000 crimes per day. Teenagers are more likely than adults to be crime victims; 6.7% of teenagers as compared to 2.6% of the population over the age of 19 are the victims of violent crime.

Violence is unquestionably becoming an accepted way of life for many kids. Suspected reasons for the increase in youth violence include: (1) neglect or abuse by parents; (2) witnessing violence at an early age at home or on the street; (3) living in a culture that glamorizes violence; (4) problems in school, including reading difficulties and learning disabilities (such academic difficulties can lead to a high level of frustration, lack of acceptance by the peer group, and school dropout); and (5) the widespread availability of guns to juveniles.

CONSEQUENCES OF GANG INVOLVEMENT

Gang-involved youth seldom perceive beyond the here and now. They often fail to consider the very real and very violent (often fatal) consequences that may result from participating in gang activity. The Texas Youth Commission (1993) has reported on both long- and short-term life-altering consequences for gang members.

Short-term consequences include trouble with the law, school problems (and likely dropout), withdrawal from family, risk of physical injury during initiation and clashes with rival gangs, and involvement in criminal activity. The long-term consequences of gang involvement are similar but more severe. They include loss of opportunity for education and legitimate employment; jail/prison terms; loss of family/friends; risking family members' lives; and endless occurrences of threats, assaults, and drive-by shootings.

Gang members have to constantly "watch their backs." The ultimate permanent consequence? Often an early and violent death. As stated previously, 60% of male gang members are dead or in prison by age 20, with the average life expectancy of a male gang member a little over 20 years. Parents and teachers would do the youth they interact with a great service by articulating these facts to potential gang members.

Speaking Up!

Some days you hate to see the sun come up. You know right then, maybe today's the day I die.

— Big city gang member

Gang Initiations

Gang initiations contribute to violence and criminal activity. These rituals are an important aspect of gang behavior. They are used to solidify the gang, bond its members through an act of violence or sex, and allow the gang member undergoing initiation to prove loyalty and dedication to the group.

Initiation into a gang is the determining factor between being a member or a wannabe. Many wannabes are reluctant or afraid to go through a gang's initiation ritual and therefore shy away from the group over the long term, or "flip-flop" from gang to gang. Flip-flopping is the term law enforcement officials use to describe people who suddenly drop their affiliation to one gang and begin associating with another.

Gang initiations come in various forms. Some initiations are very simple and nonthreatening, while others are based upon physical violence or deviant sexual activity. Following are descriptions of the various types of gang initiations commonly practiced today.

WALKIN' THE LINE

Traditional gangs often stage violent initiations referred to as "walkin' the line" or being "jumped in." In these situations the wannabe is required to fight a certain number of the gang members for a predetermined period of time. No weapons are involved, just hand-to-hand, physical combat. This initiation usually takes place in an isolated area where there is little chance that neighbors or bystanders will call the police if they see or hear the fight taking place.

In this initiation, the gang members form a circle around the individual being initiated. After the leader gives a signal to begin, the other members are expected to savagely attack the wannabe, punching and kicking in a "no holds barred" fashion. The wannabe is expected to fight back to show that he is brave and tough enough to be able to support his gang brothers in a battle with a rival gang.

Surviving this initiation proves the wannabe's loyalty to the gang. After the actual physical fight is over, the gang members show their acceptance of the newest member by embracing him, exchanging the gang hand signs/hand shakes, and congratulating him on demonstrating allegiance to the gang. However, if the wannabe fails to fight back

or gives up, he may be beaten to unconsciousness or death and left at the site of the initiation.

Speaking Up!

First, they blessed me in. Then, they said I had to walk the line. Man, they beat my ass. But I fought back. That's how you prove yourself. You fight back. You'd better man, or they'll kill ya.

– Gang member describing his initiation

TAKING 40 TO THE CHEST

Another form of physical initiation involves the wannabe standing before the higher ranking gang members and/or the gang leader and being struck with fists. A predetermined number of punches are delivered to the wannabe, and he is to offer no resistance. Gang members have told police officers that they had to "take 40 to the chest" or "take three to the mouth" to be initiated. (They are referring to the number of times that they were struck.) While the number of blows may differ from gang to gang, the ritual remains the same. The gang is using physical means to test the wannabe's toughness, dedication, and loyalty.

BEING BLESSED IN

Territorial gangs have invented another initiation ritual called being "blessed in." This initiation ritual is performed simply by having the leader place his hand on the head of the new member while reciting a prayer or an oath. They have chosen this practice over the violent beating because many members are afraid of being injured during the physical initiation.

FEMALE GANG MEMBER INITIATIONS

Female wannabes are often required to fight gang members in the same fashion as their male counterparts. In this case, both male and female gang members may be the attackers. All-female gangs hold similar types of initiations with the same purpose: to demonstrate courage, combat skills, and allegiance to the gang during battle. The actual initiation is similar to that of the males' in that the females physically attack the wannabe for a certain period of time. As with the males, she is expected to show bravery

Speaking Up!

My "in" [initiation] was to fight six of 'em for six minutes. Kickin', beatin', punchin', you name it. Anything goes. But I still wanted in, and that's what it took.

– Female gang member

and toughness by fighting back and defending herself.

Some females are given the choice of being "sexed in" to mixed-gender gangs. Those who choose the sexual initiation are required to engage in sexual activity with one or several members of the gang. (This is different from a "gang rape," as the female is a willing participant.) For example, in one documented case in San Antonio, Texas, five 14- and 15-year old female wannabes consented to have intercourse with a known HIV positive male gang member as initiation into their gang. However, female gang members have confessed to police that being "jumped in" offers them more respect from the males than being "sexed in."

Speaking Up!

Yeah, I did 'em all [had sexual intercourse with the male gang members]. I had to. That's the only way I could get in, and I wanted in real bad.

– Female gang member

SEXUAL INITIATIONS

Sexual activity has also been documented as an initiation activity of all-male gangs. In Davenport, Iowa, a gang calling themselves the "Death Row Crew" used homosexual acts between the gang's leader and wannabe members as the initiation required for gang acceptance. In September 1993, the Davenport Police Department's gang unit was tipped off to the time and location of one of this gang's meetings at a local motel. A raid was carried out in the motel room where the initiation was taking place, and arrests were made.

In the follow-up investigation of this raid, it was discovered that homosexual activity had been the ritual used for initiation. Several days later, three boys who had voluntarily participated in oral and anal sex with the gang's leader approached police investigators and provided them with information that led to the arrest and conviction of the gang leader. These boys had become so disgusted with and embarrassed about the sexual actions demanded of members for acceptance into this gang that they related details of the initiation to the police officers.

SIGNING UP

Some territorial gangs may require wannabes to "sign up," or fill out a simple application for acceptance. Others may require wannabes to pay to become a member. Police have learned that some territorial gang members were asked to contribute $20.00 for gang membership. Still others use crimes such as shoplifting, burglary, or assaults for gang initiation. Territorial gang members have told police investigators that they had to "steal a Bulls hat," or "punch out" somebody to gain acceptance by

the gang. Others have been directed to steel an item during a burglary such as a gun, jewelry, or money and deliver it back to the gang as proof that they obeyed the gang's command.

In summary, street gang initiations come in many forms and involve assorted criminal activities and degrees of violence. In contrast to the variety of initiations described, police have even discovered territorial gangs where no initiation was required of members. It's apparent that initiation rituals are more revered by the traditional gangs, and traditional gangs are much more likely to use brutality and force in their initiations than are territorial gangs. (Franchise gangs do not require initiations as they are "collaborative efforts" for a short time period only.)

Environmental Gang Indicators

There are specific indicators of gang activity that can be observed in areas where the gangs are active. The primary indicators include the appearance of graffiti, an increase in the number of individuals who dress in a similar fashion and congregate in a particular area, and an escalation of criminal activity. Each of these main indicators is explained in greater detail following.

GRAFFITI

One of the first indications of possible gang activity in an area is the appearance of graffiti. Gang graffiti will rapidly appear in any area where a gang is active. The more active the gang, the more graffiti that will be observed.

Each gang's graffiti is composed of symbols and slogans that have specific meaning to that gang. Midwest gang graffiti uses both pictures and slogans. West coast gang graffiti is composed mainly of gang names and slogans. Hispanic gangs, such as the Latin Kings, appear to have the most artistic graffiti. (It would seem that if artistically skilled gang members were channeled in the right direction, many could probably use their talents to obtain gainful employment in an art-oriented field such as graphic design, illustration, or sign painting.)

Purposes of Graffiti

Graffiti is often an informational signal from a gang communicating absolute dominance or control over an area. Youth gangs may attempt to control neighborhoods, schools, parks or other recreational areas, and various business areas such as shopping malls. For traditional gangs, the purpose of establishing control over an area is to define and establish command over drug-selling turf.

But graffiti is not only used to mark territorial boundaries. Graffiti is also a form of communication, or a "message board" of sorts. Graffiti is used to show allegiance to a certain gang. It might also serve as a warning and/or a challenge to rival gangs. Graffiti written upside down, backwards, or crossed out was written by a rival gang member. This practice is routinely employed to challenge or show disrespect to a rival gang. A name of a gang member crossed out might indicate that that person has been targeted to be killed.

Graffiti can be found anywhere a gang would like to establish turf. In the community, it is most frequently found on road or street signs, garages, walls, tunnels, and bridges. Any flat, visible surface might be used as a billboard for graffiti. (Examples of gang-related graffiti are provided in Section 2. Note, however, that those who write names, slogans, etc. on buildings or other surfaces are not always gang-related. "Class of '96" variety graffiti is a time-honored tradition among teenagers.)

Graffiti at Home and at School

In addition to graffiti drawn on community property, gang members will also write graffiti on various surfaces at school or even at home. Parents and teachers should watch for graffiti marked on school notebook covers, assignment papers, desktops, blackboards, bathroom walls, lockers, bedroom walls, furniture, and clothing.

One example of graffiti found in the home occurred after a parent attended a youth gang seminar presented by a representative of a local police department's gang unit. All of the parents attending this meeting were provided with examples of gang graffiti. Upon returning home, the parent was horrified to discover that the "doodling" all over the cover of the family telephone book was actually Black Gangster Disciple graffiti.

This case clearly demonstrates that parents and teachers must learn to recognize gang-related graffiti in order to deter children from drawing it in the home or at school. Adults should also be on the lookout for graffiti in the form of tattoos on hands, arms, or other body parts. The tattoos might be either homemade or professionally applied, and will depict gang signs/symbols.

Three R's of Graffiti: Read, Record, Remove

Parents and teachers must not allow children to write gang graffiti anywhere. Activating the "three R's" of graffiti will assist in sending this anti-graffiti message. The three R's consist of **read**, **record**, and **remove** (Goldstein & Huff, 1993).

First, it is important to **read** graffiti as opposed to simply ignoring its presence, as displays of graffiti can be thought of as a message board for gang communication.

Adults can learn to recognize the specific graffiti used by different gangs. This helps in determining which gangs are active in the area.

Second, adults should **record** or photograph the graffiti, keeping a record of each graffiti symbol observed. Polaroid cameras are useful for creating graffiti files, otherwise a likeness of the symbol can be drawn. It is helpful to identify which gang produced the graffiti. Since gangs assume they control the area that is marked by graffiti, knowing which gangs are active in an area can help track problem behaviors and crime trends. This practice might also serve to assist educators in resolving crime or vandalism committed on school property.

The third R stands for **remove**. as soon as possible after graffiti has been read and recorded, it should be removed. A solvent may be used to clean graffiti off some surfaces. In other places, it will have to be painted over. Many communities are requiring juveniles to remove graffiti as part of restitution or community service work.

Removing graffiti reduces gangs' power. Doing so sends an anti-gang mentality message (zero tolerance). Immediate removal of graffiti demonstrates to gang members that there are other more dominant and influential individuals in charge of the area. This is particularly important at school where other students might be frightened or intimidated by gang graffiti. Educators must foster a positive school climate that promotes security and a safe learning environment for all students; removing graffiti on school grounds is one positive step in this direction.

GROUPS OF SIMILAR LOOKING/ACTING INDIVIDUALS

Following the appearance of graffiti in an area, the second environmental gang indicator is that of individuals wearing similar colors and symbols congregating in specific areas on a consistent basis. There will be three notable characteristics of this group that constitute a gang.

First, gang members will often dress in the same colors, such as red and black for the Vice Lords, black and blue for the Gangster Disciples, or black and gold for the Latin Kings.

Second, gang members will display symbols or colors on either the right or the left side of the body. This is called "representing." Wearing gang identifiers on either the right or the left is a key indicator of gang affiliation. Examples of representing include hats cocked to one side or the other, jewelry worn on only the right or the left side, one sleeve or pant leg rolled up, or a colored bandanna worn on one side. (More specific information on gang colors and symbols is provided in Section 2.)

Third, gang members will flash or "throw" hand signs to communicate with each other. The hand signs are often finger representations of the initials of the letters that compose their gang name, or numbers that are pertinent to the gang. Some gangs have even adopted portions of the American Sign Language used by individuals with hearing impairments.

ASSOCIATING ON A CONTINUOUS BASIS

Members of a gang congregate together for socialization purposes as well as to conduct gang business. Some of the meetings are informal, but many are mandatory, formal meetings. Each gang enforces its own rules and regulations for its members. Typical required behaviors of gang members include successfully enduring the initiation, memorizing the gang's constitution and bylaws (if any), dressing in the gang's colors, attending meetings, obeying the gang's code of conduct, and carrying out orders of higher ranking members.

INCREASE IN CRIMINAL ACTIVITY

After graffiti appears and individuals dressed alike are associating together on a continuous basis, an increase in criminal activity is likely to develop. Since a main purpose of a gang is to carry out criminal activity for financial gain, a variety of illegal behaviors will naturally increase in any area or neighborhood where a gang is active. The most common activity of the traditional gangs is illegal drug sales. Consequently, illegal drugs will be more readily available and the incidence of drug sales will soar in areas where these gangs are found.

As drug sellers and buyers infiltrate a given area, related criminal behaviors will also escalate. Examples include weapon sales, burglaries, robberies, extortion, assaults, and intimidation. The number of assaults, especially those in and around schools, will increase as gang behavior becomes more rampant. Fighting among gang members for turf, for reputation, or for retaliation becomes common. Since many wannabe gang members still attend school, their violent behavior is brought into the schools with them. Thus athletic events, dances, school parties, and simply everyday school life can be disrupted by gang activity.

Weapons

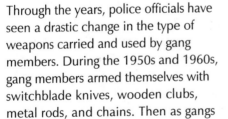

Through the years, police officials have seen a drastic change in the type of weapons carried and used by gang members. During the 1950s and 1960s, gang members armed themselves with switchblade knives, wooden clubs, metal rods, and chains. Then as gangs became more sophisticated, the degree

to which they armed themselves increased. Currently, hand guns and sawed-off shotguns seem to be the weapons of choice for gang members.

American movies and "gangster rap" music videos often show gang members wielding military-type assault weapons. Realistically, however, small, easily concealed pistols are the most popular style of firearm. The semi-automatic nine-millimeter hand gun is most referred to in gang lingo. Called either a "nine" or a "glock," this model of hand gun is favored by gang members.

HAND GUNS

Even smaller than the nine-millimeter are several models of pistols that can be held in the palm of the hand or carried in a back pants pocket without being easily detected. These .22, .25, or .32 caliber pistols are also very easily obtained on the street. A Harvard School of Public Health survey (as cited in Kantrowitz, 1993) reported that 59% of children in the sixth through the twelfth grade said that they "could get a hand gun if they wanted one." Small hand guns are the models about which teachers and parents should be most aware. Though small and easily concealed, these hand guns are lethal weapons.

MILITARY-STYLE WEAPONS

In larger cities, gangs have been known to have access to military-style weapons such as grenade launchers, "rockets" (hand-held devices with an explosive head that can be launched from a distance), machine guns, and other types of military explosives. Some of these are obtained by gang members who have served in the armed forces or who are members of military reserve units. As well as the opportunity to secure these weapons, gang members who learned their operation while in the service are later able to teach their fellow gang members how to use them.

SOURCES/USES OF GUNS

Many of the guns that fall into the hands of gang members are stolen in burglaries. Police have discovered that some street gangs require wannabes to break into a house and steal a gun for the gang as an initiation ritual. Once delivered to the gang, the gun is assigned to a gang member or stored with other weapons to be issued during times of combat.

A weapon equates to power to a gang member. Within the set it symbolizes strength and courage. To rival gang members and other citizens, possession of a weapon demands respect and instigates fear. As a gang member becomes more involved with the sale of narcotics, the weapon assumes a security role. If a member is carrying a substantial amount of drugs, he/she is likely to be carrying a substantial amount of money. Since gang members have been known to commit robberies of rival gang members, carrying a weapon decreases the

possibility that a gang member in turn will become a victim.

Sections 3 and 4 provide details on policies regarding guns and management strategies for dealing with students who bring guns to school.

The Three R's of Gang Life

The lives of gang members revolve around three vitally important traits that law enforcement officials have termed the "three R's" of gang culture. These R's stand for **reputation**, **respect**, and **retaliation**.

REPUTATION

Reputation is of critical concern to all gang members. Referred to as a "rep" by these individuals, it determines a member's status within the gang. The more violent and antisocial the reputation, the better it is considered by the gang member. During the past few years, the public's perception of gang members has automatically resulted in a negative reputation for them. Just hearing the word "gang" will conjure up feelings of fear in most people. Gang members relish this reputation, and constantly strive to make themselves look as ruthless and notorious as possible.

Territorial gang leaders usually obtain their reputation by being the biggest or toughest individual within the group. If a territorial gang leader's leadership is contested, he will have to fight the challenger to retain control over the gang. The territorial gang leader gains power through intimidating the other gang members, and might be the schoolyard bully or neighborhood "thug."

Territorial gang members earn their reputations by fighting with rival gang members, by intimidating or threatening authoritative persons (e.g., teachers, parents, police officers, adults in general), or by committing crimes that are challenging or risky.

Wannabe gang members of any gang strive to obtain the same reputation as the initiated members of the gang. Since most wannabe gang members are in their early teens or younger, a bad reputation in the eyes of their peers is not that difficult to achieve. Harassment and intimidation of others is typical behavior of young wannabe gang members—behavior that serves to enhance their negative reputations. (Parents and teachers should be on the look-out for these behaviors in order to prevent the victimization of other children.)

In **traditional** gangs, the members' reputations are often influenced by the crimes they've committed and the time they've spent in prison. The leaders of these gangs usually have extensive prison records or are incarcerated for committing felony crimes. The other gang members generally brag about time spent in jail, and are revered by younger wannabes.

Traditional gang members often obtain a reputation for violence because of their participation in gang wars. Drive-by shootings are a common practice in traditional gang life. Participating gang members are perceived as bold and daring by the other gang members and by wannabes. The more risks members choose to take, and the more violent tendencies they display, the more status and the higher the esteem in which they are held by their fellow gang members.

Inside prison, gang members' reputations are also important. If incarcerated gang members have a vicious, brutal background which is known inside the prison, they are more likely to be left alone or protected by fellow gang inmates. If members have obtained a high rank within the gang, this also helps to protect them inside prison. Those members holding rank within a gang's organizational structure usually have reputations of being violent, hardened criminals. As inmates, they find prison life easier than those who have no rank or protection from the gang.

RESPECT

The second "R" in the three R's of gang life stands for respect. This is something that gang members demand. Gang members typically will become aggressive and violent if they don't receive the respect they feel they deserve. Respect is critically important for both individual members and for a gang as a whole.

Gangs' literature, creeds, and rules and regulations demand that gang members respect their fellow gang members while continually showing disrespect to rival gang members. Respect, or disrespect, is often displayed in gang graffiti. Any signs or symbols displayed upside down, backwards, drawn in pieces, or written over demonstrates disrespect for the gang whose symbols were used.

Disrespect is considered to be a very serious violation of any gang's code of conduct. Lack of respect is also a common reason why gang wars are started. When rival gang members encounter each other, the demand for respect becomes critically significant. Flashing hand signs to show disrespect while facing off has cost many gang members their lives.

Teachers and parents need to understand how important respect is to gang members. Just as they demand respect from their own and rival gang members, they also expect respect from adults. Teachers **can** demonstrate respect for all students without condoning their inappropriate behaviors. Teachers who deliberately establish that they have no respect for gang members in their

classes risk being on the receiving end of intimidation and/or violence.

Speaking Up!

Teachers think all us kids should respect them just because they're teachers. Well we don't. They have to earn our respect. Just like I earn my respect out on the street. Teachers who are always dissin' us won't get no respect back. We hate 'em and we give 'em hell all day long.

– Zack, 17 years old

RETALIATION

The third R in the three R's of gang life is retaliation. In the gang culture, no challenge goes unanswered. In doesn't matter where that challenge comes from, be it rival members, nongang members, teachers, or parents. Gang members who feel that they have been "disrespected" (or "dis"ed) strike back.

Gang members will retaliate for each and every event that, in their perspective, shows disrespect. It does not matter whether these incidents are serious or seemingly trivial. Retaliation will be carried out for the most serious gang offenses such as disrespectful graffiti (e.g., written upside down, backwards, or crossed out), encroaching on drug turf (i.e., selling in another gang's area), or issuing a challenge (e.g., through "mad dogging," slang for intense staring, or through verbal threats). Retaliation will also occur for such minor acts as talking to a rival member's girlfriend, or making disrespectful comments about a rival gang.

Various forms of retaliation include assaults, robberies, damage to property, and drive-by shootings. In fact, drive-by shootings are one of the most common and highly publicized forms of gang retaliation. In a drive-by shooting, members of one gang will pile into a car and drive through the neighborhood/turf of a rival gang who has in some way shown them disrespect. The gang members in the vehicle may randomly select a rival gang member target, or have one individual in mind as they approach their rivals' turf. As the car passes, the gang members fire guns from within the car and then speed away.

To summarize the three R's of gang life, the following is offered: Gang members work at building a **reputation** that will hold them in high regard by their peers. They then demand the **respect** that they feel they deserve as gang members. If they don't get that respect, they **retaliate**.

Small Town Gangs

Gangs are no longer only a problem that officials in large cities must deal with. However, primary indicators of gang

activity are often ignored by city and school officials in less metropolitan communities. Many communities and schools thereby actively deny the existence of gang organization and activity in their area. This denial could be compared to an ostrich hiding its head in the sand.

Gang members would prefer to have city officials and education administrators in smaller communities continue to deny their presence. Denial facilitates a gang's ability to establish a drug-selling turf, carry out criminal activities, and recruit youth from the community for membership without hindrance. When the first signs of gang activity appear in a small town, rather than saying, "We don't have a gang problem in our town . . . ," officials must band together to address the problem proactively. It is always easier to cope with a small problem than a major crisis.

REASONS FOR GANG MIGRATION

The migration of gangs to smaller cities and rural areas is comparable to the expansion of fast food restaurants. It used to be that a person had to go to a big city to get a Big Mac. Then McDonald's restaurants discovered that they could earn satisfactory profits in smaller towns as well as the bigger cities. This economic concept has also dawned on gang leaders (many of whom have business sense comparable to legitimate corporate executives). That is, small town populations are often just as prone to the use of illegal drugs as are those who live in urban and inner city areas. Consequently, gangs are maintaining drug turf in big cities as well as migrating into suburban and rural areas.

Goldstein and Huff (1993) relate three main reasons for gang migration into smaller cities and towns, as follows.

Reduced Competition for Drug Turf

First, competition for drug turf is less intense in smaller cities as the population of gang members in these areas is less concentrated. The first gang into a specific location is able to designate its own boundaries. That is, the gang will have a monopoly; it could claim to "own" the entire town. The gang members will be able to establish "ownership" of a certain territory without having to fight another gang or negotiate for control. However, they may have to defend their turf as more gangs move into the area.

Greater Potential for Drug Profit

Second, since illegal drugs are more scarce in smaller cities, there is a greater potential for profit. This factor relates to the well-established economic principle of supply and demand: A low supply of a commodity results in a higher demand from the population, because there is less to distribute. The outcome of this situation is usually higher profits for the seller of the scarce commodity.

The distribution pipelines for illegal drugs have to this point generally bypassed smaller interior and/or midwestern cities. Thus, supplies of these drugs are simply not as readily available as in big cities on the east and west coasts. This results in exceedingly high drug sale profits in smaller towns.

Less Experienced Law Enforcement

Third, because drug problems are a relatively recent occurrence in smaller cities, law enforcement efforts to eliminate drug trafficking networks are less experienced and less intense. However, this is rapidly changing as emerging gang and drug related problems are recognized and law enforcement efforts are increased in small towns. Law enforcement officials are setting up special schools, for police officers to attend, focusing specifically on youth gang identifiers, characteristics, and management strategies. Many police departments are also establishing specialized youth gang crime patrol and investigation units to deal with the problem.

Teachers who are interested in gaining first-hand knowledge of the youth gangs in their area are encouraged to contact local police officers who specialize in gang crime or are members of a police force gang unit. A gang unit officer may be able to provide individual conferences, give a group presentation or school inservice, or schedule a "ride along." A ride along involves a civilian observer accompanying a police officer on patrol. Currently, police officers who specialize in gang crime have more practical, real-life experience in dealing with youth gang members than any other professional group.

Less Small Town Violence

Another factor related to gang migration is that some gang members are attempting to remove their families and themselves from the stress and the violence common in major cities. Retaliation is a major activity of gangs. Thus, gang members never know when one of their family members might be caught in the cross fire of gang warfare. Removing their families from cities in which the worst of the violent activity takes place is one way they try to keep their families safe.

Some gang members have professed to hoping that as their children grow up, they will not become involved in the brutal violence of gang activity. In contrast, some children grow up immersed in the gang culture as their parents and/or older siblings actually groom them to become future gang members.

Summary Box 1.5 summarizes the reasons for gang migration to smaller cities and towns.

Summary Box 1.5

Reasons for Gang Migration to Small Towns

- Less competition for drug turf

- Greater potential profit on illegal drug sales

- Less experienced/knowledgeable law enforcement officials

- Lower levels of violence and related stress for gang members' families

---

GANG FORMATION IN SUBURBS

While gang activity used to be only a problem evident in large cities, in recent years youth gangs have become a major source of concern in many suburbs and affluent communities. Law enforcement officers offer an explanation for the development of youth gangs in the suburbs and affluent communities, which seems to defy the traditional socioeconomic motivators for gang formation. Suburban youth have indicated desirable incentives such as: (1) perceived increase in peer group status; (2) self-identity needs; (3) financial gain; and (4) perceived increase in self-control or self-empowerment. The excitement of belonging to a gang was also cited as a compelling factor.

In addition, feelings of low self-esteem, lack of self-confidence, lack of proper adult role models, and a need for belonging to a group were reasons given for gang participation that are similar to the traditional motivators for joining gangs. Additionally, gangs that had been predominately organized along racial lines, such as the Latin Kings and Black Gangster Disciples, now allow membership regardless of ethnicity.

These factors send an important message to parents, teachers, and other adults who work with youth. If the basic needs (both physical and emotional) of children are not being met at home, at school, and/or in the community, they will seek to fulfill those needs in gangs.

Females in Gangs

Currently, police officers estimate that about 20% of all gang members are female. However, females are clamoring to join gangs at a rate faster than males. This is true despite the fact that female members of predominately male gangs do not have high status. In fact, they are considered the "property" of the male gang members. They will often be referred to as "queens," and are required to carry out orders of higher ranking members without question, just like their male counterparts.

Traditionally, female gang members have been used as accessories to gang crime. As members of male gangs, they might serve as lookouts while crimes are committed. They might also transport guns and drugs because they are searched less often and less thoroughly than males. They also carry information for male gang members on the street and in and out of correctional facilities and prisons.

Historically, adolescent females were allowed only a subservient role in gangs. Females still have no real decision-making rights within traditional gangs. The behavior expected by male gang members of females who desire to be gang "queens" confine them to a role that is both degrading and demeaning. The females are frequently used as sex objects by male gang members. In order to be entrusted with their gang duties, they often relinquish essentially all their moral integrity.

Some all-female territorial gangs have been organized. These gangs are usually just as ruthless and violent as their male counterparts. They establish a leadership hierarchy similar to the male gangs. Police officers consider the all-female gangs to be as heavily armed and dangerous as the male gangs.

Initiation of females as members of a gang, whether it is a predominantly male gang or an all-female gang, is typically violent. An initiate might have to take a beating from other gang members, commit a crime, or have sex with a designated number of other gang members. Alternately, a female might automatically become a member of a predominantly male gang if her boyfriend is a member. However, she would still be considered gang property and would be treated as such.

Physical and emotional abuse, substance abuse, and domestic violence are common denominators in the lives of many young women involved with gangs. Females who are at risk for gang involvement report histories of sexual and/or other abuse or by family members and peers. Most come from female-headed households living at or below the poverty line.

It is believed that many females learn violent behavior as a result of a need to protect themselves from abuse, and that female gang violence (both committing violence and tolerating violence towards themselves) may be a reaction to past sexual or physical abuse or rape. Female gang members may be violently acting out their feelings about being victimized at home and in the community. This is a societal problem that has no quick and easy solution. However, educators can help to address the problem through early intervention efforts (in the primary elementary grades, particularly) stressing self-esteem and assertiveness skills.

Profile of a Typical Gang Member

Currently, the typical gang member is an adolescent male. Only one out of every five gang members is female. The following factors are typical of most (but not all) gang members.

SCHOOL FAILURE/UNEMPLOYMENT

Gang members usually have trouble in school or are high school dropouts. As reported by the Texas Youth Commission (1993), 95% of the male gang members studied did not finish high school. Many gang members choose to drop out of school rather than to struggle on with academic subjects with which they continue to achieve only failure on a daily basis, and which are not valued by their peer group anyway.

Because of their feelings of academic inadequacy, many gang-involved students who do stay in school demonstrate negative attitudes and behaviors there. Teachers may be intimidated by the conduct of gang members in the classroom. Thus, some educators may not make the extra effort necessary to effectively teach these students. This serves to perpetuate the negative cycle, and can lead to higher dropout rates—putting youth out on the streets where they are more susceptible to gang influence.

Speaking Up!

I want to graduate so I can get a good job, like in construction. But I don't think teachers teach me as well as other kids who they know will be successful.

— Cory, 16 years old

Because gang members tend to lack an education, they generally would not have available to them many employment opportunities (even if they wanted a traditional job). This situation is further complicated by the fact that gang crime is so much more lucrative than legal employment for high school dropouts. Typically, the best job a dropout could hope to gain is one that could be described as low wage, with no benefits, and no future. Viewing the situation from a gang member's perspective, it is not difficult to understand the financial lure of profitable gang crime.

TROUBLE WITH THE LAW

Many potential gang members have trouble with the law. As a result of their criminal actions, youth gang members often end up in juvenile detention centers, then correctional centers, then prisons. Moving up through the legal system to a larger and more secure correctional institution is often viewed as a "career move" for gang members. They achieve more credibility in the eyes of their gang member peers because they have

committed more violent acts; more violence results in higher status in the gang hierarchy.

ENVIRONMENTAL PROBLEMS

Some conditions of the environment where an individual lives promote or encourage gang membership. Environmental conditions conducive to gang activity include: (1) low wages for workers in the area; (2) high rates of unemployment; (3) lack of recreational opportunities for individuals of all ages; (4) inadequate or ineffective schools; (5) a poor health care system; and (6) deteriorating or poor quality housing. Violence and high crime rates are common in these types of surroundings.

Based on the emerging anecdotal data which police departments in various communities are collecting and sharing with each other, many youth at risk for or actually involved in gang activity are from single parent or divorced families. While divorced and single parent families do not necessarily produce gang members, this does appear to be another environmental factor. Police officers who have ongoing contacts with juveniles involved with gangs report an excessive number of broken homes and single parent families, as well as various dysfunctional family systems.

Typically, gang wannabes have friends and family members in the gang. They have a history of problems and aversive experiences at school. As a result, these students do not earn much positive rein-forcement at school. By the time many of these children are in elementary school, they already idolize the gang mentality and lifestyle. They generally have no other appropriate adult role models at home or in their community.

These students tend to idolize and imitate the hostile and aggressive behaviors of initiated gang members in their neigh-borhoods or schools. Being a gang member is their main goal in life. Unfortunately, there are many youth who fit this pro-file. Too often, children who come from this representative background view gang membership as empowerment, employment, and as their ticket out of obscurity, mediocrity, and poverty.

LACK OF SELF-ESTEEM

One overriding characteristic has been identified by law enforcement person-nel who have frequent and ongoing in-teractions with youth involved in gang activity. This characteristic is more recur-rent than either environmental or school problems. Police officers who specialize in gang crime report that the most common characteristic among identified youth gang members is a lack of self-esteem.

In general, most gang members demon-strate poor social skills and have difficulty forming appropriate relationships with peers and adults outside of the gang. Their abilities are not genuinely

recognized or appreciated by other peers or adults in their environment. These gang members have generally not been able to achieve success in school, with extracurricular activities, with their families, or with community activities.

Speaking Up!

One school I went to, I can't remember where it was, I moved a lot, had a meeting, a group meet-ing for kids who had problems. We talked about peer pressure. That's hard 'cause so many kids just want to fit in. They taught us how to think more positive about ourselves and how to get positive attention. That helped me not do negative things.

– Julio, 15 years old

Based on the typical life experience of wannabe youth gang members, it is not difficult to imagine why these individu-als may suffer from low self-esteem. Most of these youth have had so many problems at home and so many aversive experiences at school that they have be-come virtual experts at failure.

Summary Box 1.6 describes the profile of a typical gang member.

Summary Box 1.6

Profile of a Typical Gang Member

- Male adolescent

- School dropout or truant

- Unemployed

- Antisocial, aggressive, hostile

- In trouble with the law/police

- Economically/socially deprived background

- Inadequate biological family support

- From a divorced/single parent home

- Lack of self-esteem

Need Fulfillment of Gangs

As many gang wannabes haven't developed the skills to establish appropriate relationships with peers and adults, they turn to a gang. Hard core gang recruiters promise to supply unconditional love, acceptance, and support often not available in the wannabe's biological family and/or community. The gang also promises employment, identity, recognition, and excitement. What adolescent who has never been accepted as a friend of a peer group, who has never succeeded at school or in the community, could turn down that offer?

A return to "old fashioned family values" (in which parents remain married, are able to adequately support their children both financially and emotionally, and value school achievement) might be one means of stemming the tide of youth gang involvement. Unfortunately, this is not very realistic for many American families today, and these influences are very difficult (if not impossible) to direct and control from outside the family. Yet an integrated home, school, and community approach to gang prevention and intervention should help, and would be the ideal manner in which to present a "zero tolerance" policy for gang activity (as detailed in Section 3).

One of the more manageable elements of that equation involves educators. Most school-age children spend upwards of six hours per day with teachers in classrooms. This is probably more time, on a consistent basis, than they spend with any other single person or activity (besides watching television). Teachers who are willing to put forth the effort could make an extraordinary impact on students' self-esteem.

All teachers should strive to be reinforcing individuals who provide a motivating and relevant curriculum for all their students. The at-risk population of potential dropouts and other students who have learned to regard school as an aversive environment and teachers as punishers would particularly benefit from interactions with these types of adults within the school.

Speaking Up!

This comment was made by a student who managed to quit one of the most violent gangs in his city:

Mrs. Johnson [his teacher] cared, she really cared. She treated me like a person, instead of just another dumb kid. Only Mrs. Johnson treated us like equals. That's how all kids want to be treated. Teachers aren't any better than me. It's funny, the one teacher I liked and respected most was white, but I never heard anyone mention her race. I think she's Jewish but none of us care. We care about her, too. She's real (pp. 61-62).

— Arthur & Erickson (1992)

Schools and community centers can establish programs that will occupy students during critical after-school hours when adolescents are typically unsupervised. Teachers can also structure activities in the classroom with which at-risk students can achieve success, in an attempt to increase their self-esteem. Building self-esteem in children does

not require special materials. It requires adults to learn to be sensitive to children and their individualized needs. All children and adolescents must learn that they are competent, that they can be successful, and that they are valued by others for the appropriate skills and abilities they demonstrate.

Speaking Up!

I got into trouble a lot after school. I done robberies, muggings, I delivered drugs. It was something to do. I got money for it. If I could get a job after school I would. If I could go somewhere, I don't know where, and work on my hobbies, or something, I probably wouldn't be a delinquent. I like music and drama and stuff.

— Matt, 15 years old

Motivational Factors: Why Kids Join Gangs

According to eminent psychologist Abraham Maslow, basic physiological needs must be met before an individual will be able to achieve "higher order" needs. The basic needs are for food, water, clothing, and shelter. Higher order needs include love or belonging, self-esteem, success, and status. For some children, particularly those from lower socioeconomic backgrounds, a gang may actually provide basic human necessities (such as food, clothing, and protection) that are not available in their homes.

Goldstein and Huff (1993) include this excerpt from R.G., a 23-year old male who literally grew up in a gang:

> . . . *When I was young, my relatives—my brothers, uncles, and cousins, all gang bangers—ran this little drug ring, and I used to hang out with them. My mom used to drink a lot, and sometimes she'd be gone for a week at a time, and my cousins and their friends—all these gang bangers—would hang out at the house and party and smoke weed and stuff and drink. . . . Gangs give you a sense of security, of belonging to the neighborhood. These guys you're growing up with, they're there; they've got the girls, they're cool . . . they have some bucks to spend on the girls. They're respected, they're feared. You get a sense of being somebody, of being respected for who you are, and you get known and praised. . . . When people are in, it's like they're part of a family, and you go from*

> *being a "peewee" or a "future" to being a full member, and you're a member for life* (p. 304).

It appears that for R.G., the gang did fulfill many higher order needs. During the course of his life, the gang provided family-like support and security in addition to a sense of belonging to a group. This is an example of how gangs easily fill in the gaps in the lives of many individuals who do not find success through more socially acceptable avenues and activities. Unfortunately, there is a high "cost" of gang membership in terms of antisocial behavior and criminal activity. These not only prevent youth from achieving to their full human potential, but gang involvement is frequently life threatening.

Youth join gangs for the same reasons other individuals join sports teams, service organizations, recreational clubs, or sororities/fraternities. Joining a group of peers provides a means of identification, belonging, and a sense of shared values. However, the benefits of membership are not as positive for youth involved in gang activity. Gang membership, unlike membership in other social organizations, submerges the individual's identity within the gang's collective identity. The gang becomes the individual's life.

In order to prevent youth from joining gangs, specific motivational factors must be identified. Teachers and parents can then provide alternative activities that will fulfill these needs. In addition to the overall need fulfillment of gangs, there are five factors that might influence an individual to join a youth gang. These factors are: (1) protection or intimidation; (2) recognition and identity; (3) financial gain; (4) excitement; and (5) family-like support.

When gangs recruit new members, these are the specific factors that they highly stress as benefits. They tell new recruits that the gang will stand by, protect, and support them at all times. Following are details of these factors that hard core recruiters use to make gang membership appear highly desirable to youth.

PROTECTION/INTIMIDATION

The first motivational factor is protection. Some youth will join a gang because they believe that the gang will be their protection from enemies. If they can help it, gang members never fight opponents alone. Members always back each other up.

Alternately, some individuals are intimidated into joining a gang. Gang recruiters often prey upon young children who are easily influenced and intimidated. Harassment, assault, and extortion are prime methods of intimidation used to coerce gang membership.

RECOGNITION/IDENTITY

The second motivational factor for joining a gang is for recognition or identity. Wannabes are usually kids who feel no sense of acceptance or belonging to any other group. Gang membership helps these youth feel like "they are somebody." They are recognized as a gang member.

Each gang has its own enforced code of conduct, colors, special dress, signs, and symbols. All gang members are required to dress in a manner that shows allegiance to the gang. Additionally, youth may perceive that gang members earn the respect or fear of others. While this recognition, or identity, may be negative, it is still a type of status that many youth have not previously experienced.

> Speaking Up!
>
> *I was nothin' before the Crips. Nothin'. Now, people know me, respect me, fear me, man. It's a real high, man.*
>
> – High school gang member

FINANCIAL GAIN

The third motivating factor is money, or financial gain. Gang members obtain a lot of money through illegal means. Typical methods of financial gain occur through extortion, burglary, weapon sales, and the sale of illegal drugs. It is not uncommon for police to find hundreds or even thousands of dollars in the possession of young gang members.

EXCITEMENT

The fourth factor is excitement. Gang members have made gang life appealing to youth by glamorizing their activities. One recruiting tactic is to describe the parties and activities that wannabes will be a part of if they join the gang. In addition, the entertainment industry has capitalized on gang life by glamorizing it in songs, music videos, and movies.

A form of rap music known as "gangster rap" promotes hostile and antisocial gang behavior. The lyrics in much of this style of music glamorize violence/murder, criminal activity, drug use, and the degradation of women. Gangster rap artists often wear gang-style clothing; flash hand signs; and show weapons, drugs, and money in their videos. These videos tend to portray gang involvement as exciting and fascinating for young people. Listening to this music and watching these music videos may excite and encourage some children into wishing to be part of a gang.

Speaking Up!

Tell kids, "don't believe the movies, don't believe the tunes, and don't buy the bulls#?@." It ain't worth it in the end.

– Incarcerated gang member
(37 years for cocaine sales)

As Russell Adams, chairman of the department of Afro American Studies at Howard University in Washington, D.C. explains (as cited in *Quad City Times,* 1993): "The kids portrayed in some of the videos [black music videos and rap programs] are poor and black, and two-thirds of the visuals in these videos are in the alleys with the graffiti—suburban white kids and even the black middle class, they still see glamour in the disaster" (p. 3T).

The criminal thrills of gang life may also become addictive to some youth. Anxiety about giving up the excitement, the identity, and the recognition that is inherent in gang membership is, for many, a compelling reason for staying in gangs. Many members sincerely believe that there are no other sources available to gratify their need for excitement other than gang activity.

Speaking Up!

I started hangin' with the GDs after I saw a drive-by shooting on TV. It looked fun to me. I wanted to do something exciting. I wanted to be like one of those guys on TV. I joined up—had to get beat in. It was pretty bad. I had broken ribs, but now I'm one of the GDs and everyone knows it. Anybody disses me now, we take care of 'em.

– "Duke Man," 17 years old

FAMILY-LIKE SUPPORT

The fifth motivational factor is for the feeling of family support. Once a wannabe has joined a gang, the gang may actually replace the child's family, thus offering a promise to deliver all of the love, loyalty, companionship, and caring that may be absent in the wannabe's biological family.

High ranking gang members use strict discipline to keep the other members in line. In effect, gang members are forced to obey rules just as children in most families are required to do so. However, there is one major difference. Most family rules are established for the benefit and safety of all the family members. Gang discipline is a practice that benefits the higher ranking members and leaders of the gang at the expense of the freedom, dignity, and safety of the lower status gang members.

SURVIVAL

Some children turn to a gang at a very young age for sheer survival. These are young children whose parents do not provide basic necessities such as food, clothing, and shelter. Gang members become surrogate parents. Young children are given the jobs lookout and courier. They are paid for their work. Many such children, even six-, seven-, or eight-years old work for a gang simply for the food and clothing that is not provided by their parents. They don't have a choice. They work to survive. They learn gang behaviors to survive.

Summary Box 1.7 lists the six main motivational factors for joining gangs.

Summary Box 1.7

Motivational Factors for Joining a Gang

- Protection or intimidation
- Recognition and identity
- Financial gain
- Excitement
- Family-like support
- Survival

Discipline Code

Law enforcement agencies have confiscated a great deal of literature created by gangs. Much of this information describes practices and expectations governing a gang member's conduct. It is a gang tradition to present a written copy of the gang codes to each new initiate.

Much of the gang literature that has been obtained has come from within the prison systems where inmate mail is monitored. While in jail, gang leaders and high ranking members organize, create, and distribute gang literature for use on the streets. Also, jailed gang members are expected to follow the same code of conduct as that which is enforced for the rest of the gang members on the streets. (**Note**: Most of the gang literature reviewed for this book was quite radical and inappropriate for reprint here. Reprinting such material might provide a convenient model for emulation by impressionable wannabes. However, interested readers could likely schedule an appointment with a local gang unit officer to review such material under supervision.)

A gang's discipline code requires members to live their lives in a particular fashion. The constitutions of all the traditional gangs specifically describe the expectations for their members. For example, associates are required to attend meetings; read and memorize the creeds, manifestoes, and codes of conduct for their gang; pay dues; and respect fellow gang members while tolerating no disrespect from rivals.

Basically all gangs demand that their members obey the orders of their superiors "no matter what." Members who do not hold rank are not allowed to question any order that is passed down from the gang's leader. Each member within the group learns the ranking order of his/her gang, and always follows the chain of command.

If members of a gang do not obey the code of conduct, violations are assessed and often brutal punishment is swiftly carried out. In gang lingo, a member is "violated," or "given a V," if the rules are broken. Punishment can range from having to pay a certain amount of money to the gang treasury to facing physical abuse at the hands of the gang leaders and/or hard core members.

Traditional gangs never digress from their written code of conduct. Their forms of punishment are formal and transcribed. Territorial gangs commonly make up their punishments as they see fit, changing the severity to match the offense of the individual. Police and medical staff in many towns have responded to assault complaints, only to find that the person injured was attacked by fellow gang members for an infraction of the rules.

Internal gang discipline is almost always ruthless and harsh. As long as gang members are thought to be beneficial and loyal to the gang, they will be protected and supported within the gang. What most gang members do not understand, however, is that they are expendable. There are always new members anxious to be recruited. If low ranking gang members die or are injured during the course of gang warfare or from gang discipline, their fellow gang members may mourn their passing, but there will always be new members to fill the positions they vacated.

Dominant Gangs Today

The dominant criminal street gangs in America today originated in Chicago and Los Angeles in the late 1950s and early 1960s. Some have developed into well-organized and highly structured groups in which rank is obtained by committing criminal acts and getting "promoted." Others are loose-knit organizations in which influence and rank

is determined merely by age and gang experience. Some of these gangs have a formal set of documents and extensive literature that must be learned by all their members, while others rely simply upon word-of-mouth to express their rules and regulations.

Each gang has specific identifiers and characteristics that are unique to that group, and all maintain their alliances through good and bad times. Following are identifiers of the dominant gangs, their characteristics and cultural behavior, and examples of how the most well-known gangs in America have grown throughout the past decades.

THE CHICAGO CONNECTION

El Rukns

Many of the gangs that are currently infesting the midwest portion of America have their roots in the Chicago, Illinois area. One of the most infamous Chicago gangs is the El Rukns (roo'-kins), and their story will explain how powerful and organized the Chicago gangs have become.

The El Rukns have been in existence in some form for the past 25 years, and at one time were one of the most sophisticated and powerful street gangs in Illinois. The original members came from a street gang of the 1950s called the "Bey Boys," run by two brothers, Ben and Kush Bey. To this day, some El

Rukns still write the word "Bey" beside their names to show respect to the group's founders.

In the late 1950s, after Kush Bey was killed, and Ben Bey went to prison, Bull Harrison took over the gang and the Bey Boys name was still used. When Harrison went to prison in 1959, Jeff Forte became the dominant force in the gang.

Forte gave the gang a new name, calling it the "Blackstone Rangers," after his address at 6536 South Blackstone in Chicago. The gang's main gathering point at that time was at 64th and Blackstone Streets. The gang came and went for the next few years, never spreading far from their original territory, and thefts and assaults were their main passion. They drew little attention to themselves so they were never taken very seriously by the police.

Within ten years, however, the Blackstone Rangers controlled the Woodlawn area of Chicago and became known as one of America's most powerful gangs. By 1969, Jeff Forte had approximately 6,000 Woodlawn youth under his control, and he gave himself the nickname "Black Prince." He then changed the gang's name to the "Almighty Black-P-Stone Nation." The Nation was comprised of a coalition of 21 of the approximately 50 Woodlawn District street gangs.

It was not uncommon for the Nation to hold meetings attended by 1,000 members. There were always 21 chairs in front of the crowd, one for each of the members who had helped Forte to organize and run the Nation. These men were given the title "the Main 21."

At the meetings, the leaders of the coalition gangs would give a report on the number of guns stockpiled, how much stolen property they had stored, and how many "Disciple" gang members had been shot or beaten. (The Disciples were the main rivals of the Nation gang throughout the early years, and still are today.) Each meeting began and ended with the slogan "Stones Run It."

In the late 1960s, Forte applied for, and was awarded, one million dollars in federal Anti-Poverty Funds, and even managed an invitation to Richard Nixon's first inaugural ball. He did not attend, but sent one of the Main 21 in his place.

In March of 1972, Forte was convicted, along with several other members of the Main 21, for defrauding one million dollars from the federal job-training program (a different million, no less!), and he was sentenced to serve five years in prison. That sentence was later reduced to six months, and he was paroled to the Milwaukee area on March 12, 1976.

The El Rukn Moorish Science Temple of America's name appeared in the media in March of 1976, coinciding with

Forte's release from prison. Forte had tried to join both this Temple and the Black Muslims, but had been turned down by both organizations because of his past gang involvement. He then created his own religious organization, the El-Pyramid Maintenance and Management Corporation, on April 14th, 1978. This organization bought the building at 3945-3959 South Drexel in Chicago, and the building was given the name the El Rukn Grand Major Temple of America, hence the current gang name, the El Rukns.

This building housed the office of Jeff Forte, meeting rooms, a television room with a large screen TV, and a kitchen and bar restaurant combination. Gang meetings were held every Friday, only now a prayer replaced the "Stones Run It" slogan.

Calling the El Rukns a street gang is really a misnomer. They are better described as an "organized crime family." They use their Moorish Temple disguise as a religious organization, and deny the claim that they are actually a gang.

The El Rukns' main source of revenue is from narcotics sales. They have a long history of violence within the black community, and crimes documented by their members include murder, rape, arson, armed robbery, extortion, and weapons violations.

In 1980, a raid conducted by the F.B.I., Chicago Police Department, and Illinois State Police revealed a plot by the El Rukns to conduct terrorist acts in order to impress Libyan leader, Muammar Khadafy. It was alleged that Forte had contacted Khadafy and was trying to negotiate a multimillion dollar deal in exchange for these terrorist acts. Forte was found guilty of plotting terrorist acts and was sentenced to 80 years in prison.

In June of 1980, the City of Chicago ordered the demolition of the El Rukn Grand Major Temple of America, which had been nicknamed "The Fort" after Forte himself.

In 1988, the State of Illinois took Forte to trial on gang activities including the ordering of a murder of a rival gang member which was committed in 1981. He was sentenced to 75 years in prison and would be more than 100 years old by the time he is eligible for parole.

El Rukns can be identified today by their red and blue colors. Their graffiti includes a pyramid with a rising star, the "all seeing eye," a samurai sword, and a five-pointed star. They represent their gang affiliation to the left, and often wear a Circle 7 medallion (which stands for the seven acts/prayers of the *Holy Koran*.)

Prison Influence

During the latter years of the 1970s, the Illinois Department of Corrections instituted an early release program. This placed many hard core, prison-educated (those who learned about their gang while incarcerated) gang members back on the streets in their home communities. During the 25 years since that time, gangs have continued to flourish in Chicago and have migrated to cities across the country. Their influence has created many problems for small communities, which are now seeking assistance from law enforcement personnel in the larger cities to combat the growing gang problem.

Many other major street gangs originated in the Chicago area, as well as the "People" and "Folk" affiliations. Some of the most notorious of these gangs are described following.

PEOPLE NATION GANGS

The gang term "People" derived from the Illinois prison system in the 1980s. It was a term used to signify specific gang affiliation inside the jail. The "Nation" is an umbrella term that encompasses a multitude of individual traditional and territorial gang sets. Even though many different gangs share the People Nation affiliation, they are still rivals of each other. Some People sets have been known to unite in times of trouble, coming to the aid of other People gangs who need assistance.

Usually the purpose of this collaboration is to fight "Folk Nation" gangs. People Nation gangs are bitter rivals of any set claiming affiliation to the "Folks."

People Nation gangs represent identifiers to the left side of the body. Their main symbol is the five-pointed star. Because of this, the number 5 is used often in their graffiti. Slogans such as "5 alive, 6 must die" show how that number is used by the gang. This means that People gang members are killing Folk members.

Some of the traditional People Nation gangs in the midwest, as identified by the Chicago Police Department, include: Vice Lords, Cobra Stones, Mickey Cobras, King Cobras, Cullerton Boys (Deuces), Insane Deuces, El Rukns (Circle 7), Gaylords, Latin Kings, Latin Brothers, Assyrian Eagles, P.R. Stones, Spanish Lords, Unknown Insanes, War Lords, Kenmore Boys, Reapers, Villa Lobos, Bishops, Jousters, Kents (Stone Kents), Latin Counts, Ghetto Brothers (GBO), Black P-Stones, and Blackstones.

Vice Lords

The largest and most powerful of the People Nation gangs is the Vice Lords. This gang originated in 1958 at the Illinois State Training School for Boys in St. Charles, Illinois (referred to as "Charlietown" by the boys sentenced there). At Hardin Cottage, where the toughest kids where housed, this gang began its long, violent history.

In 1958, several of those boys were released from St. Charles and returned to the Lawndale area of Chicago. This area was already plagued by warring Polish and Jewish street gangs. As The primary ethnic composition of Lawndale changed from white to black, fighting began between black gangs.

The once predominant black gang in that area was the Clovers. However, they were breaking up as the Vice Lords arrived. The Clovers' main rivals had been the Egyptian Cobras, who originated in the Maxwell Street District of Chicago. Later in 1958, a branch of the Egyptian Cobras was initiated in the west side ghetto called K-Town (as all the street names began with the letter K), which was very close to the Clovers' territory. They called themselves the K-Town Cobras, grew in size and power, and violently battled the Clovers.

In the fall of 1958, the Vice Lords established a small "club" and moved into the Clovers' neighborhood, which was vacated during the Clovers' decline of power. The Vice Lords' first big increase in membership came when they absorbed a gang called the El Commandos. As the Clovers became a nonentity, the Vice Lords became more powerful.

Increased pressure was being put on the Vice Lords by the Egyptian Cobras to their west, and by another gang called the Imperial Chaplins to their east. Thus, the Vice Lords had to devote time, energy, and resources to establish their territory and work on increasing their membership. To remain competitive, the Vice Lords absorbed many smaller west side "clubs" and grew in power and strength. Recruiting tactics included enticing smaller groups to join through the promise of brotherhood and power. Another method was to force members to join the Vice Lords through intimidation and violence. (These tactics are still used today in the gang's recruitment of new members.)

The Vice Lords then adopted the name the Conservative Vice Lord (or CVL) Nation, which they continue to use today. "Conservative" applies to their "reserved" manner of dress and action. CVLs want others to think that they are more sophisticated and less violent than other gangs. They wish to elevate themselves above other gangs, and feel this name projects that image.

The Vice Lords lost a great deal of their power and membership during the decade of the 1970s. Most of their leaders either went to jail or were killed in gang wars. However, during the 1980s the Vice Lords resurfaced when many of their members were released from jail back into the Chicago area. Since then, many sets have been established both in the Chicago area and throughout the midwest.

Some of the set names that comprise the Conservative Vice Lord (CVL) Nation, as identified by the Chicago Police Department, include: Unknown VLs, 4 Corner Hustlers, Cicero Insane VLs, Imperial Insane VLs, Renegade VLs, Traveling VLs, Jackson VLs, K.A.T. (Kadzia-Albany Terrible) VLs, Executioners, Undertaker VLs, 12th Street VLs, City Lords, 15th Street VLs, R.I.P. (Douglas-Ridgeway VLs), and Village VLs.

Other gang names associated with the Vice Lord Nation are the Almighty Lords of Islam Nation and the United Conservative Voters League (notice the same CVL initials, plus the appearance of a bona fide organization). Many Vice Lords falsely claim to be of the Islamic faith; some claim to be Black Muslims, as a cover-up for gang activities. Both groups will use symbols and language from that religion in their graffiti and gang literature. The *Holy Koran*, also known as the Islamic Bible, has been found in several gang house raids by police officers.

The **traditional** Vice Lord rank structure is very formal, with appointments and promotions made by the gang leader and members who have obtained rank themselves. Most of the large set leaders run their street gangs from inside Illinois prisons. On the other hand, **territorial** Vice Lord gangs may have a more relaxed leadership structure with the person with the most charisma, the "bully," or the most feared criminal as the leader.

Currently, the Vice Lords have migrated from Chicago to hundreds of smaller midwest communities. They, along with other People Nation gangs, are constantly recruiting new members and attempting to increase the power of the gang.

Latin Kings

The Latin Kings are the oldest and largest of the Hispanic street gangs from Chicago. They affiliate with the People Nation. The Latin Kings formed during the 1960s in and around two Hispanic communities in Chicago. Their original plan was to form a group maintained by ethnic boundaries. Today they do admit members from other racial groups, but remain more true to their original ethnic boundaries than the other major gangs do. Their membership is continually increasing and extending to include new members from many smaller midwest communities.

The Latin Kings' doctrine is called the "National Constitution." Each gang set may also have an individualized constitution under which they operate. Both the traditional as well as the territorial gangs' rank structure is very rigid. Appointments and promotions are made exclusively by the gang leader.

Territorial sets of the Latin Kings have been known to align themselves with territorial Vice Lord sets in some smaller midwest communities. This is possible because the Latin Kings and Vice Lords are both People Nation gangs.

FOLK NATION GANGS

The term "Folks," like People, originated in Illinois prisons in the 1980s, where it was used to signify one's gang affiliation. The main enemies of the Folk Nation gangs are any gang members who claim People Nation loyalty. There are many individual gang sets who demonstrate allegiance to the Folk Nation. Even though they are all Folk Nation affiliated gangs, they are rivals of each other under normal circumstances. However, there have been instances where rival sets of the Folk Nation aligned themselves for support, especially when that support was needed to fight a People Nation gang.

Folk Nation gangs represent their affiliation to the right side of their body. Their main symbol is the six-pointed Star of David, which makes the number 6 important to them. Folk Nation gangs will use slogans like "6 poppin' and 5 droppin'" or "6 tall Folks and 5 small People" to suggest Folk Nation gangs shooting at or killing People Nation gang members.

Some of the traditional Folk Nation gangs, as identified by the Chicago Police Department, include: Black Gangster Disciples (BGD), Black Disciples (BD), Black Gangsters (BG), Brothers of the Struggle (BOS), Ambrose, Ashland Vikings, Harrison Gents, Imperial Gangsters (White GDs), Latin Disciples (or Maniac Latin Disciples), Latin Eagles, Latin Jivers, Latin Lovers, Latin Saints, Latin Souls, Low Riders, La Raza, Insane Popes, Ridgeway Lords, Satin Disciples, Sin City Boys, Simon City Royals (also known as the Royal Disciples), Spanish Cobras, Spanish Gangster Disciples, Dragons (Latin), Black Mad Souls, Orchestra Albany, Pauline Berry Community (PBC), Braisers, Chatham BGDs, Racine Boys, Jeffrey Manor Disciples, Lun City Disciples, and Two-Six Nation (Two-Sixers).

Black Gangster Disciples

The most powerful of the Folk Nation gangs is the Black Gangster Disciples. This gang originated in Chicago in the early 1960s and were called the "Disciples." They were the main rivals of the Blackstone Rangers and the newly formed Vice Lords. (These rival gangs engaged in territorial battles throughout their early existence.) The leader of the Disciples was David Barksdale. He is credited with increasing the membership and expanding the power of the Black Gangster Disciples.

At that time, another Chicago gang, the "Supreme Disciples" were having membership problems. Their leader, Larry Hoover, also saw the need to increase membership so that they would not be eliminated by the Blackstone Rangers and/or the Vice Lords. Even though Hoover and Barksdale were enemies, their needs were similar.

Barksdale and Hoover began to meet, and eventually decided to unite the two gangs. They agreed that a coin toss would determine the gang's new name. Barksdale wanted the gang to be known as the "Black Disciple Gangsters," while Hoover liked the name the "Black Gangster Disciples." Hoover won, and the Black Gangster Disciples (BGDs) were born.

Since Barksdale's original gang was the larger of the two, it was decided that he would be the gang leader, or "King," and Hoover would be second in command. In 1974, Barksdale died from kidney failure which was the result of a gunshot wound. At his funeral, the mourning BGDs deemed him "King David," and thus the six-pointed star became their main symbol.

After Barksdale's death, Larry Hoover appointed himself the "supreme soul leader" of the Black Gangster Disciples. He fought resistance from several other members, foremost a man named Jerome "Shorty" Freeman. Freeman's original Chicago gang was the "Renegade Disciples," and he had always been loyal to David Barksdale and resented the manner in which Hoover was running the BGDs.

Several hard core members from Barksdale's original Gangsters gang pulled away from the BGDs and formed a new gang called the "Black Disciple Nation." To establish the split, Freeman removed Hoover's "Gangster" name from the gang. However, because of the original "two-king" concept, the gang's organizational structure has remained very loose knit, even today.

The pattern of the six-pointed star became the most obvious sign of distinction between the Black Gangster Disciples and the Black Disciple Nation. The star with the letter "G" in the center is for the BGDs, and that with the "D" inside stands for the Black Disciple (or BD) Nation. Both gangs' signs remain this way today.

In 1978, the "3rd World Concept" was created by the followers of Larry Hoover and Jerome Freeman in an attempt to unite the different directions the two gangs were heading. Some of David Barksdale's original ideas and concepts were included in this attempt to unite and rally the gangs. This concept involved Barksdale-Hoover-Freeman together as one, or "3 as 1," sometimes expressed as "thirty-one" (or "31"). Gang members wore three gold chains or a third world medallion. They were also issued certificates notarized by the chairman of the Board of Directors with the letter "G" in the center. But this attempt to bring the gangs together failed.

In 1985, at the Stateville Prison in Joliet, Illinois, another attempt was made to bring the Black Gangster Disciples and the Black Disciple Nation back together. Incarcerated Black Gangster Disciples developed the Brothers of the Struggle (BOS), which continues to exist in the Illinois prison system today under the leadership of incarcerated gang leader Larry Hoover. This unification attempt failed as well.

In 1986, at the Pontiac Prison in Pontiac, Illinois, a gang calling themselves the New Breed emerged. This prison gang is also a Folk Nation gang, and a set of the Black Gangster Disciples. But this group removed the word "Disciple" from the Black Gangster Disciples, similar to what Freeman did when he formed his gang. This formed yet another faction, called the "Black Gangsters." This group developed the "Gangster Concept, Laws, and Doctrines," a document which follows the gang philosophy of Larry Hoover. The Black Gangsters use the colors black and gray, rather than the original black and blue.

The **traditional** Black Gangster Disciples have a very formal leadership structure, in spite of the fact that their original leaders are still incarcerated at this time. Orders and promotions come from those with authority in prison and those with designated authority on the streets. **Territorial** Black Gangster Disciple sets try to maintain the same structure, and law enforcement officials have seen little variation from the leadership titles used by the larger, traditional gang sets.

To summarize, the Chicago-born Folk Nation faction includes the Black Gangster Disciples, Black Disciples, Black Gangsters, Brothers of the Struggle, New Breed, and 3rd World Disciples. Together they represent the largest gang membership within the Illinois Department of Corrections. Their affiliates and territorial gang sets can now be found throughout the majority of the midwest.

CALIFORNIA HISPANIC GANGS

Hispanic gangs which organized and are currently active in California were established in much the same manner as other early immigrant gangs in America. Mexican natives immigrated into southern California during the early part of the 20th century. The caucasian population regarded these immigrants as a source of cheap and unskilled labor. This attitude, combined with the political and racist views of the time, relegated the Mexican immigrants to certain barrios (neighborhoods). The population in the barrios quickly grew as more and more Mexican immigrants came to this country and preferred to live in districts where their native language was spoken and their traditions were practiced. Competition for jobs between the native Californians and the Mexican immigrants led to hatred and rivalries between the groups. Neighborhood versus neighborhood conflicts arose, and many resulted in bloodshed and even death. The accumulated prejudice and violence resulted in the formation of Hispanic gangs.

Hispanic gangs are governed by certain established traditions that today have become known as the "movidas" (rules) that Hispanic gang members live and die by. These gangs began as local neighborhood groups oriented around protection and self-preservation. But by the late 1930s and 1940s these local neighborhood groups began to solidify into what are now recognized as street gangs.

Gang rivalries became more intense and more violent as gang membership grew. Turf boundaries and rivalries that were established by the earliest Chicano gangs still exist today. Hispanic gang loyalties to turf, their barrios, are legendary. Their barrio becomes their world. Hispanic gang members retaliate violently to all challenges to their barrio. Protecting their turf from rival gang members or other intruders is an important part of life for Hispanic gang members and causes the majority of Hispanic gang violence. One turf-related problem related to education is that many such gang members will not cross turf boundaries to get to school because it is too dangerous for them to do so.

It has been reported that Hispanic gang members will remain loyal to their original barrio even if their family moves to a new neighborhood. This is a further example of how strong the bond is between a Hispanic gang member and his turf. Gang wars between rival barrios have been reported to have continued for decades.

Involvement in Hispanic gangs is generational, with many younger and older family members belonging to the same gang. Many such children grew up in the gang environment and just naturally evolved into gang members themselves. A Spanish term "carnal" or "carnalismo" is often used among Hispanic gang members, which is a friendly or affectionate term for brother/brotherhood.

Hispanic gang traditions are deeply entrenched in today's gang culture. The lifestyle of the "cholos" (male gang members) and "cholitas" (female gang members) is one of total immersion in the gang. Being a "homeboy" is not a random or part-time behavior for these individuals. Their gang identity becomes the most dominating aspect of their lives.

The "vato loco" (or "crazy life") is the goal of Hispanic gang members. They wish to be the craziest, most feared, and most fearless gang member, using whatever means necessary. Building this type of reputation gives them a higher ranking in the gang and more respect from other gang members.

California law enforcement personnel estimate that well over half of all violent crime in Los Angeles can be traced back to Hispanic street gangs. Drug use among these individuals is extensive, with PCP, marijuana, and alcohol the most popular substances.

California Hispanic gangs today all fall into one of two main factions: the Nortenos (northern California) and the Surenos (southern California). These terms are not the names of specific gangs, but simply terminology derived from the geographical area of origination of the gangs. The two factions both originated in the California prison system.

The dividing line between north and south runs horizontally in the area between San Louis Obispo and Bakersfield. Surenos and Nortenos are mortal enemies. They do not use signs and symbols the way the midwestern gangs do. Their graffiti usually includes their gang set's name, possibly identifying a particular street or neighborhood, and often the numbers "13" or "14."

Surenos use the Spanish prefix "sur," for "south," and favor the color blue. They use the number 13, which stands for the 13th letter of the alphabet, the letter "M." The letter "M" is the identifier for the Mexican Maffia, a very strong Hispanic prison gang in California. Young gang members carry the Surenos name and graffiti out on the street.

Many Surenos claim Aztec ancestry. The Aztecs were thought to be brave and respected warriors. Some dedicated Surenos gang members may study and use the ancient Aztec language.

Nortenos use the Spanish prefix "norte," for "north," and favor the color red. They use the number 14, which stands for the 14th letter of the alphabet, the letter "N." That letter is the identifier for the "Nuestra Familia" (the "Northern Structure") Hispanic prison gangs.

The major Hispanic gangs operating in California today are the Border Brothers, the 18th Street (now the largest Hispanic gang in the city of Los Angeles); the Fresno Bulldogs (or the Bulldogs); Mara Salvatrucha (or M/S); and the Sinaloan Cowboys. As more youth learn about these particular gangs, their graffiti and culture could migrate to other communities, such as those in the midwest.

BLOODS AND CRIPS

During the mid to late 1960s, the Los Angeles Police Department witnessed the birth of the most notorious street gangs in our country, the Bloods and the Crips. Both began as primarily black street gangs from the neighborhoods of south central Los Angeles. In the beginning, individuals in their twenties to early thirties joined Blood or Crip sets. Currently, wannabe members are often pre-adolescent or in their early teens.

White and Hispanic youth are still primarily excluded from traditional Crip and Blood gang sets.

The history of these two gangs is not as easy to document as the Chicago gangs. Most contend that the Crips originated at a high school in southwest Los Angeles in, or around, 1969. The Crips quickly built a violent reputation, and other loose knit black groups began to organize themselves using the Crip name.

These gangs precede the word "Crip" with their set name. The set name is usually derived from that of the neighborhood, street, or section of the city in which they live. Examples are the "Main Street Crips," the "74 Hoover Crips," or the "Rollin 60s Crips." Membership in a set was traditionally based upon residence in its neighborhood.

There is not any verified information about how the Bloods and the Crips actually decided on their names, but one story circulates about how the Crips got their name: that they liked the spooky, intimidating connotation of the word "crypt," but being largely uneducated and consequently poor spellers, these gang members called themselves Crips (rather than crypts).

It is said that the Bloods had great admiration for the African-American soldiers who were returning to their neighborhoods from the Vietnam War. The soldiers often called each other "blood"

(i.e., "relative") as a friendly greeting. Because of the great admiration they had for the veterans, the gang members began using this terminology as well.

The Bloods are the main rivals of the Crips. The first known Blood set came from West Piru Street in Compton, California, and took the name of the "Compton Pirus." The Blood gang sets formed when nonaffiliated blacks grouped together to protect themselves from the Crips, who were running rampant committing violence in their neighborhoods. These new gang sets used the Blood name along with their street, district, or neighborhood name to identify their particular set.

The Bloods and Crips are both loosely organized, and do not have the structured membership ranking system of the Chicago gangs. Those who lead the sets are those who have "bullied" their way to the top. These members' violent and ruthless reputation earned them the right to lead the gangs.

There seems to be a great deal of within-gang Crip rivalries (in other words, Crip sets fighting Crip sets). The Bloods seem to have far fewer within-gang rivalries, and spend most of their time fighting with Crip sets. Also, Crip members who have been interviewed claim that there is no Crip literature (constitutions, creeds, rules, regulations, etc.) like that which has been confiscated from the Chicago gangs.

At present, there are an estimated 300 Los Angeles-based sets who align themselves with the Bloods and the Crips. Other Crip and Blood sets have migrated across the nation and can be found in all parts of the country. When in the same geographic area, Crips align themselves with Folk Nation gangs and Bloods align themselves with the People Nation.

ASIAN GANGS

When discussing Asian gangs it is important to differentiate between the myriad of Asian cultures, which have resulted in very diverse Asian gangs. Many types of Asian gangs have been identified, including but not limited to Chinese, Japanese, Vietnamese, Korean, and Samoan. However, there is less information available about Asian gangs as compared to other traditional street gangs for two main reasons.

First, Asian gangs tend to prey upon their own people rather than people of other races and ethnicities. Because Asian immigrants often lack in trust for the American banking system, they are prime targets for gang extortion of the money and other valuables they keep in their homes. These Asian-American victims are usually not willing to report gang crimes to the authorities, either, since they typically do not trust the police force in general. Further, they often have mistrust of caucasian police officers and consequently will not

provide them with important information on gang crimes.

Second, there is simply a lack of Asian-American law enforcement personnel to gather intelligence on Asian gang activities. Asian teenagers are generally not encouraged to consider careers in police work. Because of the problems experienced historically by many Asian people with Communist governments and their associated police forces, police work is often not considered an honorable occupation in Asian families.

Some information about Asian gangs has been documented since the late 19th century when immigrants from Asian countries, particularly China, encountered ethnic prejudice, a lack of good jobs, substandard housing, few opportunities for recreational and social interactions, and a poor quality education upon arriving in this country. Much of the limited information available pertains to Chinese gangs. Drug sales (primarily heroine) and extortion are two of the main criminal activities of Chinese gangs today.

Chinese Gangs

Information about Chinese gangs dates to the latter portion of the 19th century with the immigration of large numbers of Chinese citizens to California. Segregated Chinese communities were formed there due to ethnic prejudice, differing cultural traditions, and language barriers. Religious and educational organizations, which often served as informal "social service agencies" in the late 1800s, did not provide widespread services to help the Chinese immigrants settle in and successfully adjust to life in the United States. They were left pretty much on their own to become acclimated to the new and strange customs and environment.

Tong organizations were formed by the more wealthy and powerful citizens of these Chinese communities. The original purpose of the Tong was to provide social and community support and financial assistance to Chinese families. However, some members of the Tong became involved in criminal activities such as gambling, opium dens, extortion, and prostitution.

To protect their criminal interests and to intimidate families who owed money to the Tong, "look-see boys" were recruited. The look-see boys acted as informants to the Tong leaders. In return, financial profits from their criminal activities were shared with the look-see boys.

The Immigration and Naturalization Act of 1965 allowed many more Chinese citizens to enter the United States. The great increase in the number of immigrants, in addition to the lack of social support and continued ethnic prejudice (including lack of employment and educational opportunities), resulted in an increase in criminal activities among the Chinese immigrant population. Chinese gangs were established on both the east and west coasts in California, Vancouver, New York, and Toronto.

One Chinese gang documented in California in early 1970 was called the "Wah Ching" which translates literally to "Chinese Youth." The one prerequisite for joining the gang was to have been born in Hong Kong. The Wah Ching soon developed a reputation of extreme violence and brutality which allowed them to carry out widespread extortion activities on their community businesses and citizens.

There is no standard or recognizable common dress for Chinese gang members. Some of the Wah Ching have been known to wear white T-shirts with the name of their gang on the front. Some members also have tattoos with the gang name or initials. Among some Chinese gang members, tattooing is called "branding."

Chinese gang members are predominantly young males in their late teens to early twenties. Girls will associate with the gang members but are not initiated into the gangs or allowed official membership. Like girls from other street gangs, they carry money, drugs, and weapons for their boyfriends.

Membership in Chinese gangs typically ranges from about 20-50 individuals per gang set. Since they have relatively small numbers, these gangs may recruit back-up reinforcements from other cities if conflicts with rival gangs become extreme. The Ghost Shadows and the Flying Dragons are two Chinese gangs particularly known for having memberships in numerous cities.

Chinese gangs generally have no single leader. Most Chinese gangs have two, or even up to five leaders. The Ghost Shadows are known to have four or five leaders called the "tai lou" ("big brothers"). Chinese gang leaders give orders to lower ranking members and control the gang's activities.

Ranking under the gang leaders are "lieutenants," or associate leaders. The associate leaders do not have much say in the actual administration of gang business. They follow directives from the gang leaders and control the "street soldiers" of the Chinese gangs. The Chinese name for the street soldiers is "ma jai" meaning "little horses." The ma jai are ordered by ranking members to carry out the majority of the extortion, drug sales, and other street crimes including guarding gambling places and collecting protection fees. Ma jai who commit many of the gangs' assaults may be called "shooters."

Another unique characteristic of Chinese gangs is that there may be two or more cliques within the gang who often do not like or trust the other. This is the re-sult of having more than one recognizable gang leader. It is common for these two within-gang groups to be at odds with each other over controversial matters. Because of this, there may be much internal fighting. Police intelligence shows that Chinese gang leaders are more likely to be challenged and killed by fellow gang members than rival street gang members.

Chinese Gang Recruiting and Initiation Tactics

Membership in Chinese gangs ranges from voluntary involvement to, more common today, joining because of the intimidation of or protection provided by the gang. Targets of Chinese gang recruitment are similar to those of other street gangs: isolated children and adolescents who have few friends, those who speak very little English, school drop-outs, those with too much spare time on their hands, and those who lack adequate educational and vocational skills. These youth are the most vulnerable to gangs' recruitment efforts.

Chinese gang initiations are often simplified versions of the Chinese secret societies' rituals. An initiation may include the taking of an oath, the burning of yellow paper, and drinking wine mixed with blood in the presence of the gang leaders. The oaths are often related to the traditional 36 oaths of the Chinese secret societies, while burning yellow paper is an established religious tribute to

Chinese ancestors. The physically assaultive or sexually deviant initiation activities preferred by the midwest and west coast gangs have not been evident with Chinese gangs.

Even though the membership of the Chinese gangs is relatively low in contrast with other street gangs, they are a criminal force to be reckoned with. One difference of Chinese gangs in comparison to other street gangs is that they are much better organized, and may have ongoing contacts and interactions with established community associations as well as international contacts. In fact, they may be better described as an organized crime ring than a street gang. A former captain of the New York City Police Department (as cited in Huff, 1990) relates the law enforcement interpretation of Chinese gangs:

> Chinese gangs are well-controlled and held accountable to the various associations in the Chinatown area. They are the soldiers of Oriental organized crime with strong ties to cities throughout the United States. The associations have international ties in banking, real estate, and import/export businesses and are suspected of being involved in narcotics and alien smuggling (p. 136).

Whether defined as street gangs or organized crime rings, Chinese gangs are responsible for some of the most violent and treacherous criminal activities across the nation. Law enforcement officials believe that during the 1990s Chinese criminal organizations have emerged as a significant power in gambling and racketeering activities, heroine trafficking, alien smuggling, prostitution, and money laundering.

In summary, school officials with a population of Asian students should be aware of the common characteristics of gang behavior similar to those shown by students of other races. In addition, Chinese and other Asian youth may be joining mixed-race territorial street gangs as their ethnic barriers are loosened or eliminated.

WHITE GANGS

As criminal street gangs migrate to the smaller American communities, more all-white gang sets are being documented. One of the largest, however, still has its roots in Chicago. This is an all-white gang known as the "Imperial Gangster Disciples," or IGDs.

The Imperial Gangster Disciples use all of the signs, symbols, and colors of the Black Gangster Disciples. Their main graffiti identifier is the six-pointed Star of David, sometimes with the letters "IGD" in the center. As a Folk Nation gang, they represent gang affiliation to the right side of the body, and their gang colors are the traditional blue and black. Their initiation rituals are the same as the Black Gangster Disciple sets: physical violence/beatings at the hands of gang members.

Imperial Gangster Disciple sets are a completely separate entity in Chicago. However, in smaller towns they have joined ranks with the Black Gangster Disciples. There, it is not uncommon to see black and white "Gangsters" associating together, or to see them collectively fighting with People Nation gangs, especially the Vice Lords.

Territorial white gangs are also becoming popular in small towns, suburbs, and rural communities. Since these types of locations often have a low minority representation, there are seldom enough minority youth to include when a gang is formed. In other words, primarily all-white communities are spawning all-white gangs.

These gangs often begin in schools, with a transfer student who has some knowledge of or background in a gang. Other times they begin after local youth associate in the larger cities with gang-involved kids at social events, shopping malls, or athletic competitions. In any case, the gang mentality is transported to the small town or school. Then, all the problems that are associated with youth gangs commence.

Parents and teachers who have a grasp of the main gang characteristics and ba-sic gang awareness can recognize and intervene with all-white gangs just as effectively as with gangs of mixed ethnicity. Except for the color of their skin, the gang-related behavior will be the same. Like all established gangs, criminal acts and drug trafficking are their main activities, and they can be violent and dangerous.

White Supremacist Groups

Another type of gang that operates in predominantly white areas are the white extremist, white supremacy, or "hate gangs." These gangs are based on a shared hatred of minority populations. They believe in the "superiority" of "caucasians of non-Jewish descent." Most of these groups believe that Jewish people are undermining the U.S. economy, and that African-Americans are "contaminating" the white race.

Some of the most recognized white hate groups include: Ku Klux Klan (KKK); Aryan Brotherhood; White Aryan Revolution or White Aryan Resistance (WAR); Aryan Separatist Youth Party; Northsiders; Christian Patriots Defense League; The Covenant, Sword, and the Arm of the Lord; Christian Defense League; American Nazi Party; Aryan Youth Movement; and Illinois Christian Patriots.

Like criminal street gangs, white hate gangs are recruiting young people, usually males, to join them and fight for their cause. They feast on white children who are ignorant about other races and, therefore, may be afraid of or intimidated by them.

Skinheads

"Skinheads," another form of white hate group, are also well-established in small communities across the country. They can be recognized by their shaved heads, highly polished black combat boots (often Doc Martens), dark blue denim jeans, and sweatshirts. Some will wear shirts with the country Germany displayed on the front in respect for Adolph Hitler.

The youth who are members of white hate gangs will show many of the same types of antisocial and aggressive/violent behaviors (particularly towards minorities and/or homosexuals) as individuals who belong to street gangs. Parents and teachers should look for the same warning signs of gang involvement. In addition, they also need to be aware of any "hate" propaganda materials that may turn up in the home or circulate through schools and communities.

Summary

The origins of today's street gangs stem from immigrant gangs formed more than two centuries ago. Gangs present a dilemma to communities of all sizes across the nation. They are deeply entrenched in societal inequities involving poverty, unemployment, and lack of education. In the tradition of the immigrant gangs, youth have banded together to violently seize control of "turf" and to carry out criminal activities for financial gain, regardless of the effect on the surrounding communities and citizens. Gang members demonstrate a sociopathic indifference to the severe brutality of their actions and its effects on individuals caught in the cross fire of gang warfare.

Armed with a basic knowledge of gangs and adequate preparation, youth gang activity is a problem that can be directly influenced by the two groups of adults who have the most direct influence and most contact with gang wannabes: teachers and parents.

All parents, educators, and related professionals who work in any capacity with children need to be aware of the early warning signs of gang interest or involvement. In order to most effectively prevent gang involvement or to intervene with children involved in gang activity, adults must have a working knowledge of gang motivations and formation.

Understanding the motivational factors that precipitate gang involvement is a first step in facilitating alternative and preventive programs for at-risk youth who may be lured by the gang mentality.

The history of the main American gang factions helps teachers and parents to understand how these gangs developed and how powerful they have become. Since many gang wannabes do not know the gangs' history, well-informed adults can be as "positively intimidating" as the gangs are negative and influential.

References/Resources

Arthur, R. & Erickson, E. (1992). *Gangs and schools*. Holmes Beach, FL: Learning Publications.

This book details the experiences of an educator working with gang members as a teacher, principal, and neighborhood counselor. His extensive experience provides practical insights about school and community interventions.

Gangs and Schools (ISBN #1-55691-036-3) may be ordered from Learning Publications, 5351 Gulf Drive, P.O. Box 1338, Holmes Beach, FL 34218; Phone (941) 778-6651; FAX (941) 778-6818.

Dart, R.W. (1993). *The future is here today: Street gang trends*. Chicago, IL: Gang Crime Section, Department of Police.

This publication documents current trends in street gang formation in and around the Chicago area. The early history of gangs, formation trends, gang slang, and characteristic identifiers are covered.

The Future is Here Today: Street Gang Trends may be ordered from the Gang Crime Section, City of Chicago, Department of Police, 1121 South State Street, Chicago, IL 60605; Phone (312) 746-6000.

Goldstein, A.P. (1992). *Delinquent gangs: A psychological perspective*. Champaign, IL: Research Press.

This book offers a research-based rationale that will help professionals more fully understand the youth gang phenomena. A definition and discussion of contemporary gangs are provided, as well as an interpretation of the soaring increase in gang violence. Past and present program interventions are presented along with an analysis of the psychological foundation of gang formation and behavior. Recommendations for future intervention and prevention efforts are suggested.

Delinquent Gangs: A Psychological Perspective (ISBN #0-87822-324-X) may be ordered from Research Press, 2612 North Mattis Avenue, Champaign, IL 61826; Phone (217) 352-3273; FAX (217) 352-1221.

Goldstein, A.P. & Huff, C.R. (Eds.). (1993). *The gang intervention handbook*. Champaign, IL: Research Press.

This book is an immensely useful reference manual on youth gangs. In it, Dr. Goldstein and Dr. Huff have coordinated wide-ranging contributions from a group of nationally recognized experts on youth gangs. Individual chapters were written by specialists from diverse professional fields including psychology, criminology, public policy, sociology, criminal justice, counseling and human development, special education, and law enforcement. The book provides a history of strategies used to intervene with gangs. Approaches to youth gang intervention that span both preventive and rehabilitative methods are addressed.

The Gang Intervention Handbook (ISBN #0-87822-335-5) may be ordered from Research Press, 2612 North Mattis Avenue, Champaign, IL 61826; Phone (217) 352-3273; FAX (217) 352-1221.

Huff, C.R. (1990). *Gangs in America*. Newbury Park, CA: Sage Publications.

This is an edited book of scholarly papers on the history and current status of gangs across the nation. Components of the book range from: (1) sociological and anthropological perspectives of gangs and their impact on communities, (2) gang violence, (3) the diversity of gangs, (4) assessment of the current knowledge base of gangs, and (5) public policy issues related to gangs.

Gangs in America (ISBN #0-8039-3828-4) may be ordered from Sage Publications, 2455 Teller Road, Newbury Park, CA 91320; Phone (805) 499-9774; FAX (805) 499-0871; Email: order@sagepub.com.

Kantrowitz, B. (1993, August 2). Murder and mayhem, guns and gangs: A teenage generation grows up dangerous—and scared. *Newsweek*, pp. 40-46.

This article provides a compilation of examples and statistics on teenage violence.

Metropolitan Life Insurance Company. (1993). *The Metropolitan Life survey of the American teacher*. New York: Louis Harris and Associates.

This study was based on interviews with a nationally representative sample of teachers, students, and police officers to determine their perceptions of violence in public schools.

The Metropolitan Life Survey of the American Teacher may be ordered from Louis Harris and Associates, 630 Fifth Avenue, New York, NY 10111; Phone (212) 698-9600.

National League of Cities. (1994). *School violence in America's cities*. Washington, D.C.: Author.

This study surveyed 700 communities nationwide, including urban, suburban, and rural areas to gather data on violence and its impact on schools and communities.

School Violence in America's Cities may be ordered from the National League of Cities, 1301 Pennsylvania Avenue, NW, Washington, D.C. 20004; Phone (301) 725-4299.

New York City Police Department, Fifth Precinct. (1983). *Gang intelligence information*. New York: Author.

This collection of information is not available to the general public.

Staff. (1993). *Catalog of programs and research*. Austin, TX: Texas Youth Commission, Office of Delinquency Prevention.

This publication is comprised of research-validated studies, outlines of material gathered by law enforcement personnel, summaries of community-based programs, and factual material created by the gang specialist unit of the St. Louis, Missouri Police Department for educators in the St. Louis area.

Catalog of Programs and Research may be ordered from Judy Briscoe, Director, 4900 North Lamar Boulevard, P.O. Box 4260, Austin, TX 78765; Phone (512) 483-5269; Email: prevention@tyc.state.tx.us.

Staff. (1993, September 22). Wannabes? Why suburban white kids turn to black street culture. *Quad City Times*, p. 3T.

Staff. (1986). *National crime survey*. Washington, D.C.: Center for Demographic Studies, U.S. Department of the Census, U.S. Department of Commerce.

This study was conducted to determine the number of school violence episodes inside school or on school property.

The *National Crime Survey* may be ordered from the Center for Demographic Studies, U.S. Department of the Census, U.S. Department of Commerce, Washington, D.C. 20233; Phone (301) 763-7720.

Walker, H.M., Colvin, G., & Ramsey, E. (1994). *Antisocial behavior in schools: Strategies and best practices*. Pacific Grove, CA: Brooks/Cole.

This book is a college-level text that addresses the issue of antisocial behavior in schools, as well as its prevention and remediation. Practical strategies are provided to remediate the ever increasing problem of school violence. Specific topics covered include: (1) characteristic patterns of antisocial behavior in school-age children, (2) effective interventions for antisocial behavior at school, (3) establishing a school-wide discipline plan, (4) social skills, (5) parent involvement, and (6) gangs and school safety issues.

Antisocial Behavior in Schools: Strategies and Best Practices (ISBN #0-534-25644-9) may be ordered from Brooks/Cole Publishing, 511 Forest Lodge Road, Pacific Grove, CA 93950-5098; Phone (408) 373-0728; FAX (408) 375-6414.

Identification of Youth Gang Involvement

There are a variety of observable behaviors that youth demonstrate which may be an indication of gang interest or involvement. Some of the behaviors are easy to observe and describe because they relate to visible items or details such as clothing, jewelry, haircuts, and tattoos. Other warning signs are more difficult to define qualitatively because they relate to attitudes and personality changes.

Adults who are knowledgeable about these warning signs will be able to intervene early in order to prevent more significant gang involvement. Unfortunately, many educators believe that gang awareness or gang prevention activities are most appropriate at the junior high/middle school and high school levels. This notion is becoming less and less true as gang membership rates skyrocket and the average age of gang members drops to the lower teens. Law enforcement officials report that an increasing number of children as young as seven- and eight-years old are being recruited into gangs to serve as messengers and carriers of drugs, weapons, and money for the older members. Early intervention and education programs in the **primary elementary grades** is vitally important to educate children about the dangers of gang involvement. In many communities and school districts, this educational process will be the responsibility of teachers and parents due to the lack of organized community gang intervention programs.

A Louisville, Colorado parent overheard a comment made by her son that illustrates the growing appeal of gangs to young children:

[The] six-year old was talking on the phone to a friend, trying to convince him to join the Cub Scouts. "No, Jake, it's not a club. It's a gang."

(**Source**: Staff, December 31, 1995)

This section details, for parents and teachers, the signs, colors, and symbols of the four major gang factions. Because gangs recruit members for **life**, the best way for youth to avoid the problems related to trying to gang involvement is for them to not join in the first place. Thus, adults must recognize the warning signs of gang interest and provide early intervention with the goal of preventing gang membership.

Nation and Folk Nation gangs of the midwest, and the Bloods and Crips from the west coast. All of these four gang factions have migrated to almost all parts of the country. There are many sets involved in each of these four groups, but this section concentrates on those that have proven to be the largest and most powerful. Each gang's method of representing gang allegiance is also explained.

It is important for parents and teachers to know as much as they can about the four main gang factions. This way, they cannot be intimidated or deceived by kids who think they know more. In addition, young wannabes and hard core gang members do not expect adults to know this much about the gang with which they are affiliating. Adults who are knowledgeable about gang signs will be able to suppress gang behaviors. (A "zero tolerance" policy relating to gang signs and behaviors is detailed in Section 3.) When adults are not knowledgeable about gangs, the gangs are allowed to carry out their activities unhindered.

Four Main Factions for Gang Affiliation

All of the major gangs will come under the auspices of one of the four universal gang factions. These are the People

Representing

"Representing" means that the individuals in a gang wear their gang identifiers all on one side of the body, or that gang colors are worn where they can be easily seen. Sides are defined by an imaginary vertical line drawn down the center of the body. Right or left side representation is the most important indicator for the midwest-born gangs. That is, People Nation and Folk Nation gangs specifically represent on either the left or right side of the body.

Gang members from the People Nation faction wear all of their gang symbols, colors, jewelry, and tattoos on their left side. For example, the Vice Lords and the Latin Kings are both affiliates of the People Nation. They would wear their hats tilted to the left, their earrings in their left ears, and their tattoos on their left arms.

Conversely, the Black Gangster Disciples are part of the Folk Nation, and represent all of their signs and symbols to the right side of their body. Folks represent to the right by tilting their hats to that side, as well as buckling their belts, tying bandannas, and/or rolling up one pant leg on the right side.

The style in which gang members wear their shoes can also show gang affiliation. Some members will unlace, or leave only partially laced, the shoe on their "weak side," while wearing the "strong side" shoe completely laced and tied. Members have also been known to wear gang-colored shoe laces in their strong side shoe.

Unlike the midwest-origin gangs, gangs associating with the west coast factions do not represent to a particular side of the body, but instead display their gang colors anywhere they can be easily seen. For example, the identifying colors for the Bloods is red, and for the Crips, blue. These colors may be displayed in shirts, jackets, hats, bandannas, etc.

TWO SIGNS

Gang members talk and dress in specific ways that indicate their gang affiliation, and there are a variety of fashions that gang members can use to demonstrate overt allegiance to a particular gang. However, many of the fashion fads that gangs have adopted are popular with children and adolescents in general. Plus some youth may adopt the "gang look" as a fashion statements or fad. Examples include Starter brand jackets, other types of athletic apparel, the "grunge" look, and oversized or baggy clothing (shirts and pants).

But not every individual who wears these items is a gang member! That's why police officials suggest that when looking for gang identifiers, **at least two** specific identifiers should be present **simultaneously** to indicate probable gang association. It is very important to look for combinations of identifiers, including colors, symbols, and the right/left representation that is vitally important to many gangs.

For example, an adolescent who is not in a gang might wear a red and black Chicago Bulls jacket and cap because he/she is a Bulls fan. In contrast, a Vice Lord will wear the jacket and cap because of the red and black colors. The gang member will also add other gang identifiers, such as wearing the cap cocked over to the left side, coloring the left horn of the bull on the cap black, pushing up the left sleeve of the jacket, and/or writing the numbers 22/12 somewhere on the jacket or the cap. (The 22/12 is part of the numeric alphabet code. For Vice Lords, V is the 22nd letter, and L is the 12th letter of the alphabet.)

GENERAL IDENTIFIERS

Examples of possible gang identifiers can be found from head to toe. For example, hats are usually worn tilted to the right or left. Gang colors are also displayed on the head with hair beads, barrettes, or rubber bands in assorted gang-affiliated colors.

Pony tails will often be wrapped with rubber bands of the gang's color. The right/left representation rule is adhered to with all of the various gang symbols for the midwest-origin gangs.

Many gang members wear very loosely fitted pants and oversized shirts—a look known as "saggin and baggin." This look became popular with gang members in prisons, where incarcerated gang members wore their pants very low on their hips to show gang affiliation. (This look is also very popular with children in general today.) Some gang members have related that the saggy/baggy clothing style now carries more meaning than the gangs' colors. Many gangs have reduced the wearing of their colors because it makes them easily identifiable to the police and to rival gang members. Their hand signs, and the left/right representation for the midwest-origin gangs, continues to be very important, however.

Some gang members color the inside of their pants pockets' lining to show gang loyalty. Midwest-origin gangs will then pull out the gang-colored lining and leave it hanging out on either the left or the right side. Then they are showing two gang identifiers: the color, and the left/right side representation.

West coast-influenced gang members, particularly Hispanic Blood members, may wear khaki pants and/or flannel shirts over white T-shirts. These gang members generally do not wear blue jeans.

Other gang members may wear the "new wave star." This is a scarf or bandanna in a gang color, worn under a hat, that hangs down the back. This fashion is similar to that which has been popular for quite some time with other individuals who are not associated with a gang, such as construction workers.

Haircuts may be shaved or streaked with dye in a gang color on the right or left side of the head (or eyebrows), or there may be a cut design of a gang symbol in one side of the hair such as pitchforks, arrows, stars, gang names, or nicknames. For example, Vice Lords have been observed with a gold or red streak on the left side of their head. They are also known to shave slashes or stripes in the hair or eyebrows of the left side. Gangster Disciples may add a blue streak on the right side of their hair, as well as shaving stripes or lines on the right side. Some have had the shape of a pitchfork shaved into the back, right side of their hair.

Jewelry is a popular method of showing gang loyalty. Any of the gang symbols can be made into jewelry, and many gang members demonstrate their gang allegiance through customized jewelry. For example, six-pointed stars are worn by the Gangster Disciples, and five-pointed stars are worn by the Vice Lords. Some gangs have also adopted various pieces of commercially popular jewelry. Playboy Bunny heads with straight ears are worn by the Vice Lords. The Playboy Bunny head with one ear bent over (to show disrespect to the Vice Lords) is worn by the Gangster Disciples. The Italian Horn has also been adopted by the Gangster Disciples to represent the devil's horn, which is part

of their logo. The Latin Kings have adopted the Irish Claddagh friendship ring, because it has a heart and a crown, two of their traditional gang symbols.

Earrings depicting gang symbols may be worn in either the left or the right ear. Some gang members now wear gold caps on either their right or left front tooth, engraved with gang symbols. Gang colors on beads are often worn, and "jelly" bracelets have been adopted by gang members as well. Jelly bracelets are flexible, brightly colored, "dime store" jewelry. These bracelets have been popular with many children for quite some time, and were subsequently adopted by gangs. Gang members wear combinations of these bracelets in their gang colors. Or, gang members sometimes have their symbols and/or slogans imprinted on custom-made buttons, which is another popular fad with children.

Gang members may also demonstrate gang allegiance by wearing a glove in a gang color, on either the left or the right hand. Some will also paint their fingernails gang colors. Graffiti symbols may also be drawn on the fingernails.

Summary Box 2.1 lists some clothing and other items that gang members or wannabes might wear to school to indicate their gang loyalty.

Summary Box 2.1

Gang Representing Identifiers

Look for **at least two signs** displayed **simultaneously**:

Haircuts—Shaved or streaked right or left side, or cut with significant shapes such as arrows or numbers. Right/Left eyebrows may also be partly shaved, or be streaked with dye.

Teeth—Gold caps may have gang symbols engraved on them.

Sweatshirts—Hooded sweatshirts worn under a jacket with the hood out. Hood and jacket are usually in gang colors. A sleeve pushed up on the right or the left side can indicate gang loyalty. Flannel shirts over white T-shirts are also worn by some gang members.

Buttons—Gang logos or slogans may be imprinted on them.

Jewelry—Gang symbols are made into jewelry such as a necklace, pendant, or one earring will be worn in the right or left side ear.

Pants—Rolled or pushed up on the right or left side. Some may wear blue jeans or other pants that are much too big so that they hang down low on the hips ("saggin and baggin"). These are usually worn over boxer shorts. Or, khaki pants may be worn.

Shoes (particularly "high top" basketball shoes)—Gang colors on shoes or laces. Laces tied up only on one side, or tied in an unconventional way. A shoe tongue flipped down on the left or the right side can also signify gang membership.

Hats—Worn in gang colors and/or tilted to the right or left side. Gang colors are also displayed with colored hair beads, barrettes, rubber bands, and bandannas.

Friendship Beads—Gang colors on beads. These strings of beads can be worn on clothing, shoes, in the hair, or as an earring.

Pockets—The insides of clothing pockets may be lined with gang colors. Or, bandannas in gang colors may hang out of pockets.

Tattoos—Professional or homemade tattoos showing gang colors or symbols may be worn on the right or left side of the body.

Gloves—Worn on the right or left hand, in gang colors.

Fingernails—Nails may be painted with gang colors and/or symbols on the right or left hand.

Belts—Worn buckled to the right or left side. Gang members also wear belts that are much too long and let the excess hang down on the right or left side.

ATHLETIC CLOTHING

Gangs have adopted and/or adapted many college and professional athletic teams' clothing, colors, and logos. As many schools and businesses place rigid restrictions on the wearing of gang-related clothing, by wearing popular athletic clothing gangs can represent with their colors and symbols inconspicuously. Much of this sportswear apparel is simply adopted in its commercially produced form and worn by gang members to show gang loyalty. Gangs choose athletic apparel to wear based on two main criteria. First, it must be available in their gang colors. Second, it must have symbols or letters that correspond to or can be affiliated with their gang.

For example, Black Gangster Disciples will look for apparel in black and blue colors that has symbols associated with the devil, or possibly a six-pointed object displayed on the right side of the item. The Duke Blue Devils basketball cap appears to be made to order for the Gangster Disciples. It is black and blue and has a little devil's head on the right side. Another example is the Georgetown Hoyas cap, which is also black and blue and has a bulldog on the right side with six spiky points on its collar.

Latin Kings adopted the Pittsburgh Pirates cap because it comes in their black and gold colors and has a "P" on the front, which they designate as standing for the People Nation of which they are a part.

The Vice Lords have adopted the very popular Nike Air Jordans basketball shoes because they are made in the primary Vice Lord colors of red and black.

Athletic jackets and sweatshirts from professional sports teams have also been adopted by many gangs. Some gang members wear hooded sweatshirts with a jacket over them. The color of the hood in combination with the color of the jacket represents the gang colors. The Gangster Disciples have capitalized on the Duke Blue Devils sweatshirts because of their blue color and devil logo. The Vice Lords have picked up on the Chicago Bulls jackets because of their red and black team colors. Vice Lords have also been known to wear Converse gym shoes because of the five-pointed star on their side.

Gang members will frequently personalize these items of athletic clothing by drawing or embroidering more of their gang symbols and slogans. Some clothing manufacturers and silk screeners will even custom-make gang-oriented clothing for financial profit. Gang members usually have a lot of money to spend.

Wearing a variety of athletic apparel from college and professional sports teams is more popular with gangs in the midwest than with those on the west coast. Color is important to the midwest gangs, but they are more concerned with the symbols that appear on the clothing and with right or left representation.

Midwest gang members will search for items of clothing that have identifiers relevant to their gang.

Summary Box 2.2 lists some athletic clothing items which have been adopted by gangs.

Summary Box 2.2

Sports Apparel Adopted by Youth Gangs

Proper Name/Gang Adaptation	Gang Faction/Set
Adidas shoes: Three stripes on each side; leaf pointed up	Folk Nation Gangs (specifically the Black Gangster Disciples)
Atlanta Braves: Initial "A" (used for the Almighty)	People Nation Gangs
Boston Celtics: Colors are green and white	Spanish Cobras
Charlotte Hornets: Colors are teal, black, and white	Imperial Gangsters
Charlotte Hornets: Stripes on bee; four corners on wings and feet; initials "C" and "H"	4 Corner Hustlers (Vice Lords)
Chicago Black Hawks: Colors are black and red	Vice Lords
Chicago Bulls: Colors are black and red	Vice Lords, Latin Counts, Mickey Cobras, and Cobrastones
Chicago Cubs: Initial "C"	Spanish Cobras
Cincinnati Reds: Hat is red; initial "C" can be defaced for disrespect to Crips	Bloods and 4 Corner Hustlers (they draw a "4" next to the "C" and an "H" inside the "C")
Colorado Rockies: "CR" logo	Crips and Simon City Royals (they draw a white "S" in front of the "C")

(CONTINUED)

■ *Gangs—Straight Talk, Straight Up* ■

Summary Box 2.2 (CONTINUED)

Converse shoes: Five-pointed star; . . . . . . People Nation Gangs and Vice
crescent moon   Lords

Dallas Cowboys: Five-pointed star . . . . . . People Nation Gangs

Dallas Stars (NHL): Five-pointed . . . . . . Vice Lords and People Nation
star; black, green, and gold   Gangs
uniform

Detroit Lions: Colors are silver . . . . Gangster Disciples
and royal blue

Detroit Tigers: Initial "D" (used for . . . . . . Gangster Disciples and Folk
Disciple); colors are white, black,   Nation Gangs
and orange

Georgetown: Initial "G" (used for . . . . . . Folk Nation Gangs
Gangster)

Georgetown Hoyas: Initial "G" on . . . . . . Black Gangster Disciples and
bulldog's cap; six points on dog's   Gangster Disciples
collar; colors are black, blue, and
gray

Georgia Tech: Initial "G" (used for . . . . . . Folk Nation Gangs
Gangster); colors are gold and blue

Green Bay Packers: Initial "G" . . . . Black Gangster Disciples
(used for Gangsters); colors are
green and gold

Kansas City Royals: Colors are . . . . Folk Nation Gangs
royal blue and white

Los Angeles Dodgers: Initial "D" . . . . Gangster Disciples and Crips
(used for Disciples); colors are
royal blue and white

Miami Hurricanes: Colors are . . . . People Nation Gangs and Future
orange, white, and green   Stones

(CONTINUED)

Summary Box 2.2 (CONTINUED)

Michigan: Initial "M"; colors are yellow and navy blue	Maniac Latin Disciples
Minnesota Twins: Initial "M"; colors are red, blue, and white	Maniac Latin Disciples
New York Yankees: Colors are gray, navy, and white	Gangster Disciples
Oakland A's: Initial "A" (used for Ambrose); colors are green, gold, and white	Ambrose and Spanish Cobras
Oakland Raiders: Crest has three points; the raider has his right eye covered; colors are gray and black	Black Gangster Disciples, 3rd World Disciples, Gangster Disciples, and Latin Disciples
Orlando Magic: Colors are royal blue, silver, and black	Folk Nation Gangs
Philadelphia Phillies: Five-pointed star; initial "P"; colors are red and white	People Nation Gangs and Bloods
Phoenix Suns: Initials "P" and "S"; colors are orange, blue, and red	Black Peace Stones
Pittsburgh Pirates: Initial "P"; colors are black and gold	People Nation Gangs, Latin Kings, and Piru (original Bloods)
Starter brand athletic clothing: Five-pointed star	Either People Nation Gangs or Folk Nation Gangs (Folk Nation Gangs "crack" the five-pointed star to disrespect People)
St. Louis Cardinals: Colors are red and white	Spanish Vice Lords
Tampa Bay Lightning: Colors are orange, white, and yellow	Gangster Disciples

(CONTINUED)

Summary Box 2.2 (CONTINUED)

Texas Rangers: Initial "T" . . . . People Nation Gangs
resembles an upside down
pitchfork

University of Illinois: Initials "U" . . . . . . Folk Nation Gangs
and "I" together resemble a
pitchfork

University of Indiana: Initials "U" . . . . . . Imperial Gangsters and Folk
and "I" overlapping resemble a   Nation Gangs
pitchfork

University of Texas: Logo . . . . Black Gangster Disciples
resembles a pitchfork

UNLV: Colors are red and black . . . . . . Vice Lords

White Sox: The "O" in Sox has six . . . . . Either People Nation Gangs or
points (significant to the Folks);   Folk Nation Gangs
logo has crossed canes (significant
to the Vice Lords)

(**Note:** It is interesting that so many pieces of athletic clothing are made in colors and have pertinent symbols/letters on them that are appropriate for gang use. Additionally, some teams' clothing have been distributed in locations and formats that seem unlikely. For example, St. Louis Cardinals hats have been produced and sold in a blue and white version in addition to the traditional red and white. Other teams' logos have been printed upside down and backwards! Is this simply a coincidence? Various police officers speculate that some major sports clothing corporations are catering to gangs.)

Unlike the right/left representation important to midwest gangs, gang colors, specifically red and blue, are critically important to the west coast-origin gangs. Blood gang members (red) and Crips (blue) absolutely refuse to wear any article of clothing that is their rivals' color. Some go so far as not even speaking the name of the other gang. For example, if a Crip is wounded and bleeding, he often will not say the word "bleeding." Instead, he will refer to that process as "slobbing," as Crips call Bloods "Slobs." Some Bloods will go to the extreme of not saying any word that begins with the letter "C" because Crip begins with "C," while Crips will try not to say any words that begin with the letter "B": a very difficult and complicated process indeed!

Gangs have not only adopted sports team apparel, they have also adapted the meanings of many team names or acronyms to fit their gang's mission or image. For example, in the minds of Black Gangster Disciples, Duke means "**D**isciples **U**sually **K**ill **E**verybody (or **E**nemies)." The Orlando Magic hats

have been adopted by the Vice Lords for two reasons: (1) the hat has a five-pointed star, and (2) the Vice Lord members designate the "Magic" logo on the hat as "**M**urder **A**ll **G**angsters **I**n **C**hicago." (Vice Lords and Gangster Disciples come from opposing gang nations and are rivals.)

A more complete list of gang acronyms for athletic team names is shown in Summary Box 2.3.

Summary Box 2.3
Gang Acronyms for Sports Names

Proper Name	Acronym	Gang Faction/Set
Adidas shoes	**A**ll **D**ay **I** **D**espise **A**ll **S**lobs	Crips
Boston (all teams)	**B**rothers **O**f the **S**truggle **T**aking **O**ver the Nation	Brothers of the Struggle (BOS)
British Knights	**B**lood **K**illers	Crips
Charlotte Hornets	**C**orner **H**ustlers	4 Corner Hustlers (Vice Lord Set)
Chicago Bulls	**B**loods **U**sually **L**ive **L**onger; or **B**rothers **U**nited **L**iving **L**ords **S**tyle	Bloods or Vice Lords
Chicago Bulls	**B**oy **Y**ou **L**ook **L**ike **S**tone	Black Stone Nation
Columbia Knights	**C**rip **K**iller	Bloods
Denver Broncos	Initials reversed = **B**lack **D**isciples	Black Disciples

(CONTINUED)

Summary Box 2.3 (CONTINUED)

Duke	**D**isciples **U**sually **K**ill **E**verybody . . . . (or **E**nemies); or **D**isciples **U**tilizing **K**nowledge **E**veryday	Folk Nation Gangs
FILA shoes, hats, . . . coats, etc.	**F**aith **I**n **L**ord **A**llah . . . . Members)	Vice Lords (Islamic
Georgetown Hoyas . .	**H**oover's **O**n **Y**our **As**s	Gangster Disciples
Iowa	**I** **O**nly **W**orship **A**llah . . . . Members)	Vice Lords (Islamic
Kansas City (Chiefs) . .	**KC** = **K**illing **C**rips	Bloods
Kansas City Royals . .	**R**oyals	Simon City Royals
Los Angeles Kings . . .	**K**ill **I**nglewood **N**asty **G**angsters	People Nation
Los Angeles Kings . . .	**K**ings	Latin Kings
Nike shoes	**N**igga, **I** **K**ill **E**verybody	Vice Lords
Notre Dame	**N**otorious **D**isciples	Notorious Disciples
Oakland A's	**O**rchestra **A**lbany	Orchestra Albany
Oakland Raiders . . .	**R**uthless **A**ss **I**nsane **D**isciples . . . . **R**unning **S**hit; or **R**aggedy **A**ss **I**ced **D**onuts **E**verywhere **R**unning **S**cared (used to disrespect Folks)	Either Folk Nation Gangs or People Nation Gangs
Oakland Raiders . . .	**R**emember **A**fter **I** **D**ie **E**verybody . . . **R**uns **S**cared (Folks); or **R**aggedy **A**ss **I**diotic **D**isciples **E**verywhere **R**unning **S**cared (People)	Either People Nation Gangs or Folk Nation Gangs

(CONTINUED)

Summary Box 2.3 (CONTINUED)

Orlando Magic	**M**urder **A**ll **G**angsters **I**n **C**hicago (People); **M**en **A**ssociating **W**ith **G**angsters and **I**ncoming **C**rips (Folks); or **M**aniacs and **G**angsters in **C**hicago	. . . Either People Nation Gangs or Folk Nation Gangs, and Maniac Latin Disciples
San Francisco . . . . . (any team)	**S**tone **F**reaks	. Stone Freaks, Seven Four Crips, or San Fernando Loco Crips
San Francisco Giants . .	Initials reversed = **S**uper . . . . **G**angster **F**olk	. Folk Nation Gangs
San Francisco Giants . .	Initials reversed = **F**uture . . . . . . **S**tones	. Future Stones
UNLV	Initials reversed = **V**ice **L**ord . . . . . **N**ation **U**nited	. Vice Lords

Children and Fashion Fads

Many parents experience apprehension about buying and allowing their children to wear popular athletic jackets and caps because they have been adopted by gang members. There have been documented incidents in which gang members have accosted, wounded (sometimes mortally), and stolen athletic jackets, shoes, or hats from youth. These are isolated crimes. But unfortunately, this type of assault on innocent children cannot be predicted. Thus parents must make their own individual, but informed decisions about whether to purchase and allow their children to wear these items based upon their knowledge of the level of gang activity in their area. In general, children have been able to safely wear the popular Starter jackets and other athletic team apparel. However, parents must ensure that their children wear the clothing as purchased, without adding any special signs or symbols that might indicate gang affiliation.

Gang Warning Signs

Summary Box 2.4 outlines 12 warning signs of gang involvement that have been adapted from those compiled by the Davenport, Iowa Police Department Special Operations Unit on Gang Crime (1991), each of which will be detailed

following. These warning signs have been observed in school-age children, from the early elementary grades through high school, by police officers, gang interventionists, and youth workers. Parents and teachers can use these signs to help determine if a child's unusual behavior is gang-related. One or a combination of these warning signs is usually present for every child who becomes involved with a street gang.

Summary Box 2.4

Gang Warning Signs

A child who is likely to become involved with a street gang:

- Lacks self-esteem

- Lives in a gang-oriented neighborhood

- Has relatives in a gang

- Has problems at home (is reserved, moody, abusive, etc.)

- Has problems at school (is disruptive, threatening, not performing well academically, etc.)

- Lacks recreational/leisure and vocational skills

- Wears the dress/colors and/or jewelry of a gang

- Draws gang graffiti

- Uses gang slang

- Flashes gang hand signs

- Has a gang tattoo

- Carries gang paraphernalia

LACK OF SELF-ESTEEM

A lack of self-esteem is often the common thread among all of the gang-related characteristics observed. Youth who have confidence in themselves, and who have the skills and abilities that are valued by peers and adults in their environment, will not be enticed by the gang mentality. The kids who don't have a strong family support system, who have achievement problems in school, and who have problems with peer and adult relationships are those who will look to a gang to fill the voids in their lives.

There are a variety of observable behaviors that denote lack of self-esteem in children. In the classroom, these students may make many verbal comments discounting their own abilities. When asked to name something they are good at, many will be unable or unwilling to name even one skill. They may often resist new activities because they are afraid they will fail. Thus they attempt to "save face" by refusing to try rather than trying and failing.

These students may also lack age-appropriate social skills. They may not be proficient in group interaction skills, or they might be reluctant to ask to join a group due to feelings of apprehension about being turned down by peers. It is common for students with low self-esteem to be isolated from their peer group. These students may often hang around with a younger group, or they will form relationships with others who tend to be isolates or trouble-makers.

To help combat this problem, teachers must boost the diminished sense of self-esteem many students feel by structuring classroom expectations and academic assignments for increased student success. Giving high rates of genuine positive reinforcement will also help to make school a more positive and productive environment for all students. Specific strategies teachers can use to promote the self-esteem of all students in the classroom are provided in Section 3.

LIVING IN A GANG-ORIENTED NEIGHBORHOOD

Children who show an early interest in gangs often live in neighborhoods where gangs exist. Deteriorating economic conditions produce many neighborhoods where gang activity thrives. Subsequently, children are exposed to gang life at a very early age. While originally this was a problem unique to America's larger cities, over the past decade smaller communities have begun to experience the same "rough neighborhoods."

A gang-infested neighborhood is usually effectively controlled by the gang; the gang establishes the rules/laws of the neighborhood and enforces them vigorously. Many children living in such places will feel that they have no choice but to belong to the gang in order to survive. They feel protected by being involved with the gang, and will frequently offer that security as an excuse or reason that they joined the gang in the first place. They value the unity that is created when the gang fights for their turf, and are attracted to the way in which gang members look out for each other. They are taught very early that the neighborhood belongs to the gang, and that the gang will dictate the behavior of all who live in the "hood."

Speaking Up!

I live in a bad part of the city. My ma can't get no place better for us. My dad's dead, I guess. That's what ma says. We got violence all around us everyday. Ain't nowhere I can go to get away from it. We don't got no club, no rec. center, no pool in the summer—so we hang out—we all together. It's hard, I got nowhere to go but hang out with the guys who do violence. They don't care.

– Emilio, 14 years old

One of the most effective ways that young children learn is through observation and imitation. If children are surrounded by gang activity and behavior, they too will soon behave like gang members. Many children who live in gang neighborhoods grow up as gang members because they have known no

other way of life. Often, their school is also controlled by a gang or gangs. In that case, they are surrounded by the gang 24 hours per day and there is no relief from that lifestyle. Most of such children lack appropriate role models in their environments. Consequently, they grow up idolizing and emulating the behavior of the older gang members.

Speaking Up!

Where I grew up kids steal, sell drugs, steal guns, sell guns. Most are in gangs. My mom and dad taught me not to do that. I was lucky they cared about me. I'm going to college next year. I'm going to be someone 'cause I'm getting an education. Some kids don't know anything except street violence and crime. That's what they learned when they were growing up.

– Lori, 18 years old

RELATIVES IN A GANG

Police departments are now encountering second and third generation gang members from the same family. It is becoming commonplace for children to grow up under the direct influence of gang members who are their siblings or parents. As very young children, they are introduced to the gang mentality by highly trusted individuals—fellow family members. Thus as they look up to an older member of their family, they actually revere gang behavior. In this situation, children grow up under the control and guidance of the gang itself. They have great faith and trust in their own family members and believe all that they are told pertaining to the gang.

> **Speaking Up!**
>
> *There's a family in my building—all their kids in the gang. I'm scared of them. I don't want to meet them in the hall or on the stairs. They threaten me sometimes. The whole family is like that. I guess the younger ones just do what the older ones do. Families are like that, you do what your parents and brothers and sisters do. That family—they all do bad things.*
>
> *– Jessica, 12 years old*

Police officials have heard of instances in which an older brother or sister has actually organized and/or participated in the initiation of a younger sibling into a gang. Since initiation usually requires a beating, some form of physical violence, or even deviant sexual activity, this indicates the strong loyalty to the **gang** as opposed to a family member.

> **Speaking Up!**
>
> *My older brother—he got a problem—he don't do good in school and he got in a gang. Mom says Jace is mad 'cause dad left. We ain't seen him in over two years. I know Jace is getting in trouble. My mom is worried. She worried I'll start getting in trouble, I'm not. Jace is selling rock. He's in with the VLs [Vice Lords] now. I don't want to do that. Sometimes it's hard 'cause Jace wants me to, but it makes my mom cry. I'm not gonna do it.*
>
> *– Justin, 11 years old*

The strong ties to gang life extend beyond the immediate family as well. Many times step-parents, step-siblings, aunts, uncles, and cousins who are gang members have a direct influence on a small child. Since these are often people the child spends a great deal of time with, their gang behavior is observed and frequently emulated by the child. In summary, children who grow up in families in which gang members are present are at a much greater risk of joining a gang themselves.

PROBLEMS AT HOME

Children lured by the gang mentality tend to develop a major "attitude problem" with parents, teachers, and other adults in authority. They may attempt to be physically and/or verbally aggressive, threatening, and intimidating in order to get what they want. Family rules suddenly mean nothing to them. These children also desire too much privacy. They tend to be very secretive, almost as though they are hiding out from the rest of the family. Some will stay out later than usual and/or break curfew frequently. Others will be very unwilling to tell parents where, with whom, or what they will be doing when they are out of the house. They will generally not want to introduce their friends to their parents.

Speaking Up!

My mom isn't home after school. She works 3:00–11:00 [PM] at the foundry. It's hard because I'm home alone every day. Kids try to get me to do things. I know they're wrong, some of it is gang stuff—even though they say it's not. I'm glad my mom says, "No kids in the house after school and keep the doors locked." That helps because I just tell the other kids they can't come over or my mom will ground me.

– Kylie, 13 years old

These children rebel against authority in general, and will often behave in a manner that they know will upset their parents and teachers. Parents must be constantly alert and informed as to the behavior and activities of their children. In other words, parents need to know where their children are and who they are with at all times. Open, honest, and direct communication is imperative as a means to preventing gang involvement.

PROBLEMS WITH SCHOOL

Gang members who attend school, including most wannabes and many younger hard core gang members, usually cause significant behavioral problems for teachers and administrators. They are generally disruptive in class and often challenge teachers' control. In fact, since the other students usually know who the gang members are, they will watch closely to see if their teachers or administrators show fear of, or act intimidated by, the gang members. They have come to expect the gang members to defy authority at school, and watch intently to see how the adults will handle the situation.

Real-Life Teacher Tale
The Stalemate

As a 20-year gym teacher at a big northern junior high school, I never really thought too much about gangs. People had told me there were some in our school, but they'd never bothered my class so why should I be concerned? In fact, I really thought the other teachers were overreacting.

Then one afternoon, I take a 7th grade P.E. class outdoors for flag football. You know, instead of tackle, you just pull the guy's flag off his belt and he's down, play over.

I had the kids count off by twos, with the ones on this side and the twos on that [motioning with his hands]. I then dumped the box of flags on the ground and told the ones to take the blue, and the twos the red. I figured this was pretty simple, you know.

The next thing I know about half my class is standing around and refusing to pick up any flags. I give them the order in my best military tone, and no one moves. I ask them what the problem is. This one kid says, "We don't wear blue." Another kid then tells him he can shove the red flags up his . . . . There's some words back and forth, and I realize that some of these guys are gang members and they're refusing to wear a red or blue flag. I mean, come on, who's gonna pay attention to the color of these stupid flags? They don't mean nothing. We're only gonna play for half an hour then everybody goes back inside.

By now I realize that not only are they not gonna wear the flags, they are starting to group together. Two small groups of what must have been the gang members, and then those kids who were just standing around and watching.

To show my authority, I pick up the red flags and throw them at this one group. The kids' hands never moved. They let the flags hit 'em in the chest and fall to the ground. One kid even kicks them away.

Now I'm thinking that they're taking a stand. It's me or them, and the other kids are standing by watching. I can't have them take the colors they want, or I got two teams of gang members playing each other. All the bad things I've heard

(CONTINUED)

■ *Gangs—Straight Talk, Straight Up* ■

Real-Life Teacher Tale (CONTINUED)

about gang fights and all run through my mind, and I don't wanna deal with the nonsense.

To avoid trouble, and save face, I tell them that they're all a bunch of punks and make 'em run laps around the field until the bell rings. Ya' know, these jokers would rather run till they puke than wear some stupid color. And, the kids who were just standing around not caring about the flags, they wouldn't even raise hell for having to run with them. It was amazing.

By the end of the day everyone knows about the flag deal. Some kids are laughing. I guess I don't care. It's their life.

– D.S., physical education teacher

Youth involved with gangs are usually academic underachievers with a high rate of truancy. Refusing to participate in classroom events, or simply refusing to attend school at all, are common traits among school-age gang members. Those who do attend school are usually there because their parents still exert enough control to force them to do so. Some kids do not want to deal with the consequences from their parents if they protest or are truant, so they simply attend school with no intention of paying attention or doing the required work.

LACKING RECREATIONAL/ LEISURE AND VOCATIONAL SKILLS

One of the main contributing factors that cause children and adolescents to join gangs is for the excitement they have been led to believe is part of the gang lifestyle. Gang members who recruit new associates often target children who spend a lot of time alone. Juvenile court service workers and individuals who work for youth and family service programs have reported that many children who have joined gangs said they did so because "it was something to do."

Speaking Up!

I go to school because I have to. My dad would kick my ass if I didn't. I hate it. But it's fun when me and my homies get together. When we walk the halls no one screws with us.

– High school gang member

These youth are unsupervised for long periods of time, don't know how to amuse themselves (legally), don't have the money to spend on mainstream leisure activities, and to fulfill these needs, fall into gang activity.

Part of the recruiting tactic is to describe to potential new members how much fun and excitement the gang can provide. For those kids who lack the socialization skills that most children automatically develop, the social potential hyped by the gang becomes very attractive. A promise of new friends is appealing to youth who don't have many of their own, or who have trouble making friends.

However, in deciding to join a gang for the pledge of new friends, youth overlook all of the instant enemies they make—the rival gang members! Gangs strongly support gang rivalries. Members are not allowed to associate with or be friends with rival gang members. In fact, many gangs' code of conduct requires members to associate exclusively with other members of the gang. This practice not only effectively limits their social circle, it also restricts the time members can spend with their biological families. Consequently, the gang leader's powerful and influential control over the members is enhanced.

Over time, many of these children begin to feel that they don't belong with anyone except members of their own gang.

These kids usually do not participate in sports or other extracurricular activities, do not attend or become involved with school functions, and have not developed an interest in hobbies or vocational skills. In short, many young gang members believe that they do not fit in anywhere except with the gang that recruited them.

Further, children who are at risk for gang recruitment typically are not good students. Once they become involved with gang activities, school and academic achievement take a back seat. Since most male gang members do not finish high school, their lack of a high school diploma severely limits their vocational opportunities. Consequently, these individuals find that gang "work," even though it is illegal, is the only way they believe they can make a living. The situation is reminiscent of the "no shirt, no shoes, no service" sign on many restaurant doors. In this case, it's "no education, no skills, no job."

WEARING DRESS/COLORS AND/OR JEWELRY OF A GANG

Children and adolescents who are interested in a gang will imitate the dress/colors of the gang, as discussed in detail previously. Some children may buy, or want their parents to purchase, an excessive amount of clothing in only one or two particular colors such as blue, red, black, or gold. They will exclusively choose and wear the limited colors that show affiliation with the gang.

Once youth have clothing in the gang colors, they typically associate with other kids who are also wearing the same colors. If parents notice that their children are wearing too much of a certain color combination or that they only want to wear the same colors as their friends, there is a simple test that can be tried. The parents can simply purchase one item of clothing for their children that they would probably really like. However, the item must consist mainly of the colors of the rival gang. If they refuse to wear the opposing color, parents need to confront their children with the possibility that they are affiliating with a street gang.

GANG GRAFFITI

Graffiti, or the drawing of a gang's signs and symbols, is one of the first gang warning signs youth will exhibit. Any available surface in the immediate environment can be used. Teachers should pay particular attention to notebooks, book covers, lockers, clothing, and any other material children surround themselves with during school hours. Another popular location for graffiti is in the toilet stalls in both girls' and boys' restrooms.

Teachers have recovered notes and letters passed from student to student in which gang signs and symbols were written or gang terminology was used. In particular,

teachers should look for letters of the alphabet written upside down and/or backwards, as this represents disrespectful graffiti toward a rival gang. For example, members of the Black Gangster Disciples will write upside down or backwards "V"s and "L"s on their papers to show disrespect to the Vice Lords. Students who are involved with gangs may also write their letters in that fashion on their homework assignments because they are so accustomed to writing that way when communicating with each other outside of school.

Another popular form of gang expression, often used in graffiti, is the numeric alphabet in which numbers are used in place of corresponding letters (e.g., A=1, B=2, C=3, D=4, etc.). (Often these numeric formations will look like padlock combinations.) By counting out the alphabet, the codes can be easily deciphered. Examples include: 7/4, for the "G" and the "D" of the Gangster Disciples; 22/12 for the "V" and the "L" of the Vice Lords; 3/22/12 for the "C," the "V," and the "L" of the Conservative Vice Lords; or 2/15/19 for the "B" the O, and the "S" of the Brothers of the Struggle, a Gangster Disciple affiliate.

At home, parents might simply look around their children's bedrooms to check for the presence of gang graffiti. In doing so, many parents have found posters, murals, flags, and banners all containing signs and symbols of street gangs. Police also advise parents to look inside of their children's schoolbooks and notebooks to see if gang-related drawings have eluded educators. Parents must watch for the presence of gang-oriented signs and symbols. If children think their parents will not recognize gang-related signs, they will be quite bold about writing them in obvious places about the home. Other children will be more devious and will write gang signs that may remain hidden in secret places around the house.

Summary Box 2.5 shows some examples of typical gang graffiti.

Summary Box 2.5

Gang Graffiti Examples

Vice Lords

Black Gangster Disciples

(CONTINUED)

Summary Box 2.5 (CONTINUED)

Latin Kings

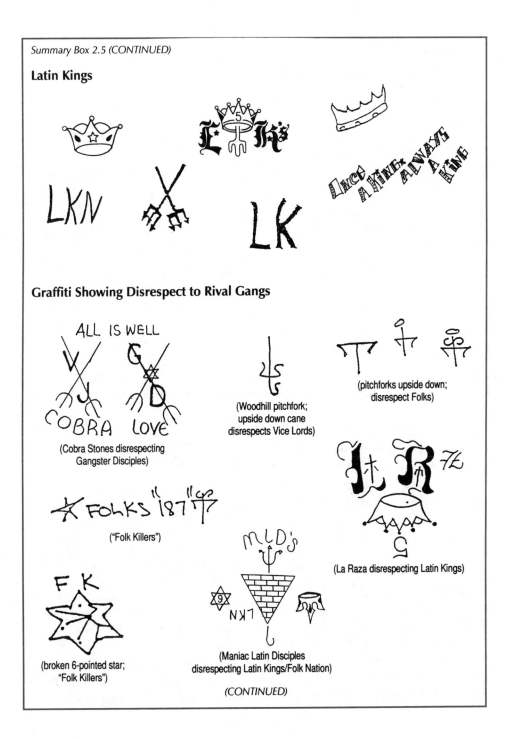

Graffiti Showing Disrespect to Rival Gangs

ALL IS WELL

COBRA LOVE

(Cobra Stones disrespecting
Gangster Disciples)

(Woodhill pitchfork;
upside down cane
disrespects Vice Lords)

(pitchforks upside down;
disrespect Folks)

FOLKS "187"

("Folk Killers")

(La Raza disrespecting Latin Kings)

F K

(broken 6-pointed star;
"Folk Killers")

(Maniac Latin Disciples
disrespecting Latin Kings/Folk Nation)

(CONTINUED)

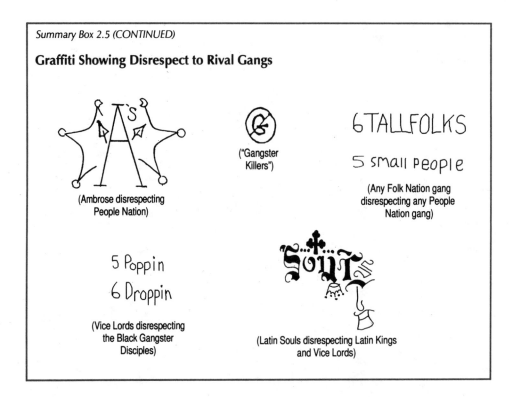

Summary Box 2.5 (CONTINUED)

Graffiti Showing Disrespect to Rival Gangs

(Ambrose disrespecting People Nation)

("Gangster Killers")

(Any Folk Nation gang disrespecting any People Nation gang)

5 Poppin
6 Droppin

(Vice Lords disrespecting the Black Gangster Disciples)

(Latin Souls disrespecting Latin Kings and Vice Lords)

GANG SLANG

Gang members have their own distinct dialect. Gang slang is used and understood by other gang members, but sounds foreign to nongang members. There are dictionary-type lists all of the jargon that police and teachers have learned have special meaning to gangs. Some of the words are specific to certain gangs, specific neighborhoods, or regional areas of the country. Since there are new words being added and deleted constantly, it is not important to maintain a dictionary of gang slang. Parents and teachers should merely listen for unique slang usage and consider it

an indicator that children who use it are being influenced by gang members who use and teach them gang slang.

Some very common examples of gang slang are words such as "trippin'" (hanging out); "hood" (neighborhood); "homies"/"homiez" (friends or fellow gang members); "dis" or "dissed" (demonstrating disrespect), "slippin'" (being caught alone by rival gang members); "5/0" (a term used for the police that originates with the old television program "Hawaii Five-0"; "Five oh" is called as a warning when police are approaching); and "packin" (has a gun). Note, however, that police caution adults **not** to try to talk to gang members in their "own language" (slang dialect), but rather to communicate in normal speech. The goal is to require gang members to deal with adults in the real world, rather than that of the gang.

Summary Box 2.6 lists some gang slang and its definitions. It is important to remember, however, that slang terms are in a constant state of change and many terms are used only by particular gangs and gang sets.

Summary Box 2.6

Gang Slang Examples

Are you straight?	Asking if you want drugs
Back up	Supporting gang members in a fight
Bangin'	Activity with gang
Barrio	Neighborhood, gang territory (Hispanic gangs)
Basehead	Crack addict
Beef	Do battle; a confrontation
B.G.	Baby Gangster
B/K	Blood Killer
Blessed in	Nonviolent initiation; reciting a prayer or oath
Blessed out	A nonviolent ceremony (rare) for quitting a gang
Bo/bow	Marijuana
Bombing	Graffiti (black gangs)
Book	To go, leave
B.O.S. order	Beat On Sight
Break	Get away

Breakdown	Shotgun
Brothers gonna work it out	Pull the trigger
Bumpin' titties	Fighting
Bum rush	Mob a person; stampede, or crash an event
Bustin'/busted	Go out shooting
Buzz	Bloods' friendly greeting to each other
Cap/popped a cap	Shoot; shoot someone in the kneecap
Clockin'	Drug dealing
CM 187	Crip murder
Colors	Logo/moniker/ primary colors of a gang
Colum	Columbian marijuana
Comin' from the pocket	Fighting with a weapon
Comin' from the shoulders	Fighting with the hands

(CONTINUED)

■ *Gangs—Straight Talk, Straight Up* ■

Summary Box 2.6 (CONTINUED)

Cop	To buy, purchase drugs	Feemer/feem . . .	Crack users
Courted	Initiation by drug use, beating, or criminal act	Firing at . . . . . someone	Throwing a punch; shooting
		5/0	Police
Crab	Derogatory name for Crips (used by Bloods)	Flashing	Using a hand signal, possibly as a challenge to a rival gang member
Crib	Apartment/home of gang member	Flying the flag . . .	Showing the colors, signs, symbols, etc. demonstrating gang allegiance/ loyalty; representing
Cuz	Short for "cousin"; implies family-like involvement among gang members; Crips' friendly greeting to each other		
		Four five	.45 caliber gun
		Gang banger	Gang member
Demonstration . .	Gang fight	Gang banging . . .	Activity with gang
Dis/dissed	Demonstrating disrespect	Gangsta/gangster .	Hard core gang member
		Gat	Gun
Double deuce . .	.22 caliber gun	Gauge	Shotgun
Down for the . . . gang	Loyalty; willing to go to blows to defend the gang	Get down	Fight
		Gladiating	Fighting
		G-ride	Stolen car
Down on	In agreement with, participating in	Gun-up	Getting ready to fight
		Head up/head . . . it up	Fighting one-on-one
Drive-by	Gang shooting	High beams on . .	High on cocaine
Drop the flag . . .	Quit a gang	Homies/homiez/ . . homeboys	Friends or fellow gang members
Deuce & deuce . .	.22 caliber gun		
Dusted	Under influence of PCP	Hood	Neighborhood, gang territory
Eight-track	2.5 grams of cocaine	In	Initiation

(CONTINUED)

■ *Gangs—Straight Talk, Straight Up* ■

Summary Box 2.6 (CONTINUED)

Jack	Hijack	Payback is a	Threat of violence
Jammed/jammin' . .	A party; also	bitch	to rival gang; act
	means a battle		of retaliation/
Jumped in	Initiated; doing a		revenge
	crime or a gang	Perico	Cocaine
	beating as initiation	Pipelead	Crack users
Jumped out	Taking a beating	Placa	Graffiti (Hispanic
	to quit the gang		gangs)
Kickin' it	Hanging out with	Play	Initiate criminal
	fellow gang		activity (Asian
	members		gangs)
Liquid juice/ . . .	PCP	Pugging	Fighting
juice		Put in work	Committing a
Lit up	Shot (with a gun)		crime for the gang
Machine	Automatic rifle	Quad	Female gang
	(AK 47; UZI)		member;
Mad dog	Stare at another		girlfriend of male
	to challenge or		member
	intimidate	Quad five	.45 caliber gun
Mad doggers . . .	Sunglasses	Quad seven	AK 47 (assault
Make a move . . .	Commit a crime		rifle)
Making bank . . .	Making money,	Queen	Female gang
	usually illegally		member; girl-
Manipulate	Commit a crime		friend of gang
Missile	Gun		member
Mushroom	Person caught in	Ride on/roll on . .	Driving to a rival
	gang crossfire		gang area to
O.G./OG	Original Gangster		attack/shoot
On the pipe . . .	Freebasing	Rock	Crack
Os	Ounce cocaine	Rock house	Drug operation
Packing/packin' . .	Gang member		base
	has a gun	Rock star	Crack users
Packing hard . . .	Carrying a gun	Roll-by	Drive-by shooting
core		Rollin'	Drug dealing
		Roscoe	Hand gun

(CONTINUED)

■ *Gangs—Straight Talk, Straight Up* ■

Summary Box 2.6 (CONTINUED)

Rush	Attack	Swag	Bogus drugs

Servin'/serving . .
   weight
	Selling drugs	Take out of . . . .
		   the box
			Kill someone

Sets	Individual groups of a gang	Talking head	Arguing
		T.G.	Tiny Gangster
Sexed in	Sex as initiation (for a female gang member)	Throw down	Fight
		Throwing a sign . .	Hand signal as a direct challenge, group-to-group or one-on-one
Sexed out	Sexual acts as a ritual for quitting a gang	Tray eight	.38 caliber gun
Shank	Jail/prison knife	Trippin'	Hanging out
Sherm	PCP	Venge	Revenge
Shermans	Marijuana; usually containing PCP	Violated/"V"ed . .	Beating by gang members as a punishment or to get out of a gang
Shermed	High on PCP		
Slangin'	Selling drugs	Violation	Breaking the laws/rules of a gang
Slippin'	Being caught alone by rival gang members		
		Wack	PCP; also crazy
Slob	Derogatory name for Bloods (used by Crips)	Wacked	High on PCP
		Water	PCP
		Wilding	Group attack on an innocent passerby, for "fun"
Smoke	Shoot someone with a gun		
Squab	Fight		
Strapped	Armed with a gun	You got four . . . . feet?	Want to fight?
Strawberry	A prostitute for drugs		

GANG HAND SIGNS

Gang members have also adopted their own form of sign language, sometimes referred to as "flagging." Hand signs can be used for three purposes. First, they can be "flashed" as a sign of allegiance to one's own gang. Second, hand signs are given to announce a specific gang's presence in an area. Third, they can also be used to show disrespect to or challenge a rival gang.

Gang hand signs are made by forming letters or numbers with the fingers to depict a gang's initials, numbers, or symbols. Hand signs are "thrown up," or pointed skyward, to show allegiance. They are "thrown down," or pointing down/used upside down, to show disrespect. Summary Box 2.7 depicts some common gang hand signs.

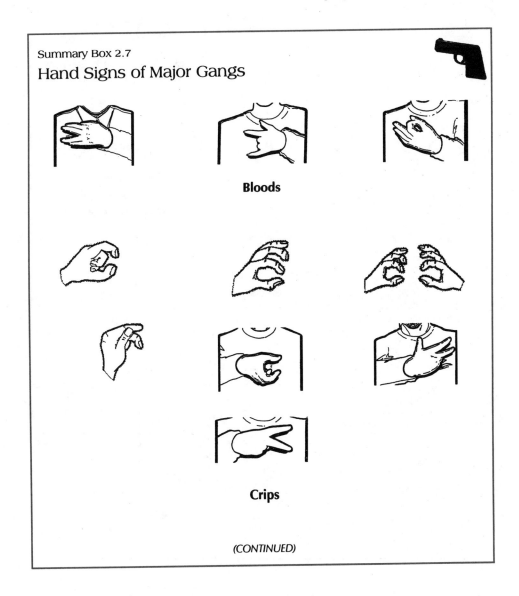

Summary Box 2.7
Hand Signs of Major Gangs

Bloods

Crips

(CONTINUED)

(when finished
shaking hands)

(one finger over the heart shows respect and loyalty to all People Nation
gangs, while Folk Nation gangs place
two fingers over their heart)

(fingers represent
the V and L)

(signifies 5; allegiance to all
People Nation gangs)

(right arm over left shows
People Nation gang membership)

Vice Lords

(**Note:** Although both Vice Lords and Latin Kings represent to the left, right handed gang members will often
throw hand signs with their right hand.)

(fingers pointing up represent
the 3 points of a crown)

Latin Kings

(white power)

White Supremacists

(CONTINUED)

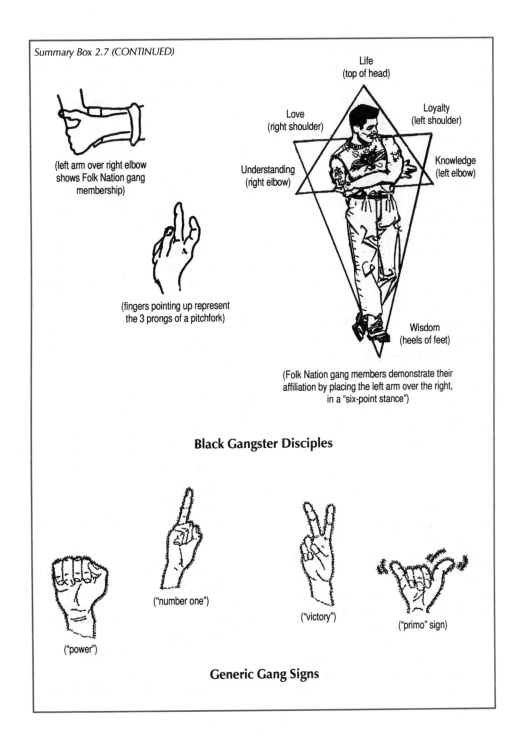

Summary Box 2.7 (CONTINUED)

(left arm over right elbow shows Folk Nation gang membership)

(fingers pointing up represent the 3 prongs of a pitchfork)

Life (top of head)

Love (right shoulder)

Loyalty (left shoulder)

Understanding (right elbow)

Knowledge (left elbow)

Wisdom (heels of feet)

(Folk Nation gang members demonstrate their affiliation by placing the left arm over the right, in a "six-point stance")

Black Gangster Disciples

("power")

("number one")

("victory")

("primo" sign)

Generic Gang Signs

Police officers providing security at teen social events have reported fights breaking out because of the exchange of hand signs between rival gang members. Throwing down hand signs has been a prelude to gang fights, shootings, and even murders.

Another danger encountered by youth using gang hand signs is when a gang member displays them in a manner called "false flagging." This occurs when gang members use a rival gang's hand sign in a crowd of people to see if they will get the same sign in return. When the sign is returned, the gang members then know that any individuals returning the sign are actually rival gang members who think they have identified themselves to a fellow gang member. False flagging has led to violence after rival gang members have unknowingly been lured into identifying themselves to their enemies.

Teachers and parents should watch the hands of children when they are with them in a setting where other kids are present, especially in and around schools. Gang hand signs are fairly easy to notice, and always signify communication between those using them. Like graffiti, it is not as important to know what the hand signs stand for as it is to know that they signify gang affiliation.

Many schools and teen centers have banned the use of hand signs on their premises. Those who are caught using them are required to leave. School administrators and teachers must make the use of gang hand signs an infraction of school rules as part of the zero tolerance policy on gangs (outlined in Section 3).

GANG TATTOOS

Gang tattoos are becoming increasingly popular because gang members see them as representative of their life-long commitment to the gang. Tattoos are permanent. Therefore, when a person decides to get a tattoo that signifies gang affiliation, he/she is promising to be a loyal gang member for life.

Gang tattoos are usually comprised of the same signs and symbols as those found in gang graffiti. Gang names, slogans, insignias, and initials are some of the most common tattoo patterns. The side of the body on which the tattoo is located is also considered to be as important at the design itself. People Nation (left side) and Folk Nation (right side) gang members will have their tattoos placed only on the side of the body that they represent with.

Some of the gang tattoos being sported by members today come from tattoo parlors and are professionally done. Traditional, hard core gang members usually have enough money from the crimes they commit to afford the best. Home-made tattoos, however, are often the variety that younger gang members and wannabes must settle for. These are often made with red-hot coat hangers, or other pieces of metal, bent to the desired pattern. This process is similar to the branding of cattle.

Another method used by gang members are tattoos made with India ink and a sewing needle or pin. In this method a design is drawn on the skin (with a ball point pen), the skin is punctured along the design line with the needle, the needle is dipped in the India ink, and then the ink-covered needle is reinserted in the previously made puncture, and so on along all the lines of the design. The closer the punctures, the more distinct the lines of the tattoo. India ink under the skin is permanent.

The least permanent form of tattooing, but one often used by gang wannabes, is to simply write the design on the skin with an ink pen or magic marker.

GANG PARAPHERNALIA

The final warning sign relates to gang paraphernalia. Certain items have been characterized as being related to gang activity. Some are stereotyped, such as pagers, portable phones, and colored bandannas. Others are articles that should cause concern if found on any child, such as alcohol, drugs, large amounts of cash, or any type of weapon. Adults should not be quick to label a young person a gang member simply because he/she has these items

in his/her possession. Possession of such items should, however, cause parents and teachers to become concerned, and to begin looking for other signs that might indicate gang influence in the child's life.

Specific Gang Identifiers

Described following are common identifiers used by the major gangs. The graffiti used by the midwest-origin gangs is recorded, along with its meanings, in these gangs' original literature. This graffiti will not change. However, territorial gang sets may adapt their graffiti symbols to better fit the mission of the particular gang set. (If the territorial gang members ever joined the more highly organized traditional gang, they would be expected to drop their previous symbols and adopt those of the traditional gang.) It isn't really important for adults to know the exact meanings of the symbols. It is important that they recognize the graffiti as gang-related and then follow the read, **record**, **remove** policy detailed in Section 1.

CRIP AND BLOOD IDENTIFIERS

Crips use the color blue as their main identifier. In athletic clothing they prefer Colorado Rockies teamwear, because the letters "CR" appear in the team's logo. They also like the Los Angeles Dodgers due to the fact that the Crips originated in L.A. and the jackets are predominately blue. British Knights apparel, especially the athletic shoes, are popular for the "BK" emblem which Crips interpret as "Blood Killer."

The Bloods use the color red as their main identifier. In sportswear they prefer the Cincinnati Reds, the Philadelphia Phillies, and the Kansas City Chiefs, as all of these jackets are primarily red in color. The Bloods' interpretation of the Kansas City ("KC") logo is that it stands for "Killing Crips."

Both the Bloods' and the Crips' graffiti tends to be very basic and unique to each gang set. They do not use signs or symbols in graffiti the way the midwest-origin gangs do. They simply write their set name before the word "Bloods" or "Crips." Examples include Outlaw Bloods, West Side Piru Bloods, Avalon Gangster Crips, or 60s Crips.

VICE LORD IDENTIFIERS

As a People Nation gang, the Vice Lords represent their gang affiliation to the left side of their body. The primary colors of the traditional Vice Lord street gangs are black and red. Some still use the gang's original colors of black and gold. Territorial Vice Lord sets will sometimes choose different colors, using yellow, orange, or any one of the warmer tones of color along with the standard black.

Summary Box 2.8 summarizes gang identifiers and graffiti that can be used to classify Vice Lord gang members.

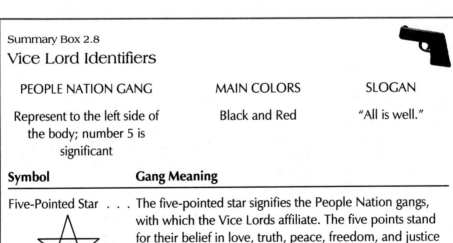

Summary Box 2.8
Vice Lord Identifiers

PEOPLE NATION GANG	MAIN COLORS	SLOGAN
Represent to the left side of the body; number 5 is significant	Black and Red	"All is well."

Symbol	Gang Meaning
Five-Pointed Star . . .	The five-pointed star signifies the People Nation gangs, with which the Vice Lords affiliate. The five points stand for their belief in love, truth, peace, freedom, and justice (within their own gang).

(CONTINUED)

Summary Box 2.8 (CONTINUED)

Bunny . . . . The Playboy Bunny with straight ears represents the awareness and quickness of Vice Lords.

Top Hat . . . . . . The top hat represents shelter for the Vice Lords.

Crescent Moon . . . . The crescent moon represents the splitting of the Black Nation into two halves, the east and the west.

Pyramid . . . . The pyramid stands for the mystery of the construction of the Great Pyramid, which was constructed by black people. The points represent mental, physical, and spiritual strength. The 21 bricks stand for the 21 days of celebration described in the *Holy Koran* (the Islamic Bible).

Champagne Glass . . . The champagne glass (also drawn as a martini glass) represents celebration and class in the Vice Lord Nation.

(CONTINUED)

■ *Gangs—Straight Talk, Straight Up* ■

Summary Box 2.8 (CONTINUED)

Staff or Cane . . . . .   The cane stands for strength in the Vice Lord Nation.
Often they will draw a cane through a top hat, which
means that Vice Lords control the area. (See the previous
illustration of the top hat.)

Circle Seven . . . . .   The circle seven stands for the seven acts/prayers of the
Holy Koran. The circle is the 360° of knowledge that black
people once ruled the world and will rule the world
again. The sun represents the rising of truth in the Black
Nation.

BLACK GANGSTER DISCIPLE IDENTIFIERS

As a Folk Nation gang, the Black
Gangster Disciples represent their gang
affiliation to the right side of their body.
The original colors of the traditional
Black Gangster Disciples are black and
blue. Most of their territorial affiliates
continue to use these colors. However,
gray and white may sometimes be used
with the main color black. Colors that
suggest cooler tones or hues such as
shades of blue or purple are also preferred. Since each gang set may adopt
their own choice of colors, parents and
teachers should be alert for any likely
combination.

The graffiti used by the Black Gangster
Disciples consists of many symbols that
are associated with the Devil. However,
it is important to note that this gang is
not cult-oriented.

Summary Box 2.9 summarizes gang
identifiers and graffiti that can be used to
classify Black Gangster Disciple members.

Summary Box 2.9
Black Gangster Disciple Identifiers

FOLK NATION GANG	MAIN COLORS	SLOGAN
Represent to the right side of the body; number 6 is significant	Black and Blue	"All is one."

Symbol	Gang Meaning
Star of David . . . . . 	The six-pointed Star of David was chosen for their late leader, David Barksdale. Each point stands for a concept: life of the Disciple Nation; love for the Nation; loyalty to the Nation; wisdom for leadership; knowledge for progress; and direction and understanding of all things and all members of the Nation.
Crown . . . . 	The crown represents leadership and acknowledgment of the Chairmen (King Hoover, King Shorty, and King David).
Signs of the Devil . . . 	The heart stands for the love they have for the Nation, the Devil's horns represent the Disciples' determination to overcome all obstacles, the pitchfork stands for the Nation's power to overcome oppression, and the Devil's tail represents the oppression that they believe all non-white people suffer.

(CONTINUED)

Summary Box 2.9 (CONTINUED)

Flame . . . . The flame stands for eternal life for the Disciple Nation.

Bunny . . . . The Playboy Bunny with one ear bent over shows
                       disrespect of the Vice Lords.

Sword . . . . The sword stands for life and death within the Nation and
                       the struggle to survive at all costs.

LATIN KING IDENTIFIERS

As a People Nation gang, the Latin Kings represent their gang affiliation to the left side of their body. Their colors are black and gold, and they use a five-pointed star predominately in their graffiti. The most favored graffiti symbol of the Latin Kings is the profile of a king, similar to that found on a deck of playing cards.

Latin King graffiti, like that of other Hispanic gangs, is very detailed and artistic when compared to the graffiti of the other gangs.

Summary Box 2.10 summarizes gang identifiers and graffiti that can be used to classify Latin King members.

Summary Box 2.10
Latin King Identifiers

PEOPLE NATION GANG	MAIN COLORS	SLOGAN
Represent to the left side of the body; number 5 is significant	Black and Gold	"Once a king, always a king."

Symbol	Gang Meaning
Five-Pointed Star . . .	The five-pointed star also represents the Latin Kings, and their affiliates. The five points stand for love, truth, justice, freedom, and peace (within their own gang).

Bunny	The Playboy Bunny with straight ears means the Kings are classy and fond of the ladies. This symbol appeals to their macho image.

Five-Pointed . . . . . Crown	The five-pointed crown stands for shelter in the Latin King Nation. The five points represent love, honor, obedience, righteousness, and sacrifice.

(CONTINUED)

■ *Gangs—Straight Talk, Straight Up* ■

Summary Box 2.10 (CONTINUED)

King's Head . . . . . . The profile of a king is a figurehead that represents the
gang as a whole.

Staff or Crane . . . . . The cane stands for strength and support of one another.

Cross . . . . The cross is a sign of their devotion to the gang; just as
others might be devoted to a religion.

WHITE SUPREMACIST/SKINHEAD IDENTIFIERS

White neo-Nazis and "hate groups," as described in Section 1, use easily recognizable symbols such as the swastika, KKK, "white power," etc.

Summary Box 2.11 summarizes gang identifiers and graffiti that can be used to classify white supremacist group members.

Summary Box 2.11

White Supremacist/Skinhead Identifiers

WHITE POWER

88

("H" is the 8th letter of
the alphabet; signifies
"Heil Hitler")

SKINS

W·A·R

Documentation of Gang Activity

Educators and law enforcement personnel would benefit by forming collaborative partnerships to share information about gangs. This practice is one strategy that helps to stem the rising tide of youth gang activity in schools and communities. Police officers who specialize in youth gang crime are able to help school personnel to identify gang graffiti/activities, and to establish a gang documentation system.

As gang activity has become epidemic, law enforcement personnel in larger cities have developed methods for collecting data on gangs, documenting levels of gang involvement, and keeping records on gang members and gang crime. Huff and McBride (cited in Goldstein & Huff, 1993) describe several such systems that track gang activity. These systems are computer-based, and may be accessed by law enforcement and probation personnel across the country.

The Los Angeles County Sheriff's Department implemented the Gang Reporting, Evaluation, And Tracking (GREAT) System procedure in the mid-1980s. It is one of the premier gang tracking systems in the country. This computerized database maintains files on more than 100,000 gang members,

color mug shots, fingerprints, and other pertinent information. Up to 150 bits of intelligence can be filed on each gang member documented. Information from GREAT has been particularly beneficial for tracking gang members as they migrate from the Los Angeles area to other regions.

DRUG TRAK

Drug Trak is a computerized, data-based system used to track gang members and gang activity in many parts of the nation. Many states have adopted Drug Trak's program in order to document criminal street gang members and share intelligence information with other law enforcement agencies in their immediate area.

For example, the state of Iowa uses Drug Trak to substantiate its charge of Criminal Gang Participation, a felony in that state. Being in a gang is not a crime there, but committing criminal acts as a gang member is. Iowa's gang charge has been challenged all the way to the State Supreme Court and has been upheld.

The bi-state area known as the Quad Cities, located on the Mississippi River between Iowa and Illinois (Davenport and Bettendorf in Iowa, and Rock Island and Moline in Illinois), recently established a criteria method, used with the Drug Trak system, to classify and document gang activity in their area. In their system, various gang-related activities are coded with a numerical point value. For example:

- Self-admission of gang membership = 9 points

- Flashing gang hand signs = 3 points

- Wearing a gang haircut or gang-related tattoos = 4 points

- Wearing gang colors, clothing, or jewelry = 3 points

Summary Box 2.12 lists all of the gang-related activities and the corresponding points assigned in the Quad Cities' criteria method. Law enforcement personnel will enter names, gang-related behaviors, and points into their own in-house computer files as they are observed. Once entered into Drug Trak, all of the Quad Cities' police departments can obtain and share that information.

Summary Box 2.12

Point System for Drug Trak

- Self-admission (**9 points**)

- Information from expert witnesses, citizens, and/or relatives (**6 points**)

- Possession of gang literature (**6 points**)

- Information from known gang affiliates or rival gang members (**5 points**)

- Gang tattoos, talk, haircuts, symbols (**6 points**)

- Admission of former membership with continued association (**6 points**)

- Photographs indicating gang association (**4 points**)

- Jail or prison correspondence identifying self as a gang member (**8 points**)

- Request at incarceration to be placed with a specific gang (**5 points**)

- Flashing gang hand signs (**3 points**)

- Observed/arrested for placing graffiti (**3 points**)

- Association with gang members (**4 points**)

- Wearing gang colors, clothing, jewelry, etc. (**3 points**)

When an individual accumulates a score of ten or more points, he/she is placed in the Drug Trak system as an active gang member. As can be determined by the point system depicted in Summary Box 2.12, no one can be classified as an active gang member on the basis of just one criterion. Two or more infractions are required before this ten-point system is activated. (Once entered, the individual retains the active gang member status until he/she is free of documented gang activity for two years.) This way, individual gang profiles can be created from Drug Trak documentation and then used in court to substantiate Criminal Gang Participation felony charges.

This system has proven to be so successful that the Iowa Department of Criminal Investigation has adopted it for state-wide gang intelligence gathering and the classification of gang membership. The computerized database will also assist researchers in determining statistics on gang membership and gang crime. Previously, the recording of gang member information and gang crime statistics has been difficult due to the lack of a consistent and widely used data collection procedure.

Summary Box 2.13 summarizes the Drug Trak procedures used state-wide in Iowa.

Summary Box 2.13
Drug Trak System Procedures

- The purpose of the system is to substantiate Iowa's Criminal Gang Participation felony charge.

- The "ten-point system" allows law enforcement personnel to classify active gang members, as follows:

  - Criteria statements are assigned a numerical value to be used in every incident in which a potential gang member is contacted.

  - One or any number of the criteria statements may apply to each contact situation. Then the accumulated value is totaled.

  - Once a person obtains a score of ten, he/she will be placed into the system as an active gang member. At that time, the Criminal Gang Participation charge may be filed when appropriate.

  - The individual will retain the active gang member status until he/she has two years free of documented gang activity.

- The incidents recorded in the Drug Trak system can be used in court to substantiate the charge of Criminal Gang Participation.

Summary

The school environment offers a "captive audience" for gang members. They can recruit, intimidate, harass, and physically threaten students. Additionally, some young gang members have contact with each other only during the school day because they are too young to drive to other locations. In such cases, gang meetings, initiations, missions (gang activity, usually criminal), and the exchange of gang literature takes place within the school building or on or near the school grounds. The environment at a school where the staff is uneducated about gang-related behavior allows the gang mentality to flourish. This in turn creates significant problems for teachers and administrators who are not aware that gang members are a part of their student population and that the problems the school is experiencing are probably gang-related.

Teachers and parents can learn to recognize gang members through awareness of the early warning signs of gang influence and a knowledge of gang representing techniques. One cannot deal with a problem if one cannot recognize it. Thus, teachers and parents must understand how and why youth become gang members if they are to be prevented from joining. It is also very important to remember that gang members show their affiliation continuously. Knowing gang hand signs, colors, dress, and symbols, and the manner in which they are displayed, helps teachers and parents to identify gang influence.

When gang influence is detected early, parents and teachers have an opportunity to positively impact students who are being lured by the gang mentality. Parents and teachers can effectively curb the rising numbers of gang members in this country by eliminating the supply of wannabes. The goal is to make kids "**don't** wannabe" in a gang.

Deterring kids from joining gangs will cut off the supply of children to the hard core gang recruiters. When this is the case, effective law enforcement and judicial processes can effectively prosecute the adults involved in the gangs. Obviously, documentation of gang behavior, through computerized systems currently being employed by the nation's police departments, is also vital if efforts to control and eliminate gang problems are to be successful.

References/Resources

Goldstein, A.P. & Huff, C.R. (Eds.). (1993). *The gang intervention handbook*. Champaign, IL: Research Press.

> This book is an immensely useful reference manual on youth gangs. In it, Dr. Goldstein and Dr. Huff have coordinated wide-ranging contributions from a group of nationally recognized experts on youth gangs. Individual chapters were written by specialists from diverse professional fields including psychology, criminology, public policy, sociology, criminal justice, counseling and human development, special education, and law enforcement. The book provides a history of strategies used to intervene with gangs. Approaches to youth gang intervention that span both preventive and rehabilitative methods are addressed.

> *The Gang Intervention Handbook* (ISBN #0-87822-335-5) may be ordered from Research Press, 2612 North Mattis Avenue, Champaign, IL 61826; Phone (217) 352-3273; FAX (217) 352-1221.

Staff. (1995, December 31). Talk of the town. *Sunday Camera*, p. 1-D.

Staff. (1991). *Gangs and special group awareness*. Springfield, IL: Illinois Department of Corrections Training Academy.

> This is a textbook provided to prison guards in the Illinois Department of Corrections (IDOC). It is not available to the general public.

Staff. (1991). *Gang warning signs*. Davenport, IA: Davenport Police Department, Special Operations Unit on Gang Crime.

> This information was compiled for educators and community members about gangs in that area, but is no longer available.

Controlling Gang Activity at School: Prevention and Intervention

This section provides step-by-step proactive management procedures that can be used to defuse a gang problem in a school and to redirect the problem behaviors into more socially appropriate channels. The main aspects of this intervention effort include: (1) administrative steps in promoting anti-gang policies school-wide; (2) establishing a positive classroom climate, including techniques for use in the classroom with students who are antisocial, hostile, and aggressive; (3) collaboration with parents; and (4) community-based options. Throughout, positive behavior management and teaching procedures are stressed rather than the more traditionally accepted punitive procedures commonly used in schools.

Assessing a Gang Problem

When gang behaviors begin to occur in a school, it is common for the school's administrators to experience a denial stage. The administrators may simply be unfamiliar with the signs of gang activity, or they may feel powerless to address such a potentially volatile problem. Another factor may be that school administrators are acutely aware of conduct or behavioral problems that are referred to the office for assistance. However, they may not be apprised of the quantity or the quality of the problems teachers handle on their own without making an office referral.

To most accurately assess a potential gang problem in a school, the administrators should survey both the teachers and the students to determine exactly where, when, and what types of gang-related problems are occurring. Incidentally, students often know more about what is happening in the school, behavior-wise, than the teachers and administrators combined. It is best to survey students anonymously and to protect the confidentiality of their responses. Students will probably be more honest and forthright if they know that the information they provide cannot be traced back to them.

Following is a copy of the "Gang Assessment Tool" (1992). This survey is useful in helping both schools and community agencies realistically measure gang activity in their area. It has been slightly adapted for use by both teachers and students. However, in order for the "Gang Assessment Tool" to be used effectively, those who answer the questions must be somewhat knowledgeable as well as honest about the gang characteristics and related activities displayed in and around their school.

To use the tool, read the questions and tally the points assigned for each question "Yes." To score the "Gang Assessment Tool," total all of the point values of the questions answered "Yes," and refer to the rating scale at the bottom of the page. The total score indicates the probability of a gang problem at the school.

The National School Safety Center, located at Pepperdine University, can be contacted for additional information about a school safety audit or assessment. They offer a continuum of services to promote safety in schools. The address is:

National School Safety Center
c/o Pepperdine University
4165 Thousand Oaks Boulevard
Suite 290
West Lake Village, CA 91326
(805) 373-9977
FAX (805) 373-9277

Gang Assessment Tool

(Developed by the National School Safety Center)

	Points	Circle Yes	No	If **Yes**, Enter Points Here
1. Do you have graffiti on or near your campus?	5	✓	✓	_____
2. Do you have crossed out graffiti on or near your campus?	10	✓	✓	_____
3. Do students wear colors, jewelry, clothing, flash hand signs, or display other behaviors that may be gang-related?	10	✓	✓	_____
4. Are drugs available in or near your school?	5	✓	✓	_____
5. Has there been a significant increase in the number of physical confrontations/stare downs within the past 12 months in or near your school?	5	✓	✓	_____
6. Is there an increasing presence of weapons in your community?	10	✓	✓	_____
7. Are beepers, pagers, or cellular phones used by students?	10	✓	✓	_____
8. Have you had a drive-by shooting at or near your school?	15	✓	✓	_____
9. Have you had a "show-by" display of weapons at or near your school?	10	✓	✓	_____

(CONTINUED)

Gang Assessment Tool (CONTINUED)

		Points	Circle Yes	No	If **Yes**, Enter Points Here
10.	Is the truancy rate at your school increasing?	5	✓	✓	_____
11.	Are there increasing numbers of racial incidents occurring in your school or community?	5	✓	✓	_____
12.	Is there a history of gangs in your community?	10	✓	✓	_____
13.	Is there an increasing presence of "informal social groups" with unusual names like "the Woodland Heights Posse," "Rip Off and Rule," "the Hit Squad," or "Kappa Phi Nasty"?	15	✓	✓	_____

TOTAL POINTS . . . .   _____

Rating Scale

0-15   Points . . . . No significant gang problem exists.

20-40   Points . . . . An emerging gang problem is evident.

45-60   Points . . . . A significant gang problem is evident. A gang prevention and intervention plan should be developed.

65+   Points . . . . An acute gang problem is evident. This level of problem merits a total gang prevention, intervention, and suppression program.

Establishing a School-Wide Anti-Gang Policy

School administrators often take ownership of and responsibility for a school's gang problem only after it has reached crisis proportions, when they can no longer ignore or deny the problem. Unfortunately, this gives the gang time to put down roots and become established in the school environment.

> **Speaking Up!**
>
> *Kings control this hall. Nobody passes by here unless we say so.*
>
> – Junior high school Latin King member

To prevent this from occurring, school administrators must take a proactive stance against the spreading of the gang mentality through the building. A school principal's strong support for anti-gang and anti-violence measures in the school is a critical element in reducing school crime and behavior problems. Proactive intervention and prevention plans have been developed in many areas across the country. Summary Box 3.1 relates some proactive anti-gang strategies. School faculty must be aware that gang activity is spreading to schools and communities of all sizes across the nation. All schools' staff need to be prepared to deal with the repercussions of gang activity.

Summary Box 3.1

Establishing an Anti-Gang Policy

- Develop basic gang awareness

- Identify gang leaders in the school

- Identify potential problems caused by transfer students

- Provide supervised youth programs after school hours

- Involve and collaborate with law enforcement officials and parents

- Encourage parents and other adults to be good role models and mentors for youth

- Cooperate to implement a community-wide anti-gang policy

In all cases the anti-gang policy must begin with basic gang awareness. Invite police, criminal justice experts, and/or university personnel to teach staff to recognize and work with potentially violent youth. School staff members should be able to recognize students who talk, act, and dress like gang members. Only after administrators and school staff are able to acknowledge the gang problem will they be prepared and able to suppress and eventually eliminate the threat of gang violence in school. Involve parent organizations, community professionals, and concerned citizens to participate in the staff training. This will help to provide a broader based anti-gang policy. The school policy will then spread from the school to homes, neighborhoods, and eventually the community at large.

School staff should identify the leaders of the gang(s) in the school, and attempt to make these students allies. These students are influential leaders of other students (gang members and wannabes). These students could be involved in planning strategies to curb gang problems in school. This form of intervention, if possible to implement, is a helpful addition to the other anti-gang steps, and may motivate the gang members and wannabes who are still in school to aim for more socially appropriate behaviors. Because the concept of respect is so critically important to gang members, school staff will be much more successful in dealing with them if they show a respectful attitude. (An attitude of basic respect for another human being in no way implies a tolerance for criminal gang activity.)

Administrators should also be aware of the potential problems of transfer students. They should know about the background of students who may be switching schools because they were expelled for gang-related problems.

Another potentially problematic situation occurs when parents voluntarily transfer their children from one school to another because they were becoming involved in gang activity. The faculty need to be advised of the potential problems with these students. It may be possible to prevent future problems of a similar type by attempting to involve the transfer students in appropriate school and community activities. However, these extra efforts can only be accomplished if school staff are apprised of past problems.

Another strategy to deal with a gang problem is to provide supervised activities during the after-school hours until dinner time. It is during this critical time period that many students get into trouble because they are unsupervised and succumb to the lure of gang activity. (More detail about such programs is provided later in this section.)

Schools will ideally collaborate with local police officers and parents in establishing an anti-gang policy. Use the knowledge of police officers to educate school staff about gang activity. Many gang unit officers will provide school in-service programs. In addition, many schools now have permanent law enforcement liaison officers. Often simply the continuous presence of a police officer in the school will curb potential gang problems. If problems do occur, the police officer can call for back-up and utilize crisis intervention, negotiation, and mediation strategies.

Parents are another source of potential support in establishing an anti-gang policy. Parent volunteers can supervise walking routes to and from the school, bus rides, playground activity, and school programs, as well as provide daily classroom and hallway supervision. Parent volunteers can be very powerful allies in reducing a gang problem at school.

In addition to volunteer duties at school, parents can be good role models for many students. One of the main reasons that many students become involved in gangs is because they do not receive adequate support from their biological families. These students are searching for a group to belong to and identify with. Having the opportunity to interact with parents while participating in appropriate school activities may provide some students with a sense of belonging and identification that is missing in their own home environments.

Various business and professional personnel in the community might also be willing to mentor youth at risk for gang involvement. A mentoring program is another method of providing positive adult role models for school age children. A program might include one or more of the following three activities. First, a mentoring arrangement might revolve around school-based activities during

which the mentor spends time at school with a specific student working on classroom/extracurricular activities, or simply building rapport. Second, the mentor/student pair might participate in business-related activities in which the student spends some time at work with the mentor gaining exposure to and possibly hands-on experience in a job or career. And finally, the mentor and student might participate together in fun, recreational, or possibly community assistance/volunteer types of activities after school hours or on weekends.

The anti-gang policy at school will be most functional if the community is involved with and supportive of the policy. School administrators will be most effective in addressing their gang problem if they collaborate with the police, all school staff, business professionals from the community, concerned citizens, and, most importantly, the parents. When all of these people work together and a provide a united front stating that individuals in their community are not going to be allowed to conduct gang activities, the anti-gang policy should be highly effective.

INSERVICE TRAINING

An important step in eliminating gangs and gang-related behaviors from a school is to promote inservice training on gang awareness for the entire school staff. There are three main groups of professionals who may be able to offer effective inservice programs on gang awareness. First, law enforcement personnel from an established gang unit are often willing to speak with teachers and parents. Second, university professors from departments of law enforcement, sociology, psychology, or special education may also be good sources of information. Third, social service agencies who work with youth at risk may have social workers or volunteers from educational organizations who conduct gang intervention/prevention activities.

Summary Box 3.2 shows a sample agenda for an inservice program on gang awareness, which can be supplemented with material from this book. This program will assist school staff in acquiring basic identification strategies regarding youth gang characteristics, behavior, and apparel. Once all the school staff are aware of and able to recognize gang-oriented behaviors, school officials can implement the anti-gang policy to effectively deal with the problem.

Summary Box 3.2

Sample Agenda: Inservice on Youth Gangs

- Brief history of gangs

- Types of gangs

- Five main characteristics of youth gangs

(CONTINUED)

Summary Box 3.2 (CONTINUED)

- Hierarchy of gang membership

- Environmental gang indicators

- Profile of a typical gang member

- Female gang members

- Reasons youth join gangs

- Four major gang factions
  - Folk Nation
  - People Nation
  - Bloods
  - Crips

- Specific gang identifiers
  - Black Gangster Disciples (BGD)
  - Vice Lords (VL)
  - Latin Kings (LK)
  - Bloods
  - Crips

- Gang identifiers: Look for at least **two**!

ZERO TOLERANCE POLICY

The next step in defusing a school gang problem is the development of a policy stating that there will be absolutely no, or "zero tolerance," for gang behavior in school. Gangs and gang activity are disruptive to the safe learning environment of both students and teachers. Thus, the policy should communicate in no uncertain terms that school will be a secure environment for staff and students. A policy statement of this type provides all students equal opportunities to learn, and can be implemented without infringing upon students' rights to freedom of expression and association under the First Amendment to the United States Constitution.

To justify the necessity of the zero tolerance policy, as well as focus its development, educators should begin to document gang activity on and near the school premises. To do so, they should log any and all gang-related activities they observe or hear about on school grounds or during school-sponsored events. Following is a copy of an "Incident Report Form" for this purpose.

Incident Report Form

_____ School/District

Student Name _____

Gender _____ Race (optional) _____

Nickname (if any)_____

DOB _____ Grade _____

Street Address _____

City _____ Telephone No. _____

Distinctive Clothing/Jewelry _____

_____

_____

Incident Date _____ Time _____

Incident Location _____

(CONTINUED)

Incident Report Form (CONTINUED)

(Check All Applicable)

- ❑ Overheard admitting/bragging about being a gang member
- ❑ Observed wearing gang-related clothing, "colors," or tattoo(s)
- ❑ Using gang hand signs
- ❑ Observed writing gang graffiti on school property
- ❑ Observed with gang signs/symbols on notebooks, papers, schoolwork, etc.

- ❑ Observed wearing gang-related jewelry
- ❑ Involved in a gang-related activity/rule infraction/crime
- ❑ Has been identified by two or more individuals as being a member of their gang
- ❑ Seen in photographs wearing gang clothing, using gang hand signs, or with known gang members

Narrative

_____

_____

_____

_____

_____

_____

_____

_____

_____

Known Gang Affiliation _____

Parents Notified? If yes, by _____

Date _____

If no, reason _____

Staff Member Filing Report _____

Date _____

Remember that gang activity includes graffiti, as described in Sections 1 and 2. If all graffiti is either photographed or drawn, then collected in a central file, a record of gang activity will soon emerge.

Teachers and administrators should also document the actions of any student who demonstrates gang affiliation. Such records should be kept as part of students' cumulative school files. Their conduct should be recorded so that documentation can be presented to support any discipline procedures necessary. This documentation may also be shared with the police in a collaborative effort to identify criminal gang activity.

If a gang-involved student moves, or is transferred, that information should be conveyed to the receiving school so that those teachers and administrators will be forewarned to effectively manage any gang behaviors that might become evident in their school. If the student is expelled, state education code may **require** this notification.

The zero tolerance policy must specifically describe expectations for conduct and behavior for all students during the school day and during all school-sponsored events. The policy should also state that gang members who attend school will not be allowed to exhibit gang-related behaviors while they are there, nor will they be allowed to represent their gang affiliation through their dress.

Speaking Up!

School's just a place to meet my homies. I hate summer because I hardly never see 'em.

– Elementary school gang member

In addition to behavioral expectations, the policy should specify the consequences for violating the rules. These consequences should be included so that everyone knows the policy and all students are treated equally under its terms.

Assigning consequences for gang-related behavior is a controversial topic. There are basically two differing opinions. Some believe in suspending or expelling students for alleged gang behaviors. Others support a more educational, or rehabilitative, approach that involves teaching students positive replacements for socially inappropriate, problem behaviors. In-school suspension (discussed in more detail later in this section) is one less severe option. If this alternative is used, the students would be completing classwork, so they don't fall behind.

We believe that rather than simply suspending students for policy infractions, school staff should try to actively teach the students new and appropriate behaviors as a component of the consequences for demonstrating gang-related behaviors at school. A main problem with employing suspension as a behavior management consequence is that in today's society there will likely be no adult supervision at home while the student is barred from attending school during the day. A a result, students who have problems with their behavior to begin with are likely to get into even more trouble when left unsupervised for long periods of time.

Furthermore, suspension is primarily a punishment. The main objective is to remove the student from school for a given period of time. However, it is only a temporary solution to the problem, and the student does not learn any new behaviors through this punishment. A consequence that involves the teaching of a socially appropriate behavior, on the other hand, increases the student's behavioral repertoire. The student gains a behavioral skill that might possibly help him/her to avoid the misbehavior in a similar situation some time in the future.

Conversely, some gang-related behaviors are potentially so severe/violent that the students may not be allowed to remain in school because they threaten the security of school staff and/or other students. Due to the need to protect the safe and secure learning environment for others, administrators sometimes have no other choice than to remove the students from school. Yet it is not enough to simply remove problem students from school for a period of days. Schools should attempt to develop other educational programs in alternative settings, as well as counseling programs, to educate students while they are suspended from the regular school program.

At times law enforcement intervention will be required for severe behaviors. This may potentially result in the arrest of students. Violating a school rule is entirely different from breaking a municipal, state, or federal law. When students simply break school rules, administrators can deal with the problem occurring utilizing established discipline policies at the school level.

However, if students break the law—such as by carrying a concealed weapon, possessing narcotics, or committing assault—it is strongly recommended that school officials request police intervention. Police officers have specialized training to deal with problems of this type. If more school officials began immediately calling law enforcement personnel when situations warranted, the incident rate of school violence could be reduced. Plus students would learn that breaking the law on school property results in their being referred to law enforcement personnel and juvenile court services.

The process of establishing an effective zero tolerance policy will require close collaboration by all school administrators, faculty, school board members, legal counsel for the district, and parents.

Once written, the policy statement should be distributed to all the students, parents, and school staff. The zero tolerance policy must also be publicized to new students when they register so that they are fully informed of the school's policy before they attend their first class.

Summary Box 3.3 provides a sample zero tolerance policy, adapted with permission from the policy document implemented in 1990 by the Davenport, Iowa Community School District.

Summary Box 3.3

Sample Zero Tolerance Policy for Youth Gang Activity at School

Policy Statement: Gangs and gang-related activities are prohibited on school property or during school-affiliated activities. No student may intimidate or harass another student for the purpose of gang recruitment, gang intimidation, or gang retaliation.

Procedures: The visibility of gangs and gang-related activities in the school setting cause a substantial disruption of and/or material interference with school and school-related activities of this district.

"Gang," as used in this policy, shall mean two or more individuals
who associate with each other primarily for criminal, disruptive, and/or
other activities prohibited by law and/or by the district's rules and regulations.

No student on or about school property or at any school-sponsored activity shall:

1. Wear, possess, use, distribute, display, or sell any clothing, jewelry, emblem, badge, symbol, sign, or other item which is evidence of membership in or affiliation with any gang.

2. Communicate membership in or affiliation with a gang either verbally or non-verbally (through gestures, handshakes, slogans, drawings, etc.).

(CONTINUED)

---

3. Commit an act which furthers gang activity, including but not limited to:

    ■ Soliciting others for membership in any gang

    ■ Requesting any person to pay for protection or otherwise intimidating or threatening any person

    ■ Committing any other illegal act or other violation of school district policies

    ■ Inciting other students to act with physical violence upon any person

Consequences: All violations of this policy will be referred to the police via the Dean of Students.

Penalties for Violations:

1. A student violating numbers 1 or 2 of these procedures will be required to attend a parent conference with the Dean of Students and a police counselor representing the local authority. The student will be required to participate in gang prevention/intervention services provided by the social service agency [such as family resources, alternative youth programs, etc., similar to services which exist in most communities], in addition to attending and completing related activities in the "Gang Education Program" provided by the school. Subsequent related violations of the policy will subject the student to in-school suspension time and related activities.

2. A student violating number 3 of these procedures will be required to attend additional hours of programming on gang intervention with the social service agency, attend in-school suspension, and complete community service activities, to be determined.

Weapons Policy

Weapons in Our Nation's Schools

- A survey conducted at 31 high schools in Illinois revealed that one in 20 students had carried a gun to school in 1990.

- The U.S. Department of Justice, Bureau of Justice Statistics (1991) reported that an estimated 430,000 students took some type of weapon to school to protect themselves at least once during a six-month period in 1989.

- The Centers for Disease Control indicated that among high school students nationwide, one in 20 had carried a gun, usually a handgun, during a one-month period in 1990.

- Results from a 1993 survey of Washington, D.C. public school teachers indicated that 30% of respondents reported a student in their classroom using a weapon in a threatening manner.

(**Source**: Center to Prevent Handgun Violence)

Gang members will often carry weapons to school. A weapon is described as any device that can be used to attack another person. Examples include any type of firearm; knife; club; slingshot; explosive; deadly or dangerous chemical; or sharp, pointed instrument.

Youth carry weapons for many reasons. For example, if members of rival gangs attend the same school, it is almost impossible to prevent conflicts between them from occurring. If a gang fight is planned ahead of time, many gang members will bring weapons to school anticipating trouble.

Speaking Up!

Sure, I've taken a gun to school. Man, I could get one anytime. Got to protect myself, ya know.

– Deon, 16 years old

Many gang members also feel that possessing a weapon in school, especially a gun, is the highest form of breaking the school rules they can achieve. Students who have been caught with weapons in schools have told police officers that they experience a "high" feeling from having the weapon with them, much like an adrenaline rush.

Another way that weapons end up in schools is by students bringing them to satisfy a dare or a bet. Gang members may make this a requirement to join their gang, or offer this as an initiation rite. For some students, gaining acceptance by taking the risk of bringing a weapon to school is more important than the risk of being caught.

Weapons are also brought to school by youth other than gang members. Many times, children who are being threatened or intimidated by gang members will arm themselves for self-protection. These children are afraid of being hurt or even killed by gang members. Weapons are taken to school with the intent of scaring gang members away.

Unfortunately, the result of this type of thinking may be fatal. Most school-age children are not capable of handling guns or other weapons safely. When they attempt to use them as protection, someone usually ends up paying the price of a human life. Parents, as well as educators, must be concerned about this because students often find these weapons in their own homes. Adults who keep guns, knives, or other weapons in the home need to take extreme measures to secure them from children.

Each school staff will need to develop a weapons policy that reflects their own unique needs based on their location, type of community, and student population. Every school is unique, and the crime and violence that a school experiences require individualized and specific solutions. In developing such a

policy, the school must follow general state and federal guidelines. (School administrators should supply this information to school staff. Educators can contact their state board of education office for specific information related to individual states.) For example, in most states: weapons need to be registered and the owner must have a permit; carrying a concealed weapon is illegal; and juveniles are not allowed to carry weapons (concealed or not) in any state.

One of the most effective methods of controlling weapons at school is to encourage the assistance of other students who may be aware of problems. In Davenport, Iowa (and other cities/states), a program called "Crime Stoppers" rewards students monetarily for reporting all school policy violations, including the presence of weapons. Student callers are assigned a number to ensure their confidentiality. The student notifies the police officer in charge of the program. Then, if an arrest is made based upon the information supplied, the student can claim his/her reward using the assigned confidential number as identification. The program is funded through contributions from the community, and has been very successful.

Student reporting can even be written into schools' weapons policies. Cooperative students can be very helpful in reducing weapon incidents at school. Encourage students to be accountable for their own and their friends' safety by reporting violence, crime, and weapons on campus. The policy might provide a reward to students who provide information that leads to confiscation of a weapon at school. The student reporting should be done in an anonymous fashion to encourage cooperation and participation without fear of retaliation. If this plan is to be successful, teachers and administrators must be visible, available, and trusted by the students. "Hot lines" for reporting weapons have proven successful, in the "Crime Stoppers" fashion.

Besides this tactic, there are five main components schools should consider when developing a weapons policy. First, the weapons policy cannot contradict any state or federal regulations. Specifically, this means that a school cannot authorize juveniles to carry firearms, or attempt to reduce or eliminate the legal charges/consequences if students do violate the law. Second, schools should assess the scope or potential of its own weapons problem. Third, schools should develop strategies, methods, and deterrents that they believe will prevent or reduce weapon incidents at the school. The number one deterrent students need to understand is that carrying a weapon is against the law and that their case will be turned over to law enforcement and juvenile services personnel. Fourth, the weapons policy should include a crisis intervention plan in case a weapons incident does occur at school (see Section 4 for more information on this subject).

Finally, if the law is broken, police intervention should be mandatory.

Summary Box 3.4 lists the factors in developing a weapons policy.

> Summary Box 3.4
> ## Components of a School Weapons Policy
>
> - Must not conflict with state and federal weapon regulations
>
> - Takes into consideration the school's own situation regarding weapons at school
>
> - Includes strategies and deterrents to eliminate weapons at school
>
> - Plans for crisis intervention during weapon incidents on campus
>
> - Collaboration with law enforcement personnel regarding weapon violations is specified

If a weapon incident does occur on campus, school authorities should deal with the problem according to state and/or federal ordinances. A typical procedure would include the following steps. First, the law violation would be reported to the police. Second, police officers would investigate the situation and possibly arrest the student for the law violation. Third, the entire case would be turned over to juvenile court services, where a juvenile court judge would dictate punishment on an individual basis. Punishment could include, but would not be limited to, assignment to a probation officer, community service hours, or incarceration in a juvenile detention facility.

In addition to processing by juvenile court services, the student may be expelled from school for a minimum of 12 months according to federal guidelines. The Gun-Free School Zone Act of 1994 makes the reception of federal funds for schools contingent upon the establishment of a school weapons policy. This law states that any student who brings, possesses, or uses a firearm on the campus of any public school receiving federal funds must be expelled from school for a minimum of one year.

Summary Box 3.5 lists the steps which should be taken if a student brings a weapon to school.

Summary Box 3.5

Dealing With a Weapon Incident at School

- Reporting of the law violation to the police

- Police conduct an investigation of the weapons incident

- Police turn the investigation facts over to juvenile court services

- Punishment is assigned on an individual basis

- Federal law mandates a one-year expulsion for weapon possession at public schools receiving federal funds

---

Summary Box 3.6 illustrates a sample school weapons policy, by permission of the Davenport, Iowa Community School District (from their policy adapted by the Board of Education in March 1990).

Summary Box 3.6
Sample Weapons Policy

VIII. **Weapons**

The Board believes weapons and other dangerous objects in school district facilities cause material and substantial disruption of the school environment or present a threat to the health and safety of students, employees, and visitors on the school district premises or property within the jurisdiction of the school district.

School district facilities are not an appropriate place for weapons or dangerous objects. Weapons and other dangerous objects shall be taken from students and others who bring them onto the school district property or onto property within the jurisdiction of the school district or from students who are within the control of the school district.

Parents of students found to possess a weapon or dangerous object on school property shall be notified of the incident. Confiscation of weapons or dangerous objects shall be reported to the law enforcement officials, and the student will be subject to disciplinary action including suspension or expulsion.

Students bringing a firearm to school shall be expelled for not less than 12 months. The Superintendent shall have the authority to recommend this expulsion requirement be modified for a student on a case-by-case basis. For purposes of this portion of this policy, the term "firearm" includes any weapon which is designed to expel a projectile by the action of an explosive, the frame or receiver of any such weapon, a muffler or silencer for such a weapon, or any explosive, incendiary, or poison gas.

Weapons under the control of law enforcement officials shall be exempt from this policy. The principal may allow authorized persons to display weapons or other dangerous objects for educational purposes. Such a display shall be exempt from this policy. It shall be the responsibility of the Superintendent, in conjunction with the principals, to develop administrative regulations regarding this policy.

Drug Policy

Gangs, crime, violence, drugs; these problems all appear to be intertwined. Gangs need to make money. Criminal activities of various types are their primary source of financial income. Many gangs sell illegal narcotics for profit, but not all of them do. The criminal activity a gang favors tends to mirror its leader's preferences. A report from the National Institute of Justice (Johnson, Webster, & Connors, 1995) indicated that the presence of gangs, gang-related violence, and gang drug trafficking are increasing in both large and small cities across the country. The illegal drugs sold by gang members include marijuana, crack, cocaine, heroine, methamphetamines, and others.

Gang members sell drugs at school. School is the environment where they have the greatest access to the largest congregation of their peers. Schools— even elementary schools—provide a large and varied clientele of drug users. Schools will need to establish a drug policy to help in managing this problem.

Speaking Up!

This comment was made by a current gang member when asked by a gang unit police officer (following his third arrest for possession of a controlled substance) why he continues to sell drugs for the gang:

It's for the money, man, the money. I don't care what nobody says, man. I see all kinds of dope at this school. An' the teachers, they scared of us. I can see it in their eyes, man. And we gonna keep 'em scared. Kids sell dope right in class when the teacher ain't lookin'. I gotta have money to keep up my rep with my homies an' the women. They expect it. An' if you ain't got money . . . you nothin' man, an' I mean nothin'.

– Tyrone, 18 years old

A drug policy should reflect the unique needs of each school and its student population. The policy should define the illegal drugs and drug paraphernalia governed by the policy. Schools might also consider addressing student possession of cellular phones and pagers on campus, as these items have been traditionally used in the sale and delivery of illegal narcotics.

There is probably no reason that the average student needs to have a cellular phone in class. But some working parents and their children are now carrying pagers for communication. The argument remains, however, that these students do not need to have their pagers turned on while in class. If necessary, parents can easily contact the school office staff who can relay messages to students when necessary.

The students themselves have the most direct line to the "pulse" of any school. As with the weapons policy, an effective method for policing illegal drugs at school would be to utilize confidential student reports with monetary rewards for tips that lead to confiscation of drugs or the arrest of students possessing illegal narcotics.

Law enforcement "k-9" units (those with dogs, or canines) can be used to literally sniff out illegal drugs in lockers and elsewhere on school premises. However, before this procedure is implemented, school officials must establish and document reasonable suspicions regarding the presence of illegal drugs on campus in order to comply with the legal methods of search and seizure (discussed later in this section). If the k-9 unit was simply used as a "fishing expedition" or preventative procedure, any evidence (drugs) found would not be admissible to document a court case. In addition, once law enforcement and/or k-9 units are involved in a search procedure, the

school authorities become agents of the state. In other words, the procedure then falls under the law enforcement agency's jurisdiction, and must follow its established procedures. The situation could no longer be handled "in-house" by school authorities.

Schools should be very strict regarding the presence of tobacco, alcohol, illegal drugs, and drug paraphernalia on school property. Offenders should be dealt with firmly, either through school disciplinary action or police intervention. While it is not necessary, nor feasible, for the police to be called every time a pack of cigarettes is confiscated from a minor, for example, school administrators should use law enforcement resources when the presence of alcohol, illegal drugs, or drug-related items are discovered at school.

Establishing an effective policy to address illegal substances on campus should be relatively simple to create. Since tobacco and alcohol are illegal for minors to possess and to use in most states, and controlled substances and drug paraphernalia are illegal to use, possess, or sell for everybody in all of the United States, the policy need only mandate that it is not allowable for students to use, sell, or have in their possession on school grounds any tobacco, alcohol, or drug product. The policy should be designed to cover all school properties, as well as private properties being used for school-related functions (hotels, motels, buses, etc.). When the policy is worded as specific rules, these can be reinforced by local, municipal, and state laws (check with the local police department for details).

Each state establishes laws that determine penalties for the possession, use, or sale of illegal narcotics. State law can also set the standards for "Drug-Free Zones," usually public school grounds, parks and playgrounds, or areas within a specified distance from such areas. Once an area is designated a "Drug-Free Zone," signs are posted announcing that the vicinity falls into this category. Anyone arrested for the possession, use, or sale of controlled substances within these areas would have their fine or penalty doubled by the courts.

Sometimes school officials will find or suspect the use of controlled substances during the school day or during school-sponsored extracurricular activities. Those possessing such items should be removed from the student setting and taken to the school office. Once there, the school administrators should determine what action is necessary. The student's parents should certainly be notified and requested to come to the school. In-school suspension, out of school suspension, or expulsion may be considered. Many school districts allow for a hearing where students involved in drug-related incidents can present their

side of the story. When adopting a drug policy, a hearing clause should be included.

The police should also be notified when alcohol or illegal drugs are found on campus. Whether a student is under their influence, attempting to sell, or merely possessing these items should not matter. All are illegal for minors, and arrest and court intervention may be necessary. Also, word will quickly spread throughout the school that being caught with these items results in arrest. This gives the school, and the school district, a tough, firm, reputation for dealing with illegal substances which will help to eliminate their presence at school.

Speaking Up!

If I could tell kids one thing? Well, just avoid the stuff [drugs], man. Stay away from it. See where it gets ya. Nowhere, man. Just the joint, and that's if it don't kill ya.

— Incarcerated gang member

The biggest advantage to involving the juvenile court services is that mandatory substance abuse programs may be included as a part of the students' sentence. This affords students the opportunity to address their use of illegal substances, and possibly begin a healing process that may have been neglected otherwise. In Davenport, Iowa, an adolescent

C.A.D.S. (Center for Alcohol and Drug Services, Inc.) program usually follows an arrest for narcotics or alcohol. There an extensive intervention program helps to assess the degree to which a student may be addicted to the substance, and recovery plans are developed. Many of the programs offer joint student and parent involvement, thus addressing problems inside the family structure that may have contributed to the child's use of alcohol or other drugs.

Summary Box 3.7 describes the recommended components of a school drug policy.

Summary Box 3.7

Components of a School Drug Policy

- School rules regarding student possession or use of illegal drugs must comply with state mandates on "Drug-Free Zones," as well as state and municipal laws.

- Define illegal drugs.

- Define drug paraphernalia.

- Also consider student possession of cellular phones and pagers.

- Define a method to promote confidential student reports of illegal drugs at school.

- Define disciplinary actions for the possession, sale of, or use of illegal drugs at school.

It is not uncommon for teachers and administrators to encounter students who are under the influence of alcohol or drugs in the classroom. While it is beyond the scope of this book to comprehensively address the signs of substance use, certain traits seem to be present in most instances. Red, watery eyes; slurred speech; a staggering walk; and the smell of the substance are present in many cases. Certain narcotics, including inhalants, can cause violent behaviors, and educators need to be aware that dangers may exist when dealing with students who are under the influence of these substances. If it becomes evident that such a student is posing a threat to others, the police should be summoned to handle the situation.

Drugs are at the root of many gang-related activities today, and to think that these substances do not show up in the nation's schools is absurd. Each school must assess it's own students' substance use, and take the necessary measures to deal with the problem. Police intervention should be mandatory when drugs or drug-related items are found, as the resources prescribed by law constitute an easy, effective measure for schools to use to control this problem on their campuses.

Dress Code Policy

Various security measures have been implemented in schools across the country in an effort to reduce gang-related violence. Many schools with severe gang problems have gone to great expense to activate security measures involving special equipment and/or personnel. Some examples include: (1) hand-held metal detectors that are used randomly, as well as fixed "airport-type" models that are permanently installed; (2) increased number of school security personnel, including the hiring of private firms; (3) police liaisons in the schools; (4) restricting and/or monitoring entrances and locking doors during school hours; (5) volunteer parent hallway patrols; (6) peer and/or staff conflict mediation teams; and (7) canceling after-school and evening events, including extracurricular activities and athletics, when the safety of students or staff may be threatened.

Restricting the representation of gang affiliation is an option utilized by many schools which is more economically feasible than some of the other alternatives just mentioned. One of the primary methods of demonstrating gang allegiance is by wearing the gang's colors and displaying gang symbols or signs on clothing. Expectations for student dress should be explicitly defined as part of

the school's zero tolerance policy. Many schools across the country have established a range of dress code policies to prohibit the wearing of items at school which indicate membership in or affiliation with any gang.

At one end of the dress code spectrum is the requirement that students wear specific uniforms, reminiscent of parochial schools. Some schools have adopted uniforms which may be worn on a voluntary basis by students. Other dress codes simply ban any type of apparel, jewelry, symbols, or signs that indicate membership in or affiliation with a gang. Additionally, as a theft and violence prevention measure, many schools are actively discouraging students from wearing inordinately expensive clothing, shoes, jackets, and jewelry. Students have been robbed of their clothing and jewelry at weaponpoint, and injured or killed, while to and from school or on school grounds.

Specific clothing items, in addition to the way the clothing is worn, can be gang identifiers, as described in detail in Section 2. Schools can usually ban gang-related items of clothing in a legal manner without violation of students' constitutional First Amendment rights of freedom of expression, or their civil rights in general. State laws grant school boards the right to take reasonable steps to provide a positive learning environment for all educational staff and students. Thus, in most cases, school boards can legally adopt a dress code for the purpose of maintaining a safe and secure school environment which facilitates effective learning.

Burke (1993) outlined the steps schools can follow to legally ban gang clothing on school grounds. First, the school must demonstrate that there is an intent to convey a particularized message through the wearing of gang clothing. Intentionally wearing gang clothing does convey a particularized message of belonging to a specific gang. Each gang has its own very meaningful colors, signs, and symbols generally depicted through their clothing styles. Gang clothing also conveys a number of other messages including intimidation and a challenge to rival gangs, and often violence. This may cause fear and thus academic disruption to other students and even to teachers.

Fights often break out in schools when gang members perceive the gang-related clothing of others as either a personal challenge or as a threat to their gang's dominance over the area. School officials should carefully document gang-related problems that occur in the school, and the dress of the parties involved. By documenting problems with gangs and gang behavior at school, school officials can substantiate that the purpose of the dress code is to provide a safe, secure learning environment for both students and teachers. (The actual purpose of the dress code is the determining factor as to whether or not it is constitutionally valid.)

To clarify, the school must be able to demonstrate that gang-related clothing has interfered with the educational rights of other students or has disrupted the learning environment. If this proof is established, then it is probable that the dress code will be upheld if legally challenged. However, if the purpose of the dress code is simply to ban the gang's message, and/or if the students are able to wear gang clothing and behave without causing any disruptions, then the dress code would quite possibly restrict the students' First Amendment rights of freedom of expression, and would therefore not be constitutionally valid. Dress codes to ban gang clothing where no documented problem exists cannot, constitutionally, be used as a preventative measure.

When used, effective dress codes for high school students must account for changing fashion fads. To do so, a provision should be made to evaluate and update the dress code on an annual basis. Collaborating with the local police is helpful in keeping up to date on gang regalia and fashions. If and when any new provisions are added to the dress code, make sure that these changes are adequately explained to the students and parents both in verbal and written form. This procedure will ensure that the dress code will not be unconstitutionally vague.

Once a dress code is established, school officials need to be able to enforce the policy. Each school should develop an enforcement policy unique to its needs and the severity of the overall gang problem. For example, students may be required to go home and change their clothes. The school may want to contact the student's parents directly. Or the policy may state that gang-related apparel at school will be confiscated by school staff and turned over to either school district or law enforcement officials to be retrieved by parents at their discretion.

Repeated violations of the dress code should have severe consequences. Schools that have successfully used dress codes to ban gang-related clothing primarily use suspension and expulsion for repeat offenders. In fairness, the policy should include an appeals process which would allow students the opportunity to rebut a charge that clothing is gang-related. The policy should afford students and their parents the opportunity and information necessary to effectively navigate this appeals process. The appeals procedure ensures that dress codes are fairly implemented and protect students from undue penalties.

Finally, the dress code policy should be specifically stated in the school handbook. The handbook should be distributed to and discussed with all the students. Then the students and their parents should be required to sign the dress code policy,

signifying that they have read and understand the dress code policy that will be enforced by the school.

Summary Box 3.8 shows a sample dress code policy.

Summary Box 3.8
Sample Dress Code Policy to Address Gang Apparel

- Students will not be allowed to remain in school if clothing: (1) creates a safety hazard; or (2) creates a serious or unnecessary disruption of the safe and secure learning environment for school staff and other students.

- If a student's clothing violates the safe and secure learning environment component of this policy, he/she will be dismissed from school to change the unacceptable clothing.

- Students will not be allowed to wear, possess, use, distribute, display, or sell any clothing, jewelry, emblem, badge, symbol, sign, or other item which indicates membership in or affiliation with any gang.

Legal Methods of Search and Seizure

While the Fourth Amendment to the United States Constitution protects citizens from illegal search and seizure, past court rulings have stipulated that teachers and school administrators do not need probable cause to search students or their personal belongings while inside the school building or on school grounds, according to New Jersey vs. T.L.O., 469 U.S. 325, 339 (1985) (as cited in Berman, 1991). This ruling is exclusive of school property such as lockers and desks where a search can be conducted at any time without prior notice upon reasonable suspicion alone. It even allows for the search of vehicles while parked on school property based upon probable cause and without a warrant. Also, the court allowed for students and their personal belongings to be searched while participating in school-sponsored extracurricular activities.

All of these circumstances are based upon the relevant needs of the school to produce a safe learning environment in relationship to the expected privacy of students. However, we suggest that teachers and school administrators develop probable cause or reasonable suspicions before conducting school searches. If contraband is discovered that violates school regulations,

appropriate consequences under the school's policy can be implemented. If the search uncovers illegal contraband, police officials should be notified to begin the law enforcement process. In order to search a student, school officials must keep the following two factors in mind.

First, they should be able to document reasonable suspicions that searching the student and/or his/her belongings will provide evidence that the student has violated a school rule or a law. Reasonable suspicion can be based on conclusions an educator can draw from sensory perceptions such as vision, hearing, or smell. Additionally, the logical and rational conclusions that an educator might draw from daily observations of student behavior can be a valid basis for suspicions.

Second, the search should be reasonable in scope. The search must be directly related to the documented suspicions that initially prompted the search. Searches that seem to be "fishing for evidence" would be judged to be inordinately intrusive. Evidence gained in such a manner would likely be disallowed in a court of law. (Such actions might also prompt lawsuits by parents.) But as long as school officials can confidently document both a reasonable suspicion and conduct a search of reasonable scope based on that suspicion, the search will be legal in most cases.

Lockers are school property and may be searched at the school's discretion. The school handbook can also be used to describe locker search policies. The handbook might state that lockers will be randomly searched. It should also state that illegal items found in student lockers will be seized, and students will be punished according to school policy and/or prosecuted according to the law as appropriate.

As with the dress code policy, placement of this information in the school handbook, plus requiring all the students and their parents to sign it, signifies that both groups have read and understand the locker search policy. This type of policy will help to make students and staff feel safe and protected in the school environment.

Due Process for Student Disciplinary Procedures

When schools establish disciplinary policies to manage student behavior, it is important to incorporate a method of due process for appeals in order to protect student rights. This gives students the chance to tell their side of the story when a problem occurs. Under this student appeals process, the school will need to provide support for the discipli-

nary procedure they are intending to implement. The school officials will need to be able to offer an objective description of the student behavior that proves that a school rule was violated.

Summary Box 3.9 contains a proactive disciplinary description of the due process procedure used by the Davenport, Iowa Community School District (used by permission). This document covers many severe problem behaviors that violate school rules, specifically drugs, weapons, assaults, and gangs. It outlines, step-by-step, how to implement a due process procedure with students and their parents. To best meet the needs of students, this policy should be in written form and clearly explained in the school handbook. All the students and their parents should be provided with a copy of this policy.

Summary Box 3.9

Sample Due Process Procedure

The following is the Board of Education statement which reaffirms existing policy 504.1:

1. The Davenport Community School District will not tolerate the possession, use, or distribution of drugs including alcohol, look-alikes, and drug paraphernalia on school grounds.

(CONTINUED)

In all cases of possession or use, the student will be removed from school and the police will be informed. The student will be required to go to the Center for Alcohol and Drug Services, Inc. (C.A.D.S.) or another comparable agency and complete the treatment, or the student will be recommended for expulsion.

The student will be suspended and recommended for expulsion in the event of a second offense.

Any student involved in the distribution of drugs (illegal or prescription) or look-alikes will be suspended and recommended for expulsion.

2. The Davenport Board of Education intends to provide a safe environment in which students and staff can learn and work. The possession of any item designed to harm people such as guns, knives, brass knuckles, martial arts weapons, etc., is prohibited. Any student in possession of any of these items on school grounds will be suspended from school, reported to the police, and recommended for expulsion in accordance with the due process procedures outlined in #7.

3. Gang-related activities growing out of the display of "colors," symbols, signals, signs, etc., will not be tolerated on school grounds. Students in violation will be suspended from school and/or recommended to the Board for expulsion.

4. Assault and Battery to school employees will result in immediate suspension of the student involved and a recommendation to the Board for expulsion from school.

5. Assault and Battery on the part of one student to another will be dealt with firmly. Staff will encourage parents to file charges with the appropriate authorities. Students engaging in this type of behavior will be subject to the discipline code of the school district, which could include suspension or a recommendation for expulsion, depending upon the severity of the act and the circumstances.

6. All students willingly participating in a fight will be suspended and their parents will be required to come to school for a hearing.

(CONTINUED)

Summary Box 3.9 (CONTINUED)

7. Due process in all cases will be followed according to Board Policy:

    a. Principal immediately informs parents of the incident.

    b. Principal schedules a meeting as soon as possible with student and parents at which time they have the opportunity to respond to the allegations. If the student is suspended, the parents and student will receive a written notice stating the reason and length of all suspensions.

    c. Principal makes decision to re-admit student to school or refer the student to the Administrative Advisory Council for an expulsion hearing.

    d. A prompt, impartial hearing shall be scheduled by written notice to the student and parents.

    e. The student shall be entitled to representation by counsel and have the right to call and cross-examine witnesses.

    f. The Council shall make written findings and recommendations to the Superintendent, and copies to the student and parents.

    g. Any recommendation for expulsion shall be forwarded to the Board of Directors through the Superintendent for action.

    h. Special procedures pertaining to the suspension or exclusion of special education students will be followed according to state and federal guidelines. Please contact the Director of Site Based Leadership PK-12 for additional explanation.

8. The procedure to follow when reporting a violation of a student's rights is to report to the:

    1. Teacher—if not resolved, then the . . .

    2. Associate Principal

    3. Principal

    4. Director of Site Based Leadership PK-12

    5. Associate Superintendent for Administrative Services

    6. Superintendent of Schools

    7. Board of Directors

Alternatives to Suspension

When students violate any of the school policies, or exhibit other problem behaviors associated with gang involvement, consequences must be applied. The most common consequence used for severe behavior problems is school suspension.

At times, suspension is warranted to protect the safe and secure learning environment for other students. As discussed in conjunction with weapons, expulsion may be mandatory under federal law for students found carrying a weapon on public school grounds. In many cases, school authorities do not have the ultimate authority to control/ choose the discipline procedures for severe behaviors through which the student actually breaks a law rather than simply violating a school rule. Suspension/ expulsion in these instances may be their only, and an appropriate, choice.

Unfortunately, suspending students from school is only a temporary solution to the misbehavior. It serves to punish the students, to remove them from school for a short period of time, but it does not teach them more appropriate replacement behaviors for those that resulted in the school suspension. Thus it is very likely that the students will repeat their offensive behaviors when they return to school.

There are alternatives to out-of-school suspension that administrators can employ in many cases. Gang-involved students often intimidate and violate the rights of other students. They need to be confronted with a specific description of their problem behavior and then taught a socially appropriate replacement behavior. Teaching requires more time and concentrated effort than simply suspending students. However, the resulting behavior change should be more long-lasting and satisfying for both the students and school staff.

Whenever possible, do not endorse out-of-school suspension. Banning students from attending school places them at risk for involvement with the juvenile justice system. Behavior problems are generally increased by putting youth out on the street. Granted, schools may need to engage in some creative planning to determine ways to keep these students in school when their behavior is unacceptable, sometimes extremely so. However there are many structured, in-school consequences that are effective in addressing problem behaviors.

In-school suspension (ISS) is one discipline strategy many schools have adopted. In-school suspension is typically a room where students are sent as a disciplinary measure. The room is monitored by a school staff member. While there, students are expected to do schoolwork and follow the school rules. However, they are not accorded social privileges/interactions. The basic idea is to make the regular school program more rewarding and motivating to attend than ISS.

There is one caution for the use of in-school suspension, however. Some schools endorse an in-school suspension plan in which the students are not allowed to complete their missed classroom assignments. The detriments of this policy far outweigh any "punishment impact" it may have on the students. The outcome is that students who are most likely already at risk for school failure and dropout are prevented from completing schoolwork while attending school, putting them even further behind the other students academically. While assigned to in-school suspension, students should be required to keep up with all their assignments while receiving none of the social perks of attending school and of their regular class schedule.

When students are assigned to in-school suspension, this is a perfect opportunity to focus on teaching them socially appropriate, positive replacement behaviors. For example, many gang members behave in a manner that is verbally or physically intimidating to staff and students in order to enhance their reputation with fellow gang members and wannabes. This type of problem behavior is likely to result in

suspension from the regular school program. But if in-school suspension is dictated instead, a school staff member could use part of that time to work with the students on prosocial behaviors.

For example, the program *Skillstreaming the Adolescent* (Goldstein et al. 1980) provides a set of 60 different social skills that can be taught individually or in small groups through role play. Emphasis is on learning new, appropriate behaviors to replace problem behaviors, and suggestions are included for the generalizing of the new behaviors beyond the learning situation (in this case, ISS). (The References/ Resources at the end of this section list some other commercially available social skills programs proven effective with at-risk students as well.)

To reiterate, it is important to structure ISS time so the students keep up with the required work in their classes. Make ISS less of a "sentence" and more of a learning experience with a high degree of structure, rules, and behavioral expectations. The social aspects of being in school are rewarding to gang members. They want to be able to hang out with their fellow gang members. So, while ISS should be a learning experience, it should not be more rewarding than regular classes. The students should not be allowed recreational, social time with their peers. The students should be motivated to work their way out of ISS and back into their regular class schedule.

Rules must be established delineating the expectations for appropriate behavior while assigned to ISS. Gang members respond to structure, discipline, and rules. Staff members can use the ISS rules to help teach the students replacement behaviors for the typical types of problem behavioral patterns that resulted in them being assigned to ISS in the first place.

After the students begin to demonstrate the new, appropriate behaviors in ISS, they should be provided with positive reinforcers/rewards. A mix of social praise, recreational activities, and small tangible items would be appropriate to use. Recreational activities might include time to work on a computer or work with a peer partner on an academic task. Small tangible items might include fast food restaurant coupons, a can of soda pop, a candy bar, or sugarless gum.

ISS should be a short-term placement. Reasonable time limits should be set for students to remain in ISS. Remember,

also, that although the emphasis is on using ISS as a learning experience, as with all positive management systems, some students will not respond to the program or the reinforcement incentives available.

Staff should set behavioral goals for students to work their way out of ISS. Examples might include following the rules, participating in social skills training role plays, and showing appropriate, respectful behaviors to the staff and students in ISS rather than intimidating types of behavior. Schedules might be established so that students would have to work their way out of ISS by showing a certain number of positive social interaction behaviors without using intimidation (or other common gang-related behaviors) with others.

Summary Box 3.10 lists the best procedures for utilizing in-school suspension to its maximum benefit.

Summary Box 3.10

Tips for Making In-School Suspension (ISS) a Learning Experience

- Set rules that establish the behavioral expectations for ISS.

- Structure the time so the students complete their academic class requirements.

- Structure time for the students to work on prosocial behaviors with staff.

(CONTINUED)

Summary Box 3.10 (CONTINUED)

- Provide positive reinforcement for prosocial behaviors:

  - Social praise.

  - Educational, recreational activities.

  - Small tangible items.

- Set time limits for ISS. Some students will not respond to the incentives of the program.

- Encourage the students to earn the privilege of returning to their regular class schedule by showing appropriate behaviors.

In addition to in-school suspension, proactive types of behavioral consequences can also support the development of prosocial skills. Most students involved with gangs have aggressive personalities and frequently attempt to bully or intimidate other students. Summary Box 3.11 lists some alternative consequences for these problem behaviors, adapted with permission from *Bully-Proofing Your School* (Garrity et al., 1993).

Summary Box 3.11

Alternatives to Suspension for Problem Behaviors

If possible, assign consequences that are prosocial and involve helping other students. For example:

- Observe the playground times of younger children and pass out rewards to those displaying kind, caring behaviors.

- Role play being the victim of one's own intimidating behavior with a teacher. Write about how it feels.

- Under supervision, do something nice for the victim of the intimidation or harassment.

- Write a report about an altruistic leader (e.g., Ghandi, Mother Teresa) and tell what kind behaviors one will demonstrate.

(CONTINUED)

Summary Box 3.11 (CONTINUED)

- Tutor a younger student in a mastered subject.

- Clean up trash or remove graffiti on the school grounds.

- Call one's parent(s) to explain the problem behavior and think of a caring act as a self-consequence.

- Stay after school to perform a helping act for a school staff member or a member of the community.

- Participate in a community service activity, such as:

  - Clean up a trash in a park

  - Visit a nursing home

  - Rake an elderly person's yard

- A "walk-a-thon" type fundraiser for a charity of choice

Safe After-School Programs

Once the school has specified for the students, in the school policy statements, everything that they **can't** do, the students should be given some positive alternatives for what they **can** do. Extracurricular activities, both during school hours and after school, would be very positive experiences for gang-involved students. Educators are asking gang members to drop their weapons. But these youth need to be offered something better to pick up! After-school programs would help fill the void for many. These types of programs would serve to occupy these students' time with legal and safe activities. Additionally, competence in extracurricular activities fosters social skill development as well as enhancing self-esteem and academic achievement.

After-school and summer programs would be effective in supplying the supervision needed during periods of the day generally unstructured for many students. Due to the large number of single parent families and families in which both parents work outside the home, a significant number of students have no adult supervision all day long during the summer and from the end of the school day until the parent arrives home from work during the school year. It is during these times that many youth will begin to "hang out" with less desirable peers and possibly become caught up in gang activity.

Speaking Up!

Response from a juvenile in a residential treatment center when asked how he will try to stay out of trouble after discharge:

At the school where I'm at now, I live here. I been here for 14 months. We talk a lot about staying out of trouble after we get out. We learn to be responsible for our own behavior. I don't wanna be in trouble all the time. I want to get a job and help out my ma. Actually we are gonna move out of the old neighborhood. My ma is already looking for a new place by my aunt. She lives in a smaller town. I think that will help me, 'cause I won't be around the old guys. To stay out of trouble I'm gonna stay away from the gang and the drug selling. That's how I first got into trouble. I'm gonna go to school every day. I kinda like school. My aunt said she'd get me a membership at the Y [YMCA] so I can do stuff there after school. I'd also like to play on the baseball team. I was pretty good in junior high before I got into trouble. My uncle works selling cars. He said I could do some work there, washing, cleaning cars and stuff to earn some money. So I'll go to school, go to the Y, work, maybe play baseball.

— Jamie, 16 years old

Schools, recreation centers, and other community organizations that provide structured, supervised, and safe after-school programs for students give them choices of various activities that are socially appropriate. Programs of this type will give students an alternative for loitering on the streets, and thus will help to prevent gang involvement.

Officers from the Davenport, Iowa Police Department's Gang Unit reported a reduced amount of "wannabe" gang activity problems in the city during the summer of 1994. The cause? There was an intentional increase in the number of structured neighborhood, school site, community, church, parks/playground, and university-sponsored programs available for children and adolescents around the city. This intervention, the wide range of structured activities for youth in the community, decreased the need for police action related to gang problems.

Structured and safe after-school programs should reflect the needs of the students. One method of determining activities in which students would like to participate would be to schedule discussion sessions with students, school staff, parents, and community members. This group could discuss and develop programs of interest to the students. Or, the staff members could survey all the students, asking them to provide suggestions for programs that would be of interest. Another idea is for the teaching staff to suggest a menu of programs that they feel qualified to provide and supervise. The after-school and summer activities must be well-planned and staffed by interested and motivated adults in order to be effective.

Program courses could be of various lengths. Some might be ongoing throughout the school year. Others could be offered as "mini-courses" periodically on a rotating schedule. Ideally, an after-school program would run from the time school was dismissed until approximately 6:00 PM.

Preplanning would be required to determine how to fund these programs for staff salaries, any necessary materials or supplies, and operating costs, if applicable. All personnel involved in planning these after-school programs could brainstorm methods of funding the activities. Funding sources might include local-, state-, or federally-funded grants; private foundations; donations from private industry; school fundraisers; collaboration with community agencies or local professional agencies; parent, teacher, or community volunteers; and charitable donations of materials or products. Be creative!

In order for the programs to remain safe, some rules would be required. First, students should not be allowed to leave the school building and return for the after-school program, as the whole

idea is to keep them off the streets. Given this, provisions would need to be made for after-school snacks for the youth involved in the programs.

Second, expectations for behavior would need to be clearly stated. The ideal structure would be just a little less formal than that expected in the classroom. The students would be allowed to choose their activities, move about freely, and would not have to raise their hands before speaking; these would be more social situations than academic. Appropriate rules might include: (1) Do what your activity supervisor asks the first time; (2) Finish the projects you start; (3) Help keep the activity area neat and organized; (4) Use appropriate language with peers and adults; and (5) Be considerate of and helpful to others.

Third, depending upon the nature of the program, the students might be required to sign a contract stating that they will complete the activities they sign up for. The contract would include an incentive reward for completion—no finish, no reward. The rewards would be dependent on the activities, age levels of the students, etc. Fulfilling their contracts should not be a problem if the activities are motivating for and relevant to the students. Upon completion of an activity or mini-course, staff should provide a certificate of merit to each participating student.

Another factor to explore is safe travel home at the conclusion of the activity, which may often be after dark. Some parents will be willing and able to transport their children home. However, many will not. Other options include public transportation (which may need to be included in the funding so students who do not have the fare are not excluded from participating), school buses, or vans owned by participating agencies and insured to transport children. Collaboration with the local police department may provide some means of safe passage home for after-school program participants.

Another suggestion would be to pair students using the "buddy system" to see each other home. Or groups of children may be escorted home (on foot or by car by older, reliable participants in the activity or by activity supervisors, either volunteer or paid. Community volunteers might be arranged to escort children safely home. The provision of safe transportation home may encourage many students to participate who might not otherwise.

Some examples of after-school programs that might be offered include homework assistance/tutoring, and educational, arts and crafts, sports, or community service activities. Other innovative and creative classes might include babysitting or child care training, creative writing, dramatics, computer use or programming, marketing or economics, magic tricks, or card/board games.

Another idea might be to create clubs that would meet after school. Some club themes might include:

- **Computer Club**. This club would teach members keyboarding skills, how to navigate the World Wide Web, or how to create computer graphics. Another component might be a professional mentoring program where students would spend some time after school or on weekends learning about a professional career involving computer operation. This could include hands-on experience in the profession (an internship).

- **Cultural Activities Club**. In this club, members would take part in cultural activities such as museum tours, art gallery events, plays, or musical productions; conduct critical reviews of movies or books; complete art, music or dance projects; and/or listen to expert guest speakers on cultural topics.

- **Vocational Skills/Employment Training Club**. Members of this club would take part in activities to increase their employability. They might participate in career discussion and experience seminars, receive on the job training, or be paired with professional career mentors.

- **Recreational Activities Club**. This club would provide experiences in safe, structured, supervised leisure time activities. A club supervisor might provide learning activities for the members on finding low or no cost (and legal) recreational activities in the community. This club might participate in a variety of recreational activities including bowling, swimming, basketball, volleyball, pool, table tennis, and other active sports.

- **Community Service Club**. This club would focus on the benefits of helping others through community service activities. Students would be paired with adults who serve as role models, and together work on community service projects such as helping the elderly, providing respite care for families with members who have disabilities or disease, taking part in neighborhood beautification, serving as a companion/mentor for younger children, planting gardens, building playgrounds or trails, working at the local animal shelter or shelter for the homeless.

- **Self-Awareness and Problem-Solving Club**. Members of this club would discuss and devise positive and appropriate alternatives to help themselves and their peers deal with current problem situations in their lives. Topics might include gangs, guns and violence, drug abuse

prevention, family issues, crime, dating, and other challenges associated with growing up in today's society.

Positive Classroom Techniques

Tremendous demands are being placed upon school systems today. Many districts are severely underfunded, the ratio of students to teachers in already overcrowded classrooms is increasing, and "nonessential" classes such as music and art are being eliminated altogether from some districts' curricula. And despite all the efforts made by educators in the face of this adversity, the dropout rate in this country is still spiraling upwards.

The nationwide dropout rate for adolescents varies across the country due to various definitions of the term itself. Yet it appears that about 25% of students without disabilities drop out of school each year (Lovitt, 1991). For individuals with mild to moderate disabilities that number is even higher. Zigmond and Thornton (1985) reported that approximately 50% of students with learning disabilities drop out annually. It is surmised that students with behavioral disorders drop out at an incredible rate of 65% (Rhode, Jenson, & Reavis, 1992). Students from minority groups are particularly at risk for school failure and dropout. For example, a 1991 report from the Illinois Criminal Justice Information Authority reported that statewide, an average of 42% of African-American males and 43% of Hispanic males fail to complete high school in Illinois annually. These figures do not even include the numbers of minority students who never enter high school.

The repercussions of school dropout are grave. Students who drop out of high school have an increased potential for personal, social, and economic failure for the rest of their lives. Drug abuse is greater among dropouts than graduates. Dropouts are more dependent upon welfare and unemployment assistance. Dropouts earn significantly less, and contribute less to their community's tax base.

Dropping out may also be a precursor to criminal activity. In 1987, Minnesota and Florida reported some interesting statistics (as cited by the Illinois Criminal Justice Information Authority, 1991). Minnesota had the highest high school graduation rate in the country and the second lowest incarceration rate, while Florida had the lowest graduation rate and the highest incarceration rate. Between 1987 and 1989, the graduation rate in Illinois dropped four percent while the incarceration rate increased by 12%. It costs approximately $4,200 annually to educate a child. The average cost of incarcerating an adult for one year is $16,200. The U.S. will

either spend the funds to effectively educate children while they are in school, or will spend upwards of four times that amount later to incarcerate many school dropouts who are unskilled, virtually unemployable, and involved in criminal activity, including gang membership.

A concerted effort must be made to keep children in school. And teacher behavior can be one of the deciding factors in making or breaking the future of a student. But not surprisingly, many teachers are intimidated by the reputations and actions of students who are hostile and aggressive in the classroom. Many gang members display behaviors that make them difficult for teachers to like. Their personalities could be described as antisocial. Students who are drawn to gang activity do not generally possess adequate social skills or abilities that are recognized by peers or adults at school.

Additionally, most of these students are not able to achieve academic success. Academic underachievement may be due to reading problems and other learning differences, fear of failure, or simply that education is not valued by their family members or gang-involved peers. These students are not involved in extracurricular activities and do not know how to form appropriate relationships with adults.

Gang members are among the types of students who teachers frequently hope will be absent. They are often truant, which is part of the reason why so many of them have school problems. When they are in school, teachers often allow them to slink to the back of the classroom hoping they will quietly "snooze" through class. That way it is less likely that disruptions will occur or that intimidating behaviors will be displayed by these students.

Speaking Up!

We're not stupid. Teachers think we are, but we're not. It's just that nobody gives a s@!# about us. They gave up on us.

— LaMont, 17 years old

Teachers need to wake up! Teachers wield great power over the students in their classrooms. Students who show violent tendencies and the hopelessness related to gang involvement are critically in need of appropriate adult role models. A startling statistic shows that annually students spend an average of 900 hours in school and 1,500 hours in front of a TV set (Keveney, 1996). During the school year, teachers probably have more contact time and interact with students more than any other human being. Teachers must reach out to the difficult students, and work hard to overcome an excess of negative environmental influences. Teachers need to make education relevant, motivating, and rewarding for all their students, even the hostile, aggressive, and often noncompliant gang members/wannabes.

Just When You Think

Just when you think,
there's no one to turn to,
there's always someone there.

In life,
you have an opportunity to succeed,
or to fail.

But anybody,
can do anything in life,
just try and you will make it.

Everyone has a teacher,
whether it is at home or at school.

We all have role models
to look up to,
and that's a teacher.

A role model
isn't a gang member,
or a drug dealer,
it is a person who cares.

The hood has no place
for a teenager,
or a child.

The hood has no place
for anybody.

Within every person
there's knowledge somewhere,
we just have to wake up
and find it.

– Lakeisha Williams, 13 years old
Edison Junior High School
Rock Island, Illinois

While it is beyond the scope of this book to address the best practices in teaching and behavior management, there are some simple steps that teachers can take which will have a profound impact on all their students, and particularly those who are at risk for school failure and/or gang involvement. These fundamentals, described following, include such strategies as creating a positive classroom climate, establishing rapport with gang members, meeting gang members' particular educational needs, addressing problem behaviors, and enhancing students' self-esteem.

Classroom Climate

I have come to a frightening conclusion that I am the decisive element in the classroom. It is my personal approach that creates the climate. It is my daily mood that makes the weather. As a teacher, I possess a tremendous power to make a child's life miserable or joyous. I can be a tool of torture or an instrument of inspiration. I can humiliate or humor, hurt or heal. In all situations, it is my response that decides whether a crisis will be escalated or de-escalated and a child humanized or de-humanized.
        – Haim Ginott (1993)

Many underachieving students find their schools and teachers to be so aversive that they would rather be any place than in the classroom. Establishing a positive classroom climate is one strategy teachers can use to make school and the curriculum a rewarding and successful experience for students, and is a factor that can be easily orchestrated by teachers. A positive classroom climate is one which is productive and reinforcing to students. It is a climate in which students are challenged to succeed, assisted in doing so, and then rewarded for their achievements. A positive classroom environment is also a preventive behavior management strategy for teachers, as less behavior problems will occur in a classroom that is managed well and structured for learning.

> **Speaking Up!**
>
> This comment was made by a former gang member, relating his impression of school and teachers:
>
> *Some teachers think we respect them just because they are teachers. I don't. I respect those who are real and respect me. I, and most of my friends, can tell a phony teacher right away. We get sick of them. Lots of kids drop out because of them. A lot of us don't go to certain classes. Sometimes going to school is like*
>
> *(CONTINUED)*

CLASSROOM RULES

Classroom rules are the foundation of a
positive classroom climate, and communicate the teacher's expectations for
student behavior. At the beginning of
the year, teachers should establish and
post about five classroom rules. These
rules should be simple, specific, and
stated **positively**. Rules stated in a positive manner teach students what **to do**.
This is in direct contrast to the most
common variety of rules, which tell students what **not to do** or what types of
behavior are not allowed.

A compliance rule such as "Follow your
teacher's instructions immediately"
should be included in the four to five
classroom rules. All of the rules must be
observable and measurable so that the
students understand exactly what is expected of them and so that the teacher
can easily monitor compliance with the
rules. Examples of positively stated rules
include:

- Follow your teacher's instructions
  immediately.

- Bring all required materials with you
  to class.

- Wait to be called on before speaking.

- Check out a hall pass before leaving
  the room.

- Keep your hands and feet to yourself.

Within reason, teachers may wish to involve their students in the selection of
classroom rules. This class discussion
will help to clarify for the students why
the rules are needed in the classroom.
Additionally, students are often more
willing to abide by procedures in which
they have participated in developing
and thus have some "ownership" in.

After establishing the rules, post them
prominently in the classroom and then
teach the students the rules. Students
need to learn the classroom rules just as
they would learn any other content material. The students should also be
aware of the consequences for both
obeying and breaking the classroom
rules. When the students follow the
rules, they should be consistently reinforced for doing so. When they break a
classroom rule, a consequence should
be immediately and consistently applied. Finally, periodically review the
classroom rules to ensure that all the students remember them.

Consistency is of paramount importance
in establishing classroom rules. Fair classroom rules are enforced consistently for
all the students in the class, including

the gifted students, those with disabilities, and those who are involved with gangs. Once teachers begin making exceptions for students based on their perceptions of the students' abilities to succeed, a double standard exists. For example, many teachers will automatically expect a student who has a behavior disorder to cause problems in the classroom. Most will also expect gang members to cause trouble, and so will not expect them to follow the rules.

When this type of double standard exists, the rule-breaking behavior of those students becomes almost a self-fulfilling prophecy as most people tend to behave in the manner that is expected of them. It is extremely important that teachers not reduce their behavioral expectations for students who demonstrate problems such as aggression, opposition, and noncompliance. Not challenging students with realistically high behavioral expectations simply leads to elevated levels of inappropriate behavior among those students, and renders the classroom rules useless.

Speaking Up!

I got a reputation. I been a Crip since I was 12. Everyone expected me to be in. My old man was in. He in prison now. I ain't seen him for a while. My brothers are all in. I used to like school. I had a couple a teachers I liked. I think a lot of adults, they jump the gun too soon. They judge a lot of us as bein' bad 'cause of who our brothers are and where we come from. A lotta teenagers could get some help from teachers if they didn't mostly think the kids were bad. After a while . . . after a couple of years of hearing that you a bad person, that you probably a gang member . . . well you become a gang member. I don't think I'm a bad person, I just do what I gotta do.

I worked my way up and I gotta keep workin' at it to stay on top. My homies, they look up to me. I gotta make the decisions, give the orders. I gotta act like a leader. Adults, teachers, even they expect me to be bad. They so used to it. I don't know any other way. This is my life, these guys are my homies. I gotta live up to my rep . . . I be the way everybody expects me to. I been doin' it so long, I don't know nothin' else. I guess I'm just doin' what everyone expects me to do.

- Raoul, 15 years old

CLASSROOM ARRANGEMENT

In addition to the classroom rules, the physical space of the classroom itself must be a safe and secure learning environment for all students. All the students in the class must receive an equal opportunity to learn. While teachers need to ensure that their expectations and behaviors are not prejudiced against gang members, they must also be diligent in ensuring that those same students are not intimidating or preventing other students from participating and achieving in class. The classroom arrangement can help to accomplish this goal, in the following ways.

The furniture and equipment of the classroom should be arranged to permit the teacher an unobstructed view of all the students working. Ideally, teachers should identify a vantage point where they can face their students while observing and assisting during various instructional periods. This face-to-face arrangement not only allows teachers to be more "tuned in" to the activities in the classroom, but it communicates "with-it-ness" (Kounin, 1970) to the students. With-it-ness means that a teacher communicates, through verbal and body language, that he/she is aware of exactly what each and every student is doing during every minute of the class. When students realize that their teacher knows what's going on all the time, they are much less likely to misbehave.

To help communicate with-it-ness, teachers should seat any students who exhibit behavior problems at the front of the classroom, and separate from other students with similar problems. This is especially critical for gang members: Don't let students involved with gangs isolate themselves in the back of the classroom. This strategy not only makes it easier for teachers to watch for problems these students might experience, but it also provides many chances for the teacher to "catch them being good" (Rhode, Jenson, & Reavis, 1992) and to consequently provide them with frequent and consistent positive reinforcement.

CLASSROOM ROUTINES AND TIME ON TASK

Establishing classroom routines is another essential to creating a positive classroom climate. Consistently adhering to a schedule will provide a predictable framework for the class. This creates an environment in which the students know what is expected of them at all times throughout the day, whether they are engaged in independent seatwork, whole class instruction, free time activities, or a transition from one activity to the next. Smooth and rapid transitions will help to prevent the behavior problems that often occur during unstructured class time.

Smooth transitions and structured classroom routines also help to maximize academic engaged time. In order for students to achieve academically, they need to spend a great amount of time on task—much more than in the average classroom. *The Tough Kid Book* (Rhode et al., 1992) offers some helpful guidelines for teachers to determine if their students are spending the amount of time focused on relevant lessons required to experience school success.

A **minimum** of 70% of the school day should be planned for academics. To determine exactly how much time students should be engaged in academic activities, simply multiply the number of minutes in the entire school day by 70%. For example, in a typical elementary school students attend school from 8:30 AM-2:30 PM, which equates to six hours, or 360 minutes. Multiplied by 70% (360 X .70 = 252), this means that 252 minutes of each school day should be scheduled for academic learning time.

Then, during the academic learning time (70% of the school day), students need to be actively engaged in the learning process and on task at least 85% of the time in order to make adequate progress. Examples of being actively engaged include, but are not limited to, activities such as reading an assignment, working in cooperative learning groups, completing worksheets, participating in a class discussion, or asking the teacher questions.

PERFORMANCE EXPECTATIONS

In order to consistently progress in school, students should be expected to achieve a minimum of 80% mastery of content material. If students are not performing at that level, they should be assisted in reaching 80% mastery before moving on to new assignments. To monitor their progress, teachers should provide daily feedback, both written and verbal, on the students' efforts.

Not all students will be able to attain an 80% mastery level immediately. Many students who become involved with gangs, particularly, have had such low achieving school careers that they have become virtual experts at failure. Achieving 80% mastery may seem as accessible to those students as walking on the moon! Their teachers must have a plan in place to support their efforts to learn. Strategies such as cooperative learning, peer tutoring, reteaching, extra practice activities, and modified learning materials could be applied for all the students who need some extra assistance. A critical component of the plan, however, will be for the teacher to encourage student effort and consistently reward any small gains made. Once students experience even a little taste of success, they will become motivated to pursue higher goals.

For students to achieve success, they need to believe that they **can** achieve success. When teachers convey their expectations for student performance, they help to build the confidence their students require in order to strive academically. Teachers can communicate their belief in the students' ability to succeed by: (1) providing opportunities for all their students to be successful with academic tasks, adapting learning activities and materials to students' abilities if necessary; (2) making many positive comments during class instruction; (3) encouraging students to participate, and supporting any of their attempts to do so; and (4) continually stressing to the students that success can be reached through sustained effort.

Success

Success is knowing that you have the ability to do almost anything you put your mind to.

Success is knowing that everywhere you go you can educate people around you.

To be successful you have to work hard.

– Lakeisha Williams, 13 years old
Edison Junior High School
Rock Island, Illinois

POSITIVE REINFORCEMENT AND MOTIVATION

Closely tied to performance expectations are motivation strategies. The use of positive reinforcement is vitally important to establishing a positive classroom climate. Teachers need to continually motivate and encourage their students to do their best work and to behave appropriately at school. Some students are very self-motivated. Those students have probably experienced success at school and are working from that foundation of accomplishment. Students who submit to the lure of gang activity, on the other hand, typically have not been successful in school academically, socially, with extracurricular activities, or in organized athletics. Plus, these students are often lacking adult role models at home who stress the value of education. For these students, their teacher may be the only person in their environment who will motivate them to succeed in school.

Providing an adequate amount of social praise is one of the quickest and easiest methods of positively reinforcing students. All students need to be praised for the good things that they do. Students in the middle school or junior high school grades are particularly vulnerable. These students are experiencing a multitude of physical, emotional, attitudinal, and behavioral changes, and this is an exceptionally critical time period in which their sense of self-esteem is developing. Students at these grade levels could benefit from some extra social reinforcement in the classroom such as a smile, a pat on the back, or a praise statement.

Verbal encouragement enables teachers to show their students that they have faith in their abilities. It is kind of funny how some students think that teachers know everything. It follows that if a teacher verbalizes faith in a student, that student will have more confidence in completing a task or meeting behavioral expectations. This is a simple procedure with a significant impact. Encouraging statements include: "I know you can do this!"; "You're a smart kid, let's give it a try!"; "Thank you for following my directions."; "That is a very good question."; etc.

Most students need much more positive reinforcement than they currently receive. Teachers should strive to make about six positive statements during each hour of the school day, and the ratio of their positive to negative comments should be at least five or six to one. What kinds of behaviors should teachers reinforce with praise statements? Any behavior that is appropriate in the classroom or any behavior pertinent to achievement at school would be a good place to start.

In addition to praise and other forms of social reinforcement, there are many other ways to motivate students. "Activity reinforcers" are easy for teachers to

deliver, and generally don't cost anything to provide. Activity reinforcers are any activities, usually carried out in the classroom, that are enjoyable for students and which they will strive to earn. The most beneficial activities will be those that are also educational, such as use of a computer program, an exciting science experiment, an interesting guest speaker, a field trip, or viewing a movie on videotape which relates to the content matter in some way. The ideas are almost endless, and limited only by the teacher's imagination. However, teachers should be careful to offer reinforcers that are truly reinforcing to the **students**. Sometimes students have different ideas than their teacher about what is or isn't a rewarding activity. (Summary Box 3.12 provides some suggestions.)

Summary Box 3.12

Suggested Positive Reinforcers for Gang-Involved Students

- Bonus cards for:

  - Extra credit points

  - Homework passes

  - Longer lunch periods

  - 1/2 homework assignments

  - Double points on assignments

  (CONTINUED)

- Positive notes to parents

- Positive phone calls to parents

- Lunch with the teacher

- Prizes/awards from local merchants

- Fast food restaurant coupons

- Coupons for local arcades or recreation activities

- Certificates of completion for specific goals, both behavioral and academic

- Letters of commendation to students and parents

- Student featured in a story in a local or school newspaper

- Ethnic or cultural activities based on holiday traditions or other special days during the year to help students understand and be proud of their heritage and celebrate the differences among them

- Special holiday activities (class parties, etc.)

- Field trips

- Guest speakers on topics of interest

Reinforcers can also be delivered on a school-wide basis, and can contribute to a positive climate in the school as a whole. For example, certificates of merit can be given by administrators to reward students for showing academic effort or kind, considerate behaviors to others at school. These certificates might include: (1) Kind Student of the Week; (2) Perfect Attendance Award; (3) Academic Achievement Award; (4) Effort in Extracurricular Activities Award; (5) No Tardies Award; (6) Most Improved Grades Award; or (7) Best Effort Award.

Whatever method of reinforcement is used, teachers should convey their enthusiasm for delivering the reinforcer and for the positive behaviors and/or academic achievement that earned the reward, such as following the rules, finishing assignments on time, using appropriate language, etc. Even an ordinary activity, presented in a "hyped-up" manner, can become reinforcing to students. Teachers need to develop a little bit of a "game show host personality" to carry this off successfully, but the students will like it. It makes school more fun and interesting for them, and motivates them to succeed. Enthusiasm is contagious. Hype involves enthusiasm. Spread it around!

Some teachers view positive reinforcement as a form of bribery, but this is not the case as the reinforcement is provided only after the class or an individual student has behaved appropriately. Most students, and particularly at-risk students such as those involved with gangs, require a great deal of motivation. The delivery of positive reinforcement encourages these students to apply themselves and, as they do so, to become more and more intrinsically motivated by their own achievement over time.

REDUCTIVE CONSEQUENCES

In order to maintain all the positive effects in the classroom of implementing procedures such as classroom rules, high expectations, and positive reinforcement, misbehaviors must be dealt with efficiently when they arise. Students should be taught the behavioral expectations and made aware of the consequences for breaking the rules. Then negative consequences must follow any rule-breaking behavior, and the consequences must be fair and consistent in order to be effective with students and to prevent or decrease the problem behavior in the future.

Inconsistent discipline is worse than none at all. If teachers do not consistently apply a consequence for a rule-breaking behavior, the students will assume that it is not important to follow the rules all of the time. Behavioral problems will actually worsen if teachers punish a certain behavior one time and not another. When this is the case, the students will persistently test the limits to determine if their teacher really means what he/she says this time.

There are many effective reductive consequences available to teachers, and the most effective will be logically tied to the misbehavior. For example, if a young student is disrupting the class with tantrumming behavior, he/she could be removed to a time-out area so that the learning of the other students is not interrupted. If an older student destroys school property in a fit of anger, he/she could be directed to clean up the mess, and then to make retribution for the damage by assisting the custodial staff for a certain number of hours.

Any discipline procedures applied will be more effective at producing long-term, durable behavior changes in students if the teaching of a socially appropriate replacement behavior is inherent in the strategy. Whatever consequence is applied, teacher are cautioned to think before promising any type of a consequence. They should **never** promise or describe a consequence that they can't (or won't) back up, as the students will lose trust in and respect for the teacher who does not follow up with promised consequences.

Establishing Rapport With Gang Members

Treating students with respect is an essential requirement for teachers to establish rapport with youth gang members in the classroom. Respect is one of the three critical elements of the gang code of conduct (respect, reputation, and retaliation). When gang members do not receive the respect they think they deserve, their reputation depends upon some sort of hostile or violent retaliation toward the individual who "disrespected"

them—even if that individual is a teacher. This does not mean that teachers should be intimidated by gang members at school. However, teachers must strive at all times to base their interactions with students who are involved in gangs upon mutual courtesy rather than fear, intimidation, or hostility. Attempting to use intimidation or threats with gang members in the classroom will only escalate any behavior problems that may be occurring.

Treating all students equally, in a fair, respectful, and consistent manner, is the key to establishing rapport with gang members in the classroom. This may be difficult, as teachers are human and will "connect" with some students (particularly well-behaved, high achieving students) more easily than others. However, as professionals, teachers must make sure all their students are provided with equal learning and social opportunities. Teachers must put aside their feelings about students' personal lives in order to give each student a fair and equal opportunity to learn. Teachers do not have to condone gang-related behaviors and violence in order to accept gang-involved students as individuals worthy of respect in the classroom.

PRAISING GANG MEMBERS

Like all the other students in the classroom, those students involved with gangs need positive reinforcement from their teachers. However, unlike most students, gang members may not be willing to acknowledge that this praise has any significance for them. In fact, these students will probably be embarrassed by public praise, and fellow gang members may ridicule the students. Their reaction to public praise may be a retaliatory act such as an inappropriate remark or action toward the teacher that will serve to reestablish the students in their more comfortable (noncompliant) role.

In order to avoid this problem, while still establishing a reinforcing relationship with these students, teachers may find that it is more effective to praise gang members privately than publicly. Some confidential methods that might be used include sending home "good behavior" notes to the students and their parents or placing telephone calls to their homes.

"Good Behavior" Notes

Teachers can write a note to a student's parent(s) relating positive behaviors the student has shown in school. Some examples may include an improved assignment score, increased homework completion, contributing to a class discussion, or showing a positive attitude. These "good behavior" notes can either be mailed directly to the student's home or given to the student to deliver to his/her parent(s).

Parents of students involved with gangs will almost always be delightfully surprised when a teacher sends a note with the sole purpose of relating positive behaviors of their child. Many of these parents have probably never had a positive contact with the school system. Unfortunately, too many educators only contact parents when students are in trouble.

Initially, the students themselves will probably be very suspicious and curious about why a teacher would want to send a "good behavior" note home. If they ask about the notes, teachers can use that opportunity to further reinforce the students for their appropriate behavior and communicate their faith in the students' abilities to continually improve. Again, teachers should be sure to have this conversation only out of earshot of the other students so that gang-involved students do not "lose face."

Calling Students at Home

Telephone calls are another option for privately reinforcing at-risk students. The teacher might call a student's parent(s) directly to tell them about a positive behavior their child exhibited at school. Or, the teacher might want to call the **students** at home to reinforce their good behavior in the classroom. One high school English teacher of a tough group of students did just that, and relates the positive effects of making those personal phone calls to students just to show that she cared about

them. This was an entirely unique experience for most of her students, as described in *My Posse Don't Do Homework*
(1992):

> . . . I tried to call at least two or
> three kids per week just to let
> them know that I was thinking
> about them. After they got over
> the initial wariness, they started to
> respond and most of my
> discipline problems disappeared.
> If I called a kid and explained, for
> example, that talking during my
> instruction was impolite and I'd
> appreciate it if he or she would try
> not to be rude, there was no
> reason for the student to create a
> power play out of the situation
> because nobody else knew what
> I had asked. Most of the kids got
> a kick out of receiving a phone call
> from a teacher and they liked to
> say casually, "Oh, yes, I was
> talking to Miss Johnson on the
> phone last night . . . ." Leroy
> Wyman was on my list, but I
> hadn't had a reason or an
> opportunity to call him and he
> grew impatient. He interrupted
> class one day to find out whether
> I had, indeed, been calling his
> classmates.
>
> "You been calling kids at home?"
> he asked.
>
> "Yes," I said.

> "What for?"
>
> "Just to talk to them, see how
> they're doing," I said.
>
> "Ha!" Leroy said. "You calling
> them to scare them and you know
> it. If they don't act right, you
> probably ask to talk to their
> mother on the spot."
>
> "No I don't," I insisted.
>
> "You say you just calling to talk,
> but you really calling to scare
> people. You can't fool me with
> that psychology."
>
> I called Leroy that night. The
> moment he heard my voice, he
> broke out in loud laughter.
>
> "Ha! Ha!" he chortled. "I psyched
> you. I knew you was gonna call
> me."
>
> "You were right," I said.
>
> "So what's on the agenda?" he
> asked. "Usually people got
> something to say when they call
> you."
>
> "I just wanted to say how much I
> enjoy having you in my class. You
> have a bright, inquiring mind and
> you are always open to discussing
> new ideas and concepts. That's a
> rare and wonderful trait and I am
> very proud of you."

Leroy didn't respond for a few seconds.

"You sure you don't want to tell that to my mother?" (pp. 150-151)

CONCEPT OF CARE

Teachers who are able to demonstrate care and empathy for students are those who will be the most effective teachers. As stated previously, this is easier said than done with many gang-involved students. Some teachers just instinctively dislike these students. Their negative feelings about students who exhibit problem behaviors are often subconsciously reflected in their actions. The verbal and body language of these teachers is then perceived by the students as, "He doesn't like me," "She is always in my face," "He treats me differently than everyone else in this class," etc. The typical response to this perception of prejudice is escalated negative behavior on the part of the students. Students generally know when their teachers are intimidated by them or simply do not like or respect them as people.

In order to make a difference in the lives of these students, teachers will probably need to tell them in words that they care about the students' well-being. This way, the students will not misinterpret their teacher's actions as mean or dogmatic when they were not intended this way. Students may not realize that their teachers do things such as assign make-up work or apply behavioral consequences because they want the students to learn academic concepts or how to behave more appropriately. Getting in the habit of saying, for example, "I do this because I care about what you learn," or, "I am concerned that you learn the appropriate behavior" is a method that teachers can use to verbally emphasize their concern for their students.

Real-Life Teacher Tale
Team Spirit

The following incident happened to a professional who was volunteering on a regular basis at his neighborhood high school in order to serve as a positive role model for the students there.

. . . I developed many relationships at the school. Most students bonded to me. But not all the students were excited about my coming. In fact, there was Paul.

I'll never forget Paul. He was a real tough-looking guy, about 6'2", 220 lbs. He had just transferred to this school. Rumor had it that he had been in and out of many juvenile detention centers. In fact, the teachers were scared of him. And why not? Two years ago, he had

(CONTINUED)

---

been sentenced for stabbing his English teacher in the chest during an argument. Everyone let him do what he wanted. He strolled to class late. Never carried a book in hand because he was just too cool for school.

From time to time, he sat in on my lunch sessions but never said anything. I think the only reason he came was to "check out the babes."

Whenever I tried to get him involved, he just stared at me with his piercing eyes. He intimidated me. He was like a bomb just waiting to explode. But I wasn't going to give up on him. Every time he came, I tried to engage him in the discussion, but he wasn't interested.

One day, I had enough and the bomb exploded.

During this particular session, we were developing our "goals collage." Students were cutting out pictures of their goals from magazines and pasting them onto a poster board. We were 20 minutes into the session when Paul strolled in.

I asked for a volunteer to share his or her goals collage with the rest of the class. Julie, a petite girl, stood up and began sharing her dreams. I was happy to see Julie stand up because, when I first met her, she was so shy.

"I'm going to go to medical school to become a doctor."

All of a sudden, laughter broke out from the back of the room.

"Please. You, a doctor? Be for real. You ain't gonna be anybody."

All heads turned to the back of the room. Paul was laughing at his statement.

I was shocked. I couldn't believe what just took place. There was complete silence. What should I do? My adrenaline was flowing strong.

"Paul, that's not right. Who are you to put somebody else down?"

"Yo, teach, you dissin' me? Are you disrespecting me? Do you know who I am? Look man, I'm an OG, original gangster. Don't mess with me; you'll get hurt."

He started walking toward the door.

"No, Paul, that doesn't fly. You have no right to put somebody else down. Enough is enough. You don't have to be here. Either you're part of the group or you're not. We've got a team here that supports one another. And, Paul, you have so much potential.

(CONTINUED)

We want your participation. You have so much to offer the group. I care about you and this entire group. That's why I'm here. Are you going to be a team player?"

Paul looked over his shoulder and gave me a stare of terror. He opened the door and walked out, slamming the door behind him.

The class was shaken by this drama, and so was I.

After class, I packed up my materials and started making my way to the parking lot. As I approached my car, someone called out to me.

I turned around and to my surprise, it was Paul. He was walking quickly toward me. A state of fear came over me. Part of me wanted to get help, but it happened so fast that I couldn't move.

"Mr. Smith, you remember what you said to me?"

"Yeah, Paul."

"Did you mean what you said about caring for me and wanting me to be part of the team?"

"Yeah, of course, Paul."

"Well, no one has ever in my life told me that they care for me. You are the first person to ever say that. I want to be part of the team. Thanks for caring enough to stand up to me. I'll apologize to Julie tomorrow in front of the entire class."

I couldn't believe my ears. I was in shock. I could hardly speak.

As he walked away, tears of joy welled up in my eyes and started rolling down my face. I had been truly touched for life. That day I decided to commit my life to empowering our young people to realize their true potential (pp. 201-203).

— Marlon Smith (Canfield & Hansen, 1995)

The School Violence Advisory Panel of the California Commission on Teacher Credentialing surveyed high school students to explore their views on teacher effectiveness (Stephens, 1993). The results of that survey showed that students typically categorize their teachers into three main groups, with only one group being consistently successful as educators.

The first group of teachers were labeled "Strict and Distant." These were teachers that the students perceived to be rigid, inflexible, following rules to the letter without concern for individual differences or needs, and appearing to have little individual interest in their students as human beings. The students said the nickname of this category of teachers could be "check collectors."

The second category of teachers were labeled "Inconsistent and Afraid." This was the group of teachers that students held in the lowest esteem. Students viewed these teachers as trying to maintain what little authority they had by not enforcing the classroom rules or implementing discipline procedures. These teachers were viewed as especially ineffectual in the classroom. They were reluctant to maintain the rules and regulations because they were afraid that the students would rebel and either physically or verbally attack them in retaliation. The students felt that these

teachers were uncaring, fearful, and timid. The nickname given to this category of teachers was "shark bait."

The third group of teachers were thought by the students to be the fewest in number, but this was also the group of teachers that students perceived to be the most effective and had the greatest chance for success with students in the classroom. This group of teachers were labeled "Tough But Caring." The students described these teachers as demanding, caring, consistent, and fair. The students also said they thought these teachers would be their advocates if the need arose.

Summary Box 3.13 summarizes the polled students' classifications of their high school teachers.

Summary Box 3.13

Categories of Teacher Behavior as Perceived by High School Students

Where do you fit?

Strict and Distant	Inconsistent and Afraid	Tough But Caring
Rigid, inflexible; little concern for students' individual differences; nicknamed **check collectors**	Little or no discipline; timid, fearful of student retaliation; nicknamed **shark bait**	Fewest in number; demanding; caring; consistent and fair; most effective with students; would act as student advocate

Meeting the Educational Needs of Gang Members

"Tough But Caring" is an apt description for the profile of a teacher who will be most successful with gang-involved students in the classroom. These teachers will have high expectations for the students' achievement and conduct, and will be respected by the gang members for their fair and consistent enforcement of the classroom rules. It is quite possible for an effective teacher to establish genuine rapport with these students and to make a profound difference in their educational careers. Teachers should keep in mind, however, that many gang-involved students will have had aversive experiences with teachers in the past. Some of these students will likely transfer their negative feelings onto all their future teachers, and these are the students that teachers will have to try the hardest with.

The most beneficial influence a teacher can have on gang-involved students is to encourage them to stay in school. There are three main components to meeting the specific educational needs of these students, and thus making school a rewarding experience for them. As stated previously, respectful teacher behavior is a prerequisite to all other interactions, with classroom rules and consequences applied to all the students in a fair and consistent manner. Second, these students will likely require additional assistance and remediation of skill deficits

Speaking Up!

There are some teachers we like and respect. They have fair rules and they're honest with us. They don't treat us bad like some teachers do. There is one teacher I would do anything for. I protect her if anything starts happening in her room. I keep my homies in line in there, teach them how to respect her. They listen to me. She treats us all good. They found out she's not like the rest of 'em. She believes in us. She really teach us stuff . . . important stuff. Some teachers we hate 'cause they don't have respect for us. They think we're stupid. I hate them. When we have a chance we hassle them all we can. We hassle any teacher who don't give us respect.

- Cameron, 15 years old

and/or some type of accommodation in order to succeed academically. Finally, both the academic and social skills taught to these students must be relevant to their real-life skill use.

Understanding that academic concepts and prosocial skills are related to real-life skills and employment opportunities is very important for students to understand, especially if they reside in low socioeconomic areas where unemployment is high. Many school-age gang members live in an environment surrounded by adults who are not employed. Some have older siblings and even parents who are gang members. Many of these students observe adults either receiving money from the mailbox (welfare or public aid checks); from selling illegal narcotics; or from other criminal activities such as theft, burglary, and/or extortion. To these students, this probably looks like "easy money." They might wonder why they should be expected to go to work for hours every day when they grow up. If those students are to acquire gainful and legitimate employment they need to

understand the connection between achievement at school and employment in the real world. They must understand that education gives them **choices** about how they can live their lives, and teachers have to establish that link in the classroom every day.

Explaining to students when, where, and how they might use a particular skill in real life is one method teachers can use to increase student motivation and time on task. One student teacher in a ninth grade algebra class used this technique quite successfully. This student teacher assumed he would simply teach algebra to the students in the class. After his first day he was anxious about his assignment, however, when he discovered that the class was composed of low achieving, at-risk students. Rather than giving up or giving in to the student apathy, low achievement, off-task talking, and truancy that ran rampant in that classroom, the teacher determined some common areas of interest among the students through observation and casual conversation. He then based many of the algebra problems assigned on those interests: sports, cooking, carpentry and construction, eating at fast food restaurants, hunting, and weight lifting.

After using that tactic to interest and motivate the students to complete the math problems, the student teacher began to relate use of the mathematical skills to real-life problem-solving situations, such as ratios for cooking when enlarging or reducing a recipe for more or less people. By making the curriculum relevant to the students' real-life needs, they were effectively engaged in math class thus increasing their achievement in math. In the process the student teacher became a more reinforcing and rewarding figure for the students. As a result they earned better grades and probably retained more real-life skills than they would have if the teacher used more traditional teaching methods such as a reliance on teaching math theory. The moral of the story? Make curricula more motivating for at-risk students by teaching real-life applications of the content.

In addition to academic skills, social skills should also be related to real-life situations in order to have any impact on gang-involved students. Teachers should stress the importance of compliance to rules using real-life examples appropriate for the students' age and developmental level. For example, the students could be engaged in class discussions and role plays to emphasize

the results of compliance/noncompliance to rules at school and/or laws in society. Younger students might role play the outcome of listening to/not listening to a lifeguard at the swimming pool or following/not following a bus driver's instructions. Older students could role play following/not following the boss' directions at a job site, for example. Or teachers might assign cooperative learning groups to identify and trace the possible consequences, both positive and negative, of various forms of rule-following/rule-breaking behavior at home, in school, and in the community. Use of these kinds of activities will stress to students the importance of following rules and obeying laws.

For an even more powerful illustration of the consequences of rule-following/rule-breaking behavior, a professional from the community, such as a police officer, juvenile justice representative, probation officer, or social worker, might be invited as a guest speaker to talk candidly to the class about his/her area of expertise. This way the students can learn that appropriate choices made consistently, and beginning at an early age while they are still in school, can positively affect their future potential, achievements, and lifestyles. Students must realize that they are more than products of their environment, and that they can direct their futures through their own responsible behavior.

(**Note:** Educators should be cautious about inviting "reformed" gang members/ juvenile delinquents to speak to students. These individuals may exhibit sensitivity about personal questions asked by the students and "clam up," or worse, feed into the perceptions of the young audience and make their former gang lifestyle sound exciting and glamorous.)

Addressing Problem Behaviors

Despite teachers' best intentions, it is likely that they will find themselves on the receiving end of some problem behaviors when they are educating students who are involved with gangs. In 1993, the School Violence Advisory Panel of the California Council on Teacher Credentialing identified the top three forms of violence teachers are likely to encounter in the classroom (Stephens, 1993). Extreme forms of physical violence were not routine. Instead, verbal harassment, bullying, and intimidation were common. Examples of these behaviors demonstrated by students included intense staring (stare downs or "mad dogging"), personal ridicule, and cursing or yelling.

This type of school violence can be termed psychological intimidation, and these are the kinds of behaviors that

administrators often expect teachers to be able to handle without reliance upon office referrals. However, the average university-level general education teacher training curriculum does not usually include behavior management or violence prevention/intervention strategies. Most teachers are not comfortable dealing with the violent or highly aggressive student behaviors that are now becoming everyday occurrences in classrooms, and if given a choice would prefer to ignore a gang problem in the classroom rather than confront the situation.

Real-Life Teacher Tale
Mad Dogging

My most scary moment came just last year. I'm a new teacher (three years) at a junior high school teaching math. Teaching was all I'd ever wanted to do, and this school made me happy.

One afternoon, I got my kids started on an assignment, and told them I had some business to take care of in the office. This had never been a disruptive bunch, so I felt comfortable leaving them unsupervised.

I was walking down the hallway and turned a corner to find three boys who were as surprised to see me as I

(CONTINUED)

---

was them. One was being held up against the lockers by another and the third was standing by and just watching.

When I saw them, I froze. I was really scared. I didn't know what to do or say, and I must have looked so pitiful. I know one thing, I certainly didn't scare them.

Two of the boys just glared at me. I felt like they were staring me down. They were intimidating, even though they were just kids. The one against the locker looked helpless, and he never took his eyes off of me.

I told them to return to their class and turned around and left in a hurry. They hadn't made a move when I left, so I never knew whether they listened to me or not.

When I got back to my class, I was sweating. I must have looked like I'd seen a ghost, because several of my kids stared at me for a minute, then went back to work.

For the rest of the day I felt terrible. I knew that I had shunned my responsibilities. The school wasn't such a happy place any more. I still don't know why the boys were there, or what they were doing, but I do know that I can't look any of them in the eye when I see them.

You know, there wasn't any training for this when I studied to be a teacher. I was so naive. I know it was part of my job to make sure these kids are safe, and I blew it. This wasn't what being a teacher was supposed to be about. Hopefully there will never be a next time because it still scares me.

– T. J., junior high school math teacher

Teachers need to learn how to safely and productively confront these behaviors rather than simply tolerating them. An accumulation of this type of behavior from students can result in feelings of burnout, isolation, and a loss of self-esteem for the teacher, as well as an out of control classroom. There are four main steps to effectively redirecting a problem behavior into a more positive, socially appropriate channel: (1) recognizing the problem behavior; (2) confronting the behavior; (3) redirecting the behavior; and (4) providing a structured choice.

Some problem behaviors that students demonstrate at school may actually serve as survival skills in the neighborhoods where they live. There are many negative home or environmental influences that teachers are simply not able to control, and teachers should concentrate on changing only those behaviors that need to be changed so that gang-involved students can achieve to their highest potential at school, without disrupting the learning environment for other students. Other problem behaviors may just need to be viewed as irrelevant and left alone.

When problem behaviors do arise, teachers should recognize that most of these behaviors are functional for the students; they serve a purpose for the students in that they are used to help get their needs met. For example, if a student is not receiving enough (or any) positive attention, that student will probably settle for negative attention and act out in order to receive it. Because the misbehaviors that prompt the negative teacher attention serve a purpose for the student, simply punishing those behaviors will not result in a durable behavior change or teach the student a more acceptable, socially appropriate behavior.

After a teacher recognizes a problem behavior that requires attention, the next step is to confront the problem behavior by acknowledging the behavior and specifically describing it for the student. For example, if a gang-involved student is staring down his/her teacher as an intimidation tactic, the teacher could verbally acknowledge and confront the behavior in the following manner: "Billy, I notice that you are staring at me. Staring is not going to make me change my mind about the assignment; you are required to make it up before you take the test."

The third step requires the teacher to redirect the student's problem behavior to an appropriate alternative. For example: "Rather than wasting your time staring at me, you need to begin the math assignment you missed. I am asking you to do it because it contains material you need to know to pass the test. I know you can pass the test with flying colors if you learn this material before you take it."

Once the problem behavior (in this example, staring) is recognized, confronted, and redirected, the final step is to give the student a structured choice between two safe and/or satisfactory outcomes, such as: "You need to get out your math book and get started on page 22. I can help you get started **or** you can start on your own and I will check to see how you are doing in a few minutes. Which would you like to do?"

Giving students a structured choice allows them the "power" to make their own decisions. Helping students to self-manage their own behavior and make appropriate choices in this way serves to reduce noncompliance, and also allows students to "save face" by not engaging them in a power struggle for which they would feel compelled to retaliate against the teacher who backed them into a corner.

Summary Box 3.14 details the four steps teachers can use to address problem behaviors in a manner that supports more socially acceptable alternatives.

When implementing the four steps of redirecting gang-involved students' problem behaviors, it will help the teacher to remember that gang members will not respect a teacher who they perceive to be weak or easy to intimidate. Even if the teacher **is** intimidated by the behavior of a gang member, he/she must project a confident, in-charge attitude. Most gang members will respond to firm

Summary Box 3.14

Steps to Redirect Problem Behaviors

- **Recognize**

  Example: The teacher must deal with intense staring.

- **Acknowledge and Confront**

  "Billy, I notice that you are staring at me. Staring is not going to make me change my mind about the assignment; you are required to make it up before you take the test."

- **Redirect**

  "Rather than wasting your time staring at me, you need to begin the math assignment you missed. I am asking you to do it because it contains material you need to know to pass the test. I know you can pass the test with flying colors if you learn this material before you take it."

- **Structured Choice**

  "You need to get out your math book and get started on page 22. I help you **or** you can start on your own and I will check to see how you are doing in a few minutes. Which would you like to do?"

and fair discipline in the classroom, and will comply with a teacher who establishes classroom rules and consistently backs them up. In fact, structured discipline is the customary pattern within a gang itself (i.e., the lower ranking members are taught to respect and adhere to the established rules of the gang leader).

Speaking Up!

This sage bit of advice was offered by a student who attended a high school populated by a number of violent gangs:

There are teachers at my school who are able to control the gang members in class and teach us at the same time. These teachers have integrity. They are fair and consistent with all of us—no matter who we are. These teachers make everyone follow the rules—and everyone knows it. Everyone knows they will be treated fairly and equally. There's no double standard. Even the gang members show respect for these teachers because they don't compromise what is right in their classrooms.

- Julia, 17 years old

Enhancing Student Self-Esteem

Perhaps the most significant positive classroom technique that a teacher can implement will be any method of enhancing students' self-esteem. A lack of self-esteem has been identified by police officers, who deal with these individuals on a daily basis on the street, as the most common characteristic of gang-involved youth. These students often have no legitimate ways to express their identity and receive recognition from their peers and adults at home, at school, or in the community. And because they have low self-esteem they have little confidence in their abilities to excel, and hesitate to try new skills (whether academic, social, or extracurricular) because of their fear of failure. The outcome is that they resort to gang activity in an attempt to fill the emptiness of their lives.

Teacher behavior can have a major impact on students' self-esteem. The process of building self-esteem in the classroom does not require special methods, materials, or techniques. Teachers need only be respectful, perceptive, approachable, and understanding of their students' feelings. Basic communication skills and lots of positive reinforcement tell students how much they are appreciated. These simple methods will help at-risk students learn that they are competent and valued human beings.

Following are suggestions that emphasize basic human values and promote a school environment where students are likely to feel appreciated and be successful. Lopez (1994) calls these the "Seven A's" for violence prevention and positive relationships:

1. **Acknowledgment**

   Teachers should identify and reinforce the unique talents and abilities of each individual student. Communicate to the students that they are valued for all different kinds of reasons. Promote and accept diversity in the classroom. Make all the students aware and proud of the talents they already have. Teach them how to build on existing skills by providing new projects and challenges that they can master.

2. **Acceptance**

   Accept and respect all students as deserving human beings. Teachers need to consistently demonstrate respect for students through both the way they speak to and behave toward them.

3. **Approval**

   Most people want to be successful at something. Provide a consistent number of genuine verbal praise statements to students. Through verbal reinforcement, instill a belief in students that they can be successful and attain their goals. Teachers will also need to provide appropriate levels of constructive criticism so that students learn positive replacement behaviors for any problem behaviors they exhibit.

4. **Appreciation**

   Create an "appreciation list" that includes qualities that can be appreciated in every student in the classroom. When a student's behavior becomes frustrating or challenging, refer to the list to help focus on more positive aspects of the student's character. Accentuate the positive!

5. **Attention**

   When students are talking, teachers need to provide their undivided attention. This is a method of showing respect for students. Create a comfortable classroom environment where students feel free to express their feelings.

6. **Admiration**

   Teachers need to recognize the many fine qualities that students embody. Then, teachers should make a specific point of telling the students why and how they are valued.

7. **Affection**

    Teachers should let students know
    that they care about them. Teach-
    ers who show their concern and
    support for all students foster a feel-
    ing of security in the classroom that
    promotes high levels of achieve-
    ment. Students feel safe to try new
    tasks and to take risks in these class-
    rooms. Smiles, pats on the back,
    supportive and encouraging com-
    ments, a warm voice tone, and ap-
    proachable body language can all
    be used to reflect affection towards
    others. An environment that is car-
    ing and supportive will encourage
    students to take risks and achieve to
    their highest potential.

Speaking Up!

This comment was made by a
student at a group session in
response to a question about
how teachers could help students:

*I would tell teachers not to get mad
at the kids; to put aside special time
for them and give them more attention and show them more affection.*

                        - Cindy, 15 years old

Note that while implementing the "Seven
A's" in the classroom, it is important for
the teacher to structure academic and behavioral goals so that the students will be
able to experience success. The activities
at which students can excel or may be
simple to learn are instant esteem build-
ers. These tasks that are easily accomplished can then be balanced with those
that are more challenging.

Working With Parents to Prevent Gang Involvement

While schools can do much to prevent
and curb the gang involvement of their
students, parents and other primary
caretakers are by far the most influential
people in children's lives. Collaboration
between educators and parents will be
critical if a gang intervention effort is to
succeed. In planning and implementing
school policies and/or programs to reduce gang behaviors, educators must remember that the majority of parents are
concerned about their children's well-
being and behavior. Most parents will
be receptive to attempts to include
them in the process; parents should always be perceived as partners in gang
intervention.

Real-Life Teacher Tale
Parental Discipline

My school is a fairly good sized elementary in the midwest. We go from "K" through fifth, mixed races, with not too many problems. I've been teaching here for 34 years, and for the last three we've been discussing gang problems. Personally, I hadn't seen any and I guess I was glad for that.

Coming back after a three-day weekend, one fifth grade kid in my class has his head shaved. He's black, and since I'd seen other black kids with shaved heads, I didn't see any big deal in it. The peculiar thing about this kid is that on that Monday, he sat real still for most of the class. No turning sideways or looking at the kid behind him. This was unusual for him because he was always, what would you say, "active" in class. Not always in a positive way, either. The kids around him were giggling and kind of secretive, so my curiosity was aroused. Several times I would walk toward the side of the room he was sitting on, and he would make eye contact with me and keep his face toward me.

I finally got behind him and saw that he had one, small braid hanging off of the lower left side of his head. He had a small black rubber band holding it together.

I asked him what it was for, and he said it was "his style." My response was that it was a gang sign since it was only on the left side of his head. He told me it wasn't, and I have to admit, he'd never shown any signs before.

Once I started talking to him, the whole class took notice. I knew I was being backed into a corner. The other kids knew it was a gang sign, and they knew you couldn't have it in school. I asked the kid to come with me to the office, and he told me no, that it wasn't a gang sign. I told him we'd leave that up to the principal. He still refused to go, until after several commands when he pushes the desk over and walks out the door.

I follow him, and he walks past the office and out the door. As the classes change, I bring this to the attention of the principal and leave it up to him.

(CONTINUED)

Well, I'm still not sure what happened after that, except that this kid is back in my class two days later with the braid cut off. The principal told me he contacted the boy's father who came to the school and took care of it. Maybe some parents do still care.

– G.S., fifth grade teacher

Parents of children who are involved with youth gangs should be concerned not only about their children's safety, but about their own and other family members' safety as well. In any home in which a child or adolescent is affiliated with a street gang, the entire household will likely be affected. Police have responded to numerous cases where houses have been the target of drive-by shootings, homes have been fire bombed or damaged by arson, family vehicles have been damaged or destroyed, parents have been threatened, and siblings assaulted. Incidents of this type occur simply because someone living in the home became involved with a gang. Rival gang members are not concerned if an innocent victim is caught in the cross fire. Consequently gang members put their family members in a very dangerous position.

The same principles that form the zero tolerance policy at school should be applied at home. Parents must inform their children that gang behavior will not be tolerated under any circumstances. Before parents can address a potential gang problem with their young wannabes, however, they need to recognize the primary indicators of youth gang involvement. Summary Box 3.15 provides a list of observable characteristics typical of gang-involved youth. Parents can use this list, created by gang unit officers very familiar with gang member behavior, to determine whether their children may be involved with a gang. Gang awareness seminars, presented either in the community by police officers or within schools, will also be helpful.

Speaking Up!

When they beat up my little brother, man, that's when I got out [of the gang]. I still have to avoid them, ya know. You're never really out.

– Sam, 13 years old

Summary Box 3.15

Warning Signs of Possible Gang Involvement (or "In a Gang . . . Not My Kid!")

If you see two of these warning signs, it is time to open the lines of communication with your child regarding street gangs. If you see three or more, the situation could be serious and you need to seek outside intervention immediately.

1. Buying, or wanting you to buy, an excessive amount of blue, red, black, or gold for their wardrobe.

2. Wearing the same color or combination of colors daily. Look for red and black, blue and black, gold and black, or all blue or all red. Don't overlook colored shoes or shoe laces.

3. Wearing their pants "sagging down" over their hips. Often, boxer shorts of a particular color (see #1 and #2) are worn under the pants so their color can be seen.

4. Wanting only a certain brand of clothing (e.g., Nike, FILA), or an abundance of sports apparel, particularly of one team. Make sure they are true fans: many athletic teams' merchandise contains logos, colors, or numbers significant to gangs.

5. Wearing a lot of gold or silver jewelry. Where did they get it/how did they afford it? Or wearing commercial or customized jewelry with gang symbols.

6. Getting tattoos, professional or homemade, containing gang terms or symbols.

7. Drawing gang graffiti on school books, clothing, or in their bedroom.

8. Using gang slang in their conversations with friends or family members.

9. Withdrawing from family members; not wanting to be around family. Desiring too much privacy.

10. Having trouble at school; lower grades, fighting, suspensions, skipping classes.

11. Associating with "undesirables," especially those wearing gang colors.

(CONTINUED)

Summary Box 3.15 (CONTINUED)

12. Not willing to let you meet their friends, or not willing to provide information about who they're with, where they're going, or what they'll be doing.

13. Staying out later than usual or breaking curfew often. (Ask why.)

14. Developing a major "attitude problem" with you, teachers, or other adults in a position of authority. This includes verbal and/or physical aggression or threats.

15. Using hand signs while in the presence of other young people.

16. Starting to use alcohol, tobacco, or other drugs, or carrying drug-related items.

17. Carrying large amounts of cash, drugs, or drug-related items.

18. Carrying, or talking about, weapons such as guns, knives, etc.

19. Being caught with, or arrested with, other young people in gang-related activities.

20. Talking about being initiated, being "jumped in," being "blessed in," wanting to be in a gang, or actually saying they're a gang member.

21. You're told they are in a gang by other people!

The fight against gangs begins in your own home!

ACTIVE PARENTING

There are several steps that parents can take to become better equipped to deal with any gang behaviors exhibited by their children. First and foremost, parents need to act like parents. Parents need to consistently ask their children where they are going, when they will be home, and who they will be with. Then, parents should check to see whether their children are actually where they say they will be.

Adequate adult supervision of school-age children must be in place at all times: This is a primary gang prevention method. For example, parents should call other parents to arrange after-school visits or sleepovers rather than simply taking their children's word that the other parents will be at home. If their children want to attend a special event, the parents can drop them off and pick them up. Parents might also want to act as chaperons at various school and community events.

Parental intervention/prevention procedures may take a variety of forms. Parents need to spend time with their children. Identify activities and outings that all the family members will enjoy and do these as a group. Parents should provide structured and consistent limits and routines for their children's time and activities. They should structure family rules that are fair and consistent for all, and enforce the rules. Time for family meetings designed to share opinions, concerns, and implement problem solving when necessary should also be set aside.

> **Speaking Up!**
>
> *Man . . . my mom don't care. My old man, he kicked me out. These guys, the VLs [Vice Lords], are my homies, my family. They take care of me. They have love for me. I know I can trust them. We have rules. We have discipline. My parents never cared enough to have any rules for me or my brothers. We could get away with anything. Parents have to be more strict and stick to the rules so their kids will know they care.*
>
> – Shannon, 17 years old

Parents need to help their children identify and participate in after-school clubs, music programs, sports, city recreation, or church programs of interest. This helps occupy their time in a supervised manner. Using this strategy, youth are much less likely to have excess time on their hands which often leads to trouble.

Parents need to be active with their children in activities outside the home. If possible, they could sponsor or supervise youth programs. They could encourage other children and families to join. If parents are not aware of local supervised activities, they could call their neighborhood school, social service agencies, recreation center, or law enforcement department. They should make sure that programs and other functions at school, at home, or or in the community that their children participate in are closely supervised by responsible adults.

After joining activity groups, parents can help their children set goals for progress, whether the goal concerns athletics, academics, learning a new skill, or a challenge of some other type. Then, they could monitor and support their children's progress made toward the goal. Accomplishing goals will help to enhance children's self-esteem, and make them less susceptible to the lure of gangs.

Finally, all parents must have an open line of communication with their children. All children need to be educated about the dangers and repercussions of gang involvement.

Love

If you love me you would teach me the right way to live, not the wrong way.

If you love me you care, and if I love you I would do the same.

If I love you I would respect you.

If you love me you would make me feel special.

If you teach me right, if you love me, then you care.

I care; I love you; I respect you. That means we love each other.

– Lakeisha Williams, 13 years old
Edison Junior High School
Rock Island, Illinois

Some youth will not like this regime of adult supervision. Some will accuse their parents of "being unfair" or of "spying on them." In this case, the parents can explain that supervision, guardianship, and protection of children is their job, and continue to stand firm with their expectations of always knowing where their children are, who they are with, what they are doing, and when they will be home. As Dr. Mitchell

Rosenthall (1972), a child psychiatrist, stresses:

Nothing today is as important to parents to recognize as the need to set limits. Parents have to be able to take positions about bed time or drinking or sleepovers. They've got to know where they stand on curfews, school night dating, chaperons, or study time. They've got to hold that line in the face of bickering and blackmail and all the other tactics youngsters use to get their way. The great thing is that the payout is that their children will be under control and they will feel better about themselves and feel better about their parents.

Without a doubt, it is the parents' job to set goals, behavioral expectations, and limits for their children. However, this may not be an easy task for all parents. For example, single or divorced parents may have a particularly difficult time of arranging for adequate supervision of their children. In these cases, parents might make efforts to reorganize work and social schedules so that they are better able to monitor their children's activities or participate more actively in their children's lives. Or, enlisting the aid of a relative or forming a child care partnership with other parents in the neighborhood may provide a solution. Simply spending time with at-risk children is an important step in discouraging them from becoming involved in gang activity.

Some parents might also require assistance with behavior management techniques. The same behaviors that are intimidating to teachers are often frightening to parents as well. Students who exhibit antisocial or aggressive behaviors in the classroom are rarely polite, well-behaved children at home. Their parents may be no better equipped to correct their children's misbehaviors than are school staff members. The strategies described in this book can be used by parents to help reduce noncompliance, aggression, and even violence at home.

Another option is structured parenting classes, which can empower parents and help them to learn effective discipline strategies that focus on reducing problem behaviors while increasing desired, socially appropriate behaviors in their children. Parenting classes may be provided by local social service agencies, universities, or by the public school system.

One important point for educators to keep in mind, however, is that not all youth involved with gangs come from broken or dysfunctional homes. Misbehavior on the part of children is not necessarily a reflection of a lack of concern and/or discipline on the part of the parents. Collaborative intervention will be much more likely to succeed if school staff do not fall into the all too common mistake of blaming the parents.

Getting Out of a Gang

(**Note**: Adults should be aware of the fact that while not impossible, attempting to quit a gang is extremely dangerous for youth—quite possibly deadly. In 1991, a 15-year old named Regnaldo Cruz was executed in a park in Wichita, Kansas with a .410-gauge shotgun. Police there believe he was killed for trying to quit a gang called the Vato Loco Boyz [Hull, 1992]. What happened to Cruz is not an isolated incident. Anyone acting as an interventionist, working with youth who desire to leave a gang they're already affiliated with, should proceed very cautiously. It is recommended that such individuals consult with their local police department before advising youth or taking any action.)

One aspect of gang affiliation that gang specialists and gang members alike agree upon is the difficulty members have in "getting out" if they want to quit their gang. In gang terminology, members "drop their flag" when they make the decision to leave their gang. Most gang members concede, as one 15-year old gang member told a police officer, "once you're in, you're in for life." In fact, some gang members claim the name "Crip" is an acronym for their perception of the duration of gang membership: "from the **C**radle to the grave (or **RIP**)".

Wannabes are told up front that they cannot leave the gang; that they will suffer severe consequences if they try. In the beginning, however, the desire to join is usually so powerful that new members don't stop to think about the life-long and possibly fatal commitment they are making when they join a gang.

Members are then convinced to remain in a gang through intimidation and fear. Since the wannabes and new members are usually very young (pre-teen to early teens), they are easily influenced and scared by the older members who recruit them and who enforce the rules. One gang member related to a police officer that his gang told him they would "hunt him down" and "take care of him" if he dropped his flag. As a result, he maintained his affiliation with his gang, even participating in their criminal activities when he no longer had any desire to be involved.

> Speaking Up!
>
> *Once you're in, you're in. Don't even think about droppin' your flag. You're never out.*
>
> – Jackson, 15 years old

Besides fearing for their physical safety, the pressure to remain in a gang can be observed in a students' schoolwork. The students may be so overwhelmed by the threats being made to them by their own gang that they have little energy left over to think about class assignments and school responsibilities. This same effect is seen at school when gangs try to recruit new members through intimidation; there is an overwhelming feeling of constant fear and anxiety among students.

The threat of retaliation is not an idle one. Police officers have encountered many youth who have been violently assaulted for trying to leave their gang. Most were afraid they would be repeatedly attacked if the gang caught them alone, as gang rules and regulations often require those in the gang to assault any members who have quit every time they see them. In some cases, houses have been the targets of drive-by shootings, cars and other property have been damaged with gang graffiti, and family members have been threatened and assaulted simply because a member was trying to leave a gang.

> Speaking Up!
>
> *It [a firebomb] hit right here, man [pointing to the back of his house]. They wanted all of us. My mom, my sisters, my brothers. All of us. That's why they used the bomb. Beats tryin' to shoot us.*
>
> – Zachary, 19 years old

The common gang rule is that no one walks away without a violent and often brutal penalty. Through gang investigations, police officers have discovered that some territorial gangs tell members that they could be "beat out" or "violated" if they wanted to quit. This is similar to the initiation ritual of being "jumped in," only it usually lasts longer and is more severe because those administering the beating are angry.

One 18-year old former member of a Crip set in Los Angeles, Thomas R., reported this outcome when he said no to his gang (as cited in Hull, 1992):

> *"They did me pretty bad," he says softly. Bad meaning a broken arm, a broken wrist, two teeth knocked out, lots of cigarette burns on his face and a few dozen bruises, which really isn't too bad for the Crips. But Thomas cautions, "You bet they ain't done with me yet"* (p. 38).

Some female gang members have been allowed to be "sexed out" of their gang, a requirement to perform sexual acts with as many male gang members as the gang leader sees fit. Some territorial gangs comprised of young male members have allowed their members to be "blessed out," a simple process of taking an oath (a promise that they will never reveal the gang's activities, secrets, etc.) and then quitting. However, on several occasions these gangs assaulted their former members anyway. This supports the theory that "you're never really out" in the eyes of a gang.

This "in for life" mentality is one of the major stumbling blocks of gang intervention for parents, teachers, police officers, and social service representatives. Even when youth express a desire to leave their gang, they may be hesitant to work with supportive adults because of the fear instilled in them by their fellow gang members. Older gang members know that they need the younger members to assist in the gang's criminal activities and for the perpetuation of the gang. Thus they will say or do anything to keep the gang's members from straying. Ironically, some members who do successfully leave their gang eventually join a rival gang seeking protection from the gang they quit. Then they're right back where they started.

The most effective gang intervention begins in the home. Parents need to be educated about the gang culture in order to provide convincing information to their children. With a great deal of determination and effort, some families may be able to extricate their children from the fanatical hold of gangs. In order to do this their children must first **want** to leave the gang. Second, their parents and family members must be able to provide an adequate replacement for whatever motivated the children to join the gang in the first place.

For example, if the gang has been a substitute for the love, support, and acceptance missing in the biological family, then structured, consistent family counseling is probably in order to remediate the situation.

Parents might also help by providing surveillance of their children during critical times. This might include walking to and from school and during after-school hours and in the evenings. It might also be beneficial to organize a neighborhood watch program. If there has already been gang activity in a neighborhood, many of the neighbors would probably be appreciative of the collaborative effort. Parents can also assist their children in joining in community, school, church, or other extracurricular activities. Chances are, other active gang members will not participate in programs of this type. Above all, parents need to monitor the whereabouts of their children and to spend time with them.

Some parents attempt to remove their children from the clutches of a gang through relocation. Sometimes the whole family moves—ideally to another state. Another option is to send the gang-involved child to live with a distant relative. Again, in order for this plan to be successful, the child must be determined to leave the gang. Otherwise what often happens when the child is relocated is that he/she creates a gang

or joins an already existing gang in the new environment.

One somewhat impractical, but creative and effective intervention strategy that's worked for one community in Wichita, Kansas is similar to the desperate measures employed in the late 1800s to liberate slaves:

> . . . members of Pastor Chuck Chipman's congregation descended on a gang-infested neighborhood to rescue a 12-year old boy being forced to work as a drug courier for a gang that was threatening him and his family. Before gang members could react, the entire family of four and all its belongings were whisked away to a safe house.
>
> That evacuation prompted a local group called Project Freedom to construct a network dubbed the underground railroad to funnel gang members and their families to safety in cases where all else fails. Six former gang members and two families have been shuttled to safety through a patchwork of churches both in and out of the state. The relocations are coordinated with the Wichita police, who check for outstanding warrants. Project Freedom pays for the initial move, while local congregations agree to assume housing costs and arrange

for jobs and education for as long as two years (Hull, 1992, p. 40).

Police officers can also be involved in helping a child to quit a gang through the use of informal counseling—weighing the options available and providing information on alternative activities and resources in the community. Sometimes a "scared straight" conversation with a police officer can be an effective method of gang prevention and intervention. But it must be remembered that youth who want to get out of a gang are likely to be scared, to feel hopeless, and need reassurance that the interventionist will be willing to help them in any way possible.

Without a doubt, the most effective form of gang intervention is early gang **prevention**. Teachers, parents, and community members must attempt to reach children at the wannabe stage, before they're initiated and firmly entrenched in a gang and the associated gang mentality. Often this means intervening with children in the **primary** grades—redirecting their interests toward more socially appropriate channels and educating them about the dangers of gang involvement throughout elementary school. Initiating gang intervention programs at the high school level will be too late for most youth. By this time, youth involved with gangs will be so indoctrinated into gang beliefs, behaviors,

and coping mechanisms that it will be extremely difficult to change them.

An effective method of dissuading wannabes from joining a gang is to inform them of the harsh realities of gang life. The statements following are examples of how parents, teachers, police officers, or any other interventionist can approach young people to combat the lure of gang membership. For the best results, children who are not already connected with a gang need this education before they fall victim to gang involvement. Some facts that have been most successful—which will never be told to them by gang recruiters—include:

- "If you're involved in a gang, your family is involved as well." This statement warns youth about the dangers their families can face because of their gang involvement. Many cities have had drive-by shootings and fire-bombings of houses where the target was a gang member who lived there. Most of the time, the individuals' parents and siblings had no idea why they were targeted for violence.

- "Your future as a gang member will likely include being dead, in jail, a career criminal, or a substance abuser." These are the outcomes for most hard core gang members, and if young people can see that their future is bleak when involved with a gang, they might decide there are better paths to follow. It is important to convince youth that gang life is a dead-end road.

- "Gang money is fast money, but it's here today and gone tomorrow." Many youth are lured by "big bucks" when they consider gang membership. The fact is that the young gang members receive very little money for the risks they take, they have to give most of what they make to the older members, and are sometimes even charged a "street tax" to stay in the gang.

- "If you're a gang member, you are a suspect in any crime that the gang commits." As an example, in one gang-motivated homicide in Davenport, Iowa, six juvenile gang members were convicted of the crime, and three sentenced to life in prison, even though only two of them drove the victim to the murder scene, and only one shot her. If young people can be convinced that they may have to pay, and pay dearly, for the actions of their fellow gang members, they may think twice about joining a gang when they consider the reputation of those who are already members.

- "If you are arrested, and go to jail, you start on the bottom." Many gang members try to convince themselves and their peers that being sent to prison is a status symbol within the gang. They talk about rank and the

status that can be obtained simply by doing time in jail. However, many young gang members who are incarcerated learn quickly that once in jail there actually is no status. They start at the bottom where they are required to do what the gang tells them to do, when they say to do it, and with swift punishment if orders are not complied with. Gang life in prison is far different from gang life on the streets. In jail, there is no way to escape the gang environment. There is no home to go to, and none of the creature comforts that most young people today have become accustomed to having. Jail is a rude awakening for young people, and this should be pointed out to youth who have aspirations of joining a gang.

Many communities already provide programs designed to give youth a positive alternative to gangs. Parents and educators should explore any community intervention programs that may be relevant to the needs of the youth in their area. But because many communities currently have no formal gang intervention process in place, parents and teachers may be faced with the task of gang prevention/intervention themselves. The more information they have on the signs, symbols, and dress of the gangs; the reasons youth join; and the dangers they face afterward, the better equipped adults will be to assume the task of educating children about why they should stay away from gangs.

Collaborative Methods of Gang Prevention/ Intervention

Goldstein and Huff (1993) reported that community efforts to rehabilitate juvenile delinquents have been largely unsuccessful. Unfortunately, the same may be true of most community efforts to rehabilitate youth gang members. Recidivism rates are high and statistics suggests that there is not a single, viable approach to consistently deal with the gang problem.

Historically, punitive methods of dealing with problem behavior in the community, in particular, have not been successful. Incarceration is the number one current punitive method employed. Yet, as with out-of-school suspensions commonly used to punish school problems, prison time simply keeps certain individuals off the streets for a while. It generally does not teach new, socially appropriate replacements for the illegal behaviors. It is also very expensive for society as a whole. In addition to using prison as a method to keep violent criminals off the street, a comprehensive program of rehabilitation to teach problem-solving, conflict resolution, and improved social skills, as well as moral reasoning, is imperative.

"Boot camp" forms of incarceration have also been suggested as an alternative to keep first time offenders out of the prison system where these individuals learn more criminal behaviors by spending extended periods of time in the prison system amongst only criminal role models. Boot camp incarceration reduces a convicted youth's sentence time dramatically in exchange for the inmate's agreement to complete the boot camp requirements. Boot camp programs entail hard labor, much physical conditioning, and military-like maneuvers and discipline strategies.

Yet at this time follow-up studies of boot camps are necessary to determine their effectiveness in reducing recidivism rates among participants. Too many ex-boot camp inmates are still finding the lure of gangs and the financial profits of criminal activity too strong to resist. In fact, according to many law enforcement officers, many gangs are recruiting right out the "front door" of the boot camps!

After completing the boot camp program, these individuals are highly desirable as gang members. They are physically fit, well-trained, disciplined, and they can take orders and follow through. They are used to the military-like discipline hierarchy enforced by gang leaders. This personality profile is just what gangs are looking for.

There is little data available to document specific community-based strategies successful in reducing gang crime rates. However, law enforcement personnel experienced with gangs maintain that collaboration between community agencies to address the gang problem is critical to success. The collaborative programs should involve criminal justice workers, educators, and community-based social service agencies to produce programs that address vocational, recreational, social, and educational skills.

Youth gang intervention cannot be assigned the responsibility of any one service agency. For example, gangs are not just a police problem, a school problem, or a family problem. Increased family involvement is one very important piece of the puzzle. However, families alone cannot be made the main effective change agent responsible for this epidemic societal problem. Likewise, police officers and/or teachers cannot successfully address the problem in an isolated fashion. Intervention efforts are likely to be more quickly and efficiently effective if they are initiated when the signs of gang activity first appear, in a collaborative manner.

The first organization to deal with street gangs in any community is usually the police, when they respond to citizens' complaints about gang crime. Police officers provide a tremendous service when they lend their law enforcement expertise to education/prevention

efforts in order to successfully address a gang problem. This marks the beginning of a collaboration effort in a community. First police departments should educate their own officers about gangs. Second, they could then set the stage for prevention/intervention by creating a zero tolerance policy concerning gang crime. When that policy is strictly followed, local gang members soon learn that their activities are the target of specific enforcement efforts by the police.

For example, the state of Iowa has established the Criminal Gang Participation Act (its tracking system, Drug Trak, was described in Section 2). Through this sort of legislation and law enforcement procedures, individuals can be prosecuted for **gang activity**, from representing gang affiliation, writing graffiti, and flashing gang hand signs. Yet even communities without such laws can establish a zero tolerance policy and make it as difficult as possible for youth to talk and act like gang members in public places. A community-wide anti-gang mentality may make gang activity so uncomfortable for gang members (and wannabes) that they will decide it's not worth the effort to establish themselves in the area. It is important to remember that local gangs are only as powerful as the community allows them to be!

Police officers can also help to educate the public about gangs by providing gang awareness seminars to groups of interested citizens and community agencies. These programs could include the early warning signs of gang activity and the basics of the zero tolerance policy that has been adopted by the police department. Such seminars might be provided at parent teacher association (PTA) meetings, church gatherings, Neighborhood Watch meetings, professional business organization training sessions, school inservices for teachers and administrators, college and university classes, town meetings, or any other setting where members of the community can collectively receive the information.

Gang intervention efforts must certainly extend to the schools. As stated previously, explicit rules and regulations should be established in each school's handbook reflecting the school district's stance on gang activity. To be most effective, the written zero tolerance (anti-gang) disciplinary policies must be distributed and explained to all staff members, the students, and their parents.

Since gang involvement must also be addressed at home, parents must be able to recognize and consistently contribute to the effort of decreasing their children's opportunities to affiliate with gang members. Parental and school collaboration is imperative. Parents can become actively involved with their children's education by volunteering at school, attending school functions, and demonstrating that they are interested in what happens at school. PTA groups

are an excellent vehicle for parents and school staff to work together toward the goal of reducing gang membership and associated violence.

The most successful gang suppression endeavors will result from cooperation between members of school, community, and parent groups, as a gang "intervention team." Suggestions for team members include educators, law enforcement officers, parents, social service workers, counselors, parks and recreation employees, probation and corrections officers, business professionals, and elected community officials. Each group or member of the gang intervention team will play a unique role, and will supply novel and innovative alternatives and solutions, representative of their unique viewpoints, to remedy the gang problem specific to their community.

Most states process arrested juveniles separately and differently from adult offenders. Thus juvenile court services personnel are another group that should be invited to participate on the gang intervention team. Many of these professionals serve as gang interventionists due to the nature of their profession and the fact that they frequently interact with gang-involved youth. Again, they will have a wealth of pertinent information to share with other team members.

Ideally the gang intervention team will meet on a consistent basis to share information and plan for intervention procedures. The team should brainstorm a multitude of educational, recreational, vocational, and appropriate social opportunities designed to be more appealing than gang activity to potential gang members (as described previously in this section). Schools and the community can work together to establish a variety of constructive activities to keep youth busy and off the street. The gang intervention team could also form partnerships with local businesses. Job placement for adolescents is a powerful gang prevention strategy. As Goldstein and Huff point out, "Young people are bound to work at something whether it be criminal activity on the streets or employment activity where they can learn specific skills with responsible adult supervision and positive role models" (1993, p. 231).

> Speaking Up!
>
> *I was in a lock-up before this place. I didn't have to go to school there—I didn't have to do nothin'. I lifted [weights], I hung out with my homies. After I got outa there I got in trouble again and I got sent to this place. Here, I have to go to school, an' my social worker here and my teacher, they really try to help us. We have to work on goals. My teacher, she tries to tell us about what's out there in the world. She takes us to places and shows us real stuff, ya know? She has a lot of people come in and talk about their jobs—and we go to see some—so we know what kinds of jobs they do—and maybe learn more about what jobs we want. I want to get a good job, I want people to respect me for what I do—not for my rep—like I used to. I don't want to be in jail. This place is helping me get my education. I want to be somebody . . . somebody good.*
>
> — Justin, 17 years old

Using this collaborative effort, gang intelligence can be gathered and distributed to all the parties involved. During this process, each community will be governed by their individual state's right to privacy and confidentiality ordinances. For example, while only law enforcement agencies, prisons, and selected social service agencies can share the names of adjudicated (i.e., have been charged with a crime and processed through the courts) gang members, typical gang characteristics and behavior can be related to **everyone** involved in addressing the gang problem.

Gang intervention teams may wish to explore one method of collaboration that has helped some communities to successfully manage street gang crime: Neighborhood Watch. Many Neighborhood Watch programs are organized and assisted through the educational efforts of the local police departments. Through this program, individuals in a neighborhood are encouraged to get into the habit of watching for gang behavior and reporting any suspicious activities to the police. Neighborhoods with such programs established near schools also help by watching for strangers who may loiter around the area before or after school.

Another organization that can contribute to the success of the team effort is the state Department of Corrections (DOC), or other prison officials. Jails and prisons are an excellent source for gathering gang intelligence. Employees of these agencies have been dealing with incarcerated gang members, and their associated behavior problems, for many years. These professionals are typically very well-informed and willing to share pertinent information about gangs.

There are a variety of programs across the country that have been created specifically to suppress and eliminate gangs. Yet there is no reliable data to suggest that any of the variety of existing programs will be successful in reducing gang activity for all communities. There is no one tried and true method, nor is there a "cookbook" approach to dealing with gangs. A list of such programs is included in the Appendix, but gang intervention teams are urged to begin by defining their own unique gang problem and community needs.

The individuals participating in the gang intervention team effort will also need to focus on identifying possible sources of funding for program supervision and implementation. Their suggestions should be based on the team members' understanding of their own community's resources. Federal and state grant proposals could be written to fund gang intervention programs. Funding possibilities might also be available through police departments, social service agencies, state agencies such as the state board of education, or the state criminal justice authority. Local public librarians and college or university professors might also be able to provide reference information on funding sources.

In the event that assistance from outside the community is deemed necessary, police officers from larger cities with more extensive gang problems, university or research personnel, school staff or community organizations that have established successful anti-gang policies, or federal criminal or juvenile justice agencies might be contacted. Personnel from these organizations and agencies are often able to describe the strategies that have proven successful in their own communities and schools. It is important to keep in mind, however, that the composition of a gang problem in each community is somewhat unique, and what works in one are is not guaranteed to be successful in another. Yet a collaborative prevention/intervention effort, through any of these avenues, is bound to increase a community's chances for success.

Summary

The initial step in dealing with gangs in a community is to recognize that there is a problem, and assess its severity. Each individual community will need to use gang awareness information to honestly appraise what types of activity are being observed. Next, individuals and agencies in the community will ideally collaborate to provide a zero tolerance, or anti-gang, policy to be implemented on a community-wide basis. Using this strategy, gang members will not be given free rein to carry out their criminal activities. Collaboration to implement a zero tolerance policy on a community- and school-wide basis is key to eliminating the epidemic problems of gang violence. Using this cooperative method, each individual community, regardless of size, will be able to honestly assess and then construct an appropriate plan to decrease and eliminate its criminal gang activity.

At school, written policies on gang activity, weapons, drugs, dress code, and legal methods of search and seizure can all contribute to establishing and implementing the comprehensive anti-gang policy. These various policy components, documented in the school handbook, delineate behaviors that will not be tolerated and include consequences for violations of the school rules. Law enforcement officials and representatives from social service agencies can be of assistance to school personnel in determining these policies.

School administrators should become comfortable working with the local police department. These officers are specially trained to deal with individuals who break municipal, state, and federal laws. Some of a school's policies may be based on federal mandates, such as the weapons policy and the drug-free school zone policy. Thus if students violate these mandates, they are breaking the law rather than just a school rule. In these cases, it is an administrator's prerogative to turn these students over to the police for prosecution.

Strategies for establishing a positive class-room atmosphere have been provided with the goal of keeping more kids motivated to stay in school. The national dropout rate is upwards of 25%, with the rates for adolescents with mild disabilities ranging from 50-65% (Woods, 1996). Dropouts suffer economic, social, emotional, and vocational stress for the rest of their lives. Many find crime, including gang activity, much more lucrative than a minimum wage, no benefits, no future-type job. The Illinois Criminal Justice Authority, in 1991, established that 72% of inmates in that state were high school dropouts (as cited in Woods, 1996). It is imperative that schools provide a motivating and relevant curriculum in a positive atmosphere in order to keep these adolescents at risk for school failure in school.

Teachers and administrators can plan creatively for ways to educate students. The alternative is that society may pay to incarcerate them later. Appropriate classroom management and behavior management strategies have been addressed for this purpose. Likewise, self-esteem problems seem to run rampant in gang members. Teachers can reduce this problem by establishing activities in the classroom through which all students can experience success. It is also important to establish a positive rapport with gang-involved youth and to treat all students with basic human respect. This is not to be confused with tolerating gang behaviors or gang violence.

Recommendations for establishing safe after-school programs are provided to assist school staff in providing supervised activities for youth during critical time periods. After school, in the evening, and on weekends are times when many students are unsupervised and may get into trouble by "hanging out" in the wrong places with the wrong kids.

Proactive parenting is one of the keys to combating a gang problem. A common motivator for joining gangs is the feeling of consistent family-like support that is provided by the gang to the members. Parents should be aware of their children's friends, activities, and whereabouts at all times. They need to establish open, honest, and direct lines of communication with their children. Parents can also help educate their children about the dangers and inevitable negative and dangerous outcomes of gang affiliation. Above all, parents need to demonstrate an active interest in their children's lives, and spend time with them. Strong family support may be enough to discourage youth from gang activity.

Once youth are initiated into a gang, it is extremely difficult for them to "drop their flag," or get out of the gang. In most cases, quitting a gang will require a violent beating that may have no time limit. The other gang members view any violent beating that may have no time limit. The other gang members view any individual who wants to quit as a traitor to the gang. They usually have orders from higher ranking members to physically assault the ex-member every time he/she is seen. Police officers, teachers, other professionals, and parents acting · as gang interventionists will need to be able to provide support and protection for individuals who want to "retire" from a gang.

References/Resources

Arthur, R. & Erickson, E. (1992). *Gangs and schools*. Holmes Beach, FL: Learning Publications.

This book describes the youth gang problem from an educator's firsthand experience. The authors promote the idea of teachers and students "bonding" in order to form social relationships that will make gang membership less attractive to youth. Suggestions for establishing such relationships are described, and a strong emphasis is placed on preparing students with the knowledge, skills, and values for making appropriate choices.

Gangs and Schools (ISBN #1-55691-036-3) may be ordered from Learning Publications, 5351 Gulf Drive, P.O. Box 1338, Holmes Beach, FL 34218; Phone (941) 778-6651; FAX (941) 778-6818.

Berman, S.C. (1991, October). Student Fourth Amendment rights: Defining the scope of the T.L.O. School search exception. *New York University Law Review, 6*, 1077-1129.

This article explains the parameters allowed by law for searching students and their belongings, school property including desks and lockers, and student vehicles parked on school premises.

Black, D.D. & Downs, J.C. (1993). *Administrative intervention: A school administrator's guide to working with aggressive and disruptive students* (2nd ed.). Longmont, CO: Sopris West.

This manual utilizes the findings of discipline research with aggressive and disruptive students to provide a step-by-step approach to dealing with out of control students, from onset to reentry into the classroom. With this process, administrators model appropriate behavior, show students how to be success-ful, engage in consensus-building regarding appropriate and inappropriate behavior, and provide consistent feedback during the intervention.

Administrative Intervention: A School Administrator's Guide to Working With Aggressive and Disruptive Students (ISBN #0-944584-57-8) may be ordered from Sopris West, 1140 Boston Avenue, Longmont, CO 80501; Phone (800) 547-6747; FAX (303) 776-5934; http://www.sopriswest.com.

Burke, N.D. (1993). Restricting gang clothing in the public schools. *West's Education Law Quarterly, 2*(3), 391-404.

This article provides a concise explanation of the legalities underlying the establishment of dress codes to ban gang apparel in schools.

Canfield, J. & Hansen, M.V. (Eds.). (1995). *A 2nd helping of chicken soup for the soul: 101 more stories to open the heart and rekindle the spirit.* Deerfield Beach, FL: Health Communications.

This delightful collection of stories contributed by readers across the country includes a section on "Learning and Teaching," designed to inspire, motivate, and sustain the reader in times of frustration.

A 2nd Helping of Chicken Soup for the Soul: 101 More Stories to Open the Heart and Rekindle the Spirit (ISBN #1-55874-331-6) may be ordered from Health Communications, 3201 Southwest 15th Street, Deerfield Beach, FL 33442-8190; Phone (954) 360-0909; FAX (954) 360-0034.

Fad, K. (1996). *Reaching out to troubled kids: 15 helpful ways to bridge the gap between parents, teachers, and kids* (2nd ed.). Longmont, CO: Sopris West.

This handbook provides ideas for adults who want to develop trust and positive communications with the at-risk youth in their lives. Detailed are 15 areas in which parents and teachers can work to improve their relationships with young people, based on the premise that change is possible and that positive approaches are more effective than punitive approaches in bringing about long-term change.

Reaching Out to Troubled Kids: 15 Helpful Ways to Bridge the Gap Between Parents, Teachers, and Kids (ISBN #1-57035-075-2) may be ordered from Sopris West, 1140 Boston Avenue, Longmont, CO 80501; Phone (800) 547-6747; FAX (303) 776-5934; http://www.sopriswest.com.

Fister, S.L. & Kemp, K.A. (1995). *The one-minute skill builder: Improving student social skills*. Longmont, CO: Sopris West.

This powerful videotape increases a teacher's repertoire of methods for keeping a class socially on track by correcting social skill errors. This simple four-step process, which takes about a minute to implement with a student, can be used school-wide or by an individual staff member. A workbook that clearly illustrates the procedure accompanies the video.

The One-Minute Skill Builder: Improving Student Social Skills (ISBN # not required for purchasing) may be ordered from Sopris West, 1140 Boston Avenue, Longmont, CO 80501; Phone (800) 547-6747; FAX (303) 776-5934; http://www.sopriswest.com.

Garrity, C., Jens, K., Porter, W., Sager, N., & Short-Camilli, C. (1993). *Bully-proofing your school: A comprehensive approach for elementary schools*. Longmont, CO: Sopris West.

This is a fully inclusive inservice manual for elementary educators on preventing bullying behavior. This school-wide approach incorporates five main components, addressing staff training, student instruction, support of victims, intervention with bullies, and collaboration with parents. The approach used is positive rather than punitive, and involves teaching both groups of children socially acceptable behaviors.

Bully-Proofing Your School: A Comprehensive Approach for Elementary Schools (ISBN #0-944584-99-3) may be ordered from Sopris West, 1140 Boston Avenue, Longmont, CO 80501; Phone (800) 547-6747; FAX (303) 776-5934; http://www.sopriswest.com.

Ginott, H.G. (1993). *Teacher and child: A book for parents and teachers* (pp. 15-16). New York: Simon & Schuster.

This is a book on strategies for forming positive teacher/student relationships at school. Tips are also provided for parents on assisting with the most beneficial and successful school adjustment for children. Teachers are provided with many suggestions for humanizing the classroom environment and classroom management.

Teacher and Child: A Book for Parents and Teachers (ISBN #0-02-013974-8) may be ordered from Simon & Schuster, Order Department 200, 200 Old Tappan Road, Old Tappan, NJ 07675; Phone (800) 223-2348; FAX (800) 445-6991.

Goldstein, A.P. (1990). *Delinquents on delinquency*. Champaign, IL: Research Press.

This book is unique in that it provides responses from delinquent youth on their thoughts regarding causes of juvenile delinquency, prevention, and remediation. Youth from 19 different facilities in seven states were interviewed. The interviews provide a fascinating firsthand view of life experiences of the youth themselves.

Delinquents on Delinquency (ISBN #0-87822-308-8) may be ordered from Research Press, Department 95, P.O. Box 9177, 2612 North Mattis Avenue, Champaign, IL 61826; Phone (217) 352-3273; FAX (217) 352-1221.

Goldstein, A.P. & Huff, C.R. (Eds.). (1993). *The gang intervention handbook*. Champaign, IL: Research Press.

This book is an immensely useful reference manual on youth gangs. In it, Dr. Goldstein and Dr. Huff have coordinated wide-ranging contributions from a group of nationally recognized experts on youth gangs. Individual chapters were written by specialists from diverse professional fields including psychology, criminology, public policy, sociology, criminal justice, counseling and human development, special education, and law enforcement. The book provides a history of strategies used to intervene with gangs. Approaches to youth gang intervention that span both preventive and rehabilitative methods are addressed.

The Gang Intervention Handbook (ISBN #0-87822-335-5) may be ordered from Research Press, 2612 North Mattis Avenue, Champaign, IL 61826; Phone (217) 352-3273; FAX (217) 352-1221.

Goldstein, A.P., Sprafkin, R.P., Gershaw, N.J., & Klein, P. (1980). *Skillstreaming the adolescent*. Champaign, IL: Research Press.

This book provides a step-by-step plan for teaching prosocial skills to adolescents. The manual covers 60 different skills. Each skill is described in a lesson plan format and includes role play options. Suggestions are given for transfer of training, homework assignments, and record-keeping systems.

Skillstreaming the Adolescent (ISBN #0-87822-205-7) may be ordered from Research Press, Department 95, P.O. Box 9177, 2612 North Mattis Avenue, Champaign, IL 61826; Phone (217) 352-3273; FAX (217) 352-1221.

Huggins, P. (1994). *Building self-esteem in the classroom*. Longmont, CO: Sopris West.

Through these lessons, elementary students refine their self-descriptions and acquire an appreciation for their uniqueness. They learn the concepts of multiple intelligences, self-encouragement, and their own responsibility for their academic success. Over 600 pages of scripted lessons, transparency masters, and creative student handouts are included in this manual, available in two versions: *Primary* and *Intermediate*.

Building Self-Esteem in the Classroom (ISBN # not required for purchasing) may be ordered from Sopris West, 1140 Boston Avenue, Longmont, CO 80501; Phone (800) 547-6747; FAX (303) 776-5934; http://www.sopriswest.com.

Hull, J.D. (1992, August 17). No way out. *Time*, pp. 38-40.

Illinois Criminal Justice Authority. (1991). *Trends and issues: Education and criminal justice in Illinois*. Chicago: Author.

This publication is a compilation of statistics in the areas of: (1) education and criminal justice, (2) special education, (3) crime in schools, (4) educational experiences of inmates, and (5) truancy and dropout issues.

Trends and Issues: Education and Criminal Justice in Illinois may be ordered from the Illinois Criminal Justice Information Authority, 120 South Riverside Plaza, Chicago, IL 60606-3997; Phone (312) 793-8550.

Johnson, L.A. (1992). *My posse don't do homework*. New York: St. Martin's Press.

This book was written by a high school English teacher about her experiences teaching very tough students in a California high school. The methods Ms. Johnson use emphasize her belief in the ability of all students to succeed even though they may never have had a single successful experience before entering her classroom. This is an excellent example of a teacher who really cares about her students.

My Posse Don't Do Homework (ISBN #0-312-95163-9) was reprinted under the title *Dangerous Minds* (ISBN #0-312-95620-7), and may be ordered from St. Martin's Press, 175 Fifth Avenue, New York, NY 10010; Phone (800) 446-8923.

Johnson, C., Webster, B., & Connors, E. (1995). *Prosecuting gangs: A national assessment*. Washington, D.C.: National Institute of Justice.

This document provides the findings of a National Institute of Justice (NIJ) sponsored nationwide survey of local prosecutors' approaches to gang prosecution, a review of state legislation targeted at street gang activity, and case studies of prosecution efforts at four sites.

Prosecuting Gangs: A National Assessment (as well as other NIJ documents) may be ordered from the National Institute of Justice, U.S. Department of Justice, Washington, D.C. 20531; Phone (800) 851-3420; Email:

askncjrs@ncjrs.aspensys.com.(**Note:** The National Institute of Justice [NIJ] catalog is sent free to all registered users of NCJRS (the National Criminal Justice Reference Service). To become a registered user, contact NCJRS, P.O. Box 6000, Rockville, MD 20849-6000; Phone (800) 851-3420.

Keveney, B. (1996, March 17). A V-chip Q & A: How TV's latest feature works and when it will be available. *The Sunday Camera*, p. 8-C.

This article details the proposed V-chip to allow the programming of children's television viewing by parents.

Kounin, J.S. (1970). *Discipline and group management in classrooms*. San Francisco: Holt, Rinehart, & Winston.

This book describes management strategies that are appropriate for any teacher to use in the classroom. There is a focus on teacher behavior as preventive management. Although it is a relatively "older" book, the content and strategies are still effective.

Discipline and Group Management in Classrooms (ISBN #0-03-078210-4) may be ordered from Holt, Rinehart, & Winston, 6277 Sea Harbor Drive, Orlando, FL 32887; Phone (800) 225-5425; FAX (800) 874-6418.

Lopez, L.L. (1994, Winter). Enhancing self-esteem. *School Safety*, p. 16.

This article discusses seven basic human values that teachers need to be aware of in order to enhance students' self-esteem.

Lovitt, T.C. (1991). *Preventing school dropouts: Tactics for at-risk, remedial, and mildly handicapped adolescents*. Austin, TX: Pro-Ed.

The purpose of this book is to educate teachers on causes and ramifications of the dropout problem. It suggests practical tactics for application in the classroom. The tactics provided are meant to be used as a method to enhance and make academic content more relevant and motivating for adolescents. Teachers are not directed to alter the material they present, just the way they deliver that material. This book could be used at the college level in teacher training, or for inservice staff development and training.

Preventing School Dropouts: Tactics for At-Risk, Remedial, and Mildly Handicapped Adolescents (ISBN #0-89079-454-5) may be ordered from Pro-Ed, 8700 Shoal Creek Boulevard, Austin, TX 78757-6897; Phone (512) 451-3246; FAX (512) 451-8542.

McGinnis, E. & Goldstein, A.P. (1984). *Skillstreaming the elementary school child.* Champaign, IL: Research Press.

This book provides a step-by-step plan for teaching prosocial skills to students in elementary grades. The manual covers 60 different skills. Each skill is described in a lesson plan format and includes role play options. Suggestions are given for transfer of training, homework assignments, and record-keeping systems.

Skillstreaming the Elementary School Child (ISBN #0-87822-235-9) may be ordered from Research Press, Department 95, P.O. Box 9177, 2612 North Mattis Avenue, Champaign, IL 61826; Phone (217) 352-3273; FAX (217) 352-1221.

Moriarity, A. & Fleming, T.W. (1990). Youth gangs aren't just a big-city problem anymore. *The Executive Educator, 12*(7), pp. 13, 15-16.

This article outlines the reasons for gang migration to smaller towns and communities. The three main reasons cited are an attempt to evade law enforcement pressure, to acquire more drug selling turf, and the possibility of higher drug selling profits.

National School Safety Center. (1992, March). Gangs vs. schools: Assessing the score in your community. *School Safety Update* (National School Safety Center News Service), p. 8.

The Raoul Wallenberg Committee of the United States. (1996). *A study of heroes: A program that inspires and educates through the example of heroes* (2nd ed.). Longmont, CO: Sopris West.

This comprehensive multidisciplinary program, presented as a reproducible kit, helps to revitalize the tradition of heroes by studying the lives of true heroes—positive role models from many different periods of history, ethnicities, nationalities, and areas of accomplishment. This program teaches students about character development. They discover that heroes can be figures they encounter daily—parents, public officials, teachers, neighbors, classmates, and even themselves.

A Study of Heroes: A Program That Inspires and Educates Through the Example of Heroes (ISBN #1-57035-072-8) may be ordered from Sopris West, 1140 Boston Avenue, Longmont, CO 80501; Phone (800) 547-6747; FAX (303) 776-5934; http://www.sopriswest.com.

Rhode, G., Jenson, W.R., & Reavis, H.K. (1992). *The tough kid book: Practical classroom management strategies*. Longmont, CO: Sopris West.

This book is a resource for both regular and special education teachers. The research-validated solutions provided include assessment information, unique positive procedures for student reinforcement, and practical reductive techniques to decrease "Tough Kids'" disruptive behavior without big investments on the teacher's part in terms of time, money, and emotion. The solutions also provide "Tough Kids" with the behavioral, academic, and social survival skills they lack.

The Tough Kid Book: Practical Classroom Management Strategies (ISBN #0-944584-54-3) may be ordered from Sopris West, 1140 Boston Avenue, Longmont, CO 80501; Phone (800) 547-6747; FAX (303) 776-5934; http://www.sopriswest.com.

Rosenthal, M.S. & Mothner, I. (1972). *Drugs, parents, and children: The three-way connection*. Boston: Houghton Mifflin.

This book provides parents with information on parenting skills for helping their children deal with issues related to growing up.

Drugs, Parents, and Children: The Three-Way Connection (ISBN #0-39-312718-1) may be ordered from Houghton Mifflin, 215 Park Avenue South, New York, NY 10003; Phone (800) 225-1464; FAX (800) 733-1810.

Sheridan, S.M. (1995). *The tough kid social skills book*. Longmont, CO: Sopris West.

Part of the "Tough Kid" series by Rhode, Jenson, and Reavis, this manual offers detailed, specific methods for teachers, school psychologists, counselors, social workers, and school support staff to identify and assess "Tough Kids," and provides effective techniques for turning these kids around. Included are flexible outlines for conducting social skills sessions with students.

The Tough Kid Social Skills Book (ISBN #1-57035-051-5) may be ordered from Sopris West, 1140 Boston Avenue, Longmont, CO 80501; Phone (800) 547-6747; FAX (303) 776-5934; http://www.sopriswest.com.

Staff. (1993, November). Weapons: A deadly role in the drama of school violence. *The National School Safety Update*, pp. 1-4. West Lake Village, CA: National School Safety Center News Service.

This article describes how the increased number of students with weapons at school has raised the rate and intensity of school violence. Self-protection, rather than intimidation or aggression, is cited as the most common reason students offer for carrying a gun to school.

Stephens, R.D. (1993, Fall). Preparing tomorrow's teachers. *National School Safety Center Update*, p. 2.

This short article describes results reported on a state-wide survey of teachers and students in California. The survey was conducted over an 18-month period by the School Violence Advisory Panel of the California Commission on Teacher Credentialing (CTC). The purpose of the survey was to examine school crime and violence issues with the goal of identifying strategies and techniques to better prepare teachers for their role and responsibilities in the public schools.

Stephens, R.D. (1995). *Safe schools: A handbook for violence prevention*. Bloomington, IN: National Educational Service.

This handbook written for school administrators provides a process for assessing their school climate, as well as clear descriptions of the key elements involved in developing, implementing, and evaluating a comprehensive and systematic safe school plan. This manual emphasizes the effects of the law on school policy decision making, and includes many sample policies from schools across the country.

Safe Schools: A Handbook for Violence Prevention (ISBN #1-879639-32-7) may be ordered from the National Educational Service, 1610 West Third Street, P.O. Box 8, Bloomington, IN 47402; Phone (800) 733-6786; FAX (812) 336-7790.

Woods, E.G. "Reducing the dropout rate," *Close Up #17,* 12/17/96 [on-line]; available from http://www.nwrel.org/scpd/c017.html.

This publication (on-line) provides background information on school dropout, including a definition of the problem, risk factors, a short literature review, and a compilation of dropout statistics based on a variety of data collection methods. The author indicates that the dropout rate varies widely across the country due to differences in definitions of "dropout," different time periods during the school year when data are collected, different data collection methods, different ways of tracking youth no longer in school, and different methods used by school districts and states to calculate the dropout rate.

Zigmond, N. & Thornton, H. (1985). Follow-up of postsecondary age learning disabled graduates and dropouts. *Learning Disabilities Research, 1*(1), 50-55.

This article provided summary data comparing outcomes for adolescents with learning disabilities who had either finished high school by obtaining a diploma or dropped out prior to graduation.

Developing Crisis Management Plans

Even when proactive behavior management strategies are implemented on a building-wide basis, gang influence within a school can result in violence, either in the classroom or in common areas of the school. This section provides a simple structure that educational staff and students may follow in crisis situations related to gang violence. The focus is on preplanning and preparation in order to best manage crisis situations. Strategies address: (1) predicting a crisis; (2) managing a crisis, including formulating a crisis management plan; and (3) self-protection. Although these strategies were written with school situations in mind, they would also be effective for parents to use at home (with only minor modifications), if necessary.

For the purposes of this section, crisis situations are defined as any circumstance involving student violence (whether gang members or other students who demonstrate antisocial behaviors). Violence is defined as any act of aggression against school staff or students in which the violator attempts to intimidate, hurt, or abuse the victim. School violence usually includes force, such as the use of a weapon or physical assault, and is often accompanied by intense emotions.

Defining a Crisis

Most teachers prefer to believe that a crisis will never occur in their classroom. A crisis situation is something that most think will only happen to someone else. But all teachers need to realize that in every classroom there is likely one (or more) student who has the potential to demonstrate out of control behaviors that might constitute a crisis situation. As described in Section 3, the most efficient type of behavior management system in the classroom is proactive (meaning that specific methods are used to reduce the probability that problems will occur). At times, however, these may fail. When students' behavior is out of control and they have become a danger to themselves or others, a crisis situation has developed.

In order to competently manage crisis situations if and when they occur, school personnel must be prepared with a crisis management plan which details exactly what actions the administrators, teachers, and students would take in a crisis. Having a preplanned crisis management strategy will enable them to behave appropriately in the face of an emergency. Otherwise, they are likely to feel overwhelmed, victimized, and/or terrified in a crisis situation—strong emotions that interfere with logical responses to dangerous situations.

Once developed, crisis management plans should be rehearsed in a manner similar to school drills for fires and tornadoes. The plans will need to address both teacher self-defense and student safety. In addition, the students must be able to carry out their part in the plan without their teacher's guidance or supervision if necessary. (Specific steps for formulating this plan will be covered elsewhere in this section.)

Predicting a Crisis

Crisis prediction may sound like an oxymoron, as crises seem to "come out of nowhere," generally taking school staff by surprise. But like the tornado mentioned previously, crises are often the violent climax of smaller storms that can be "tracked" (i.e., predicted) with "teacher radar." That is, there should be an almost constant surveillance of student behavior in the classroom. The teacher should be aware of the moods, attitudes, peer interactions, and general behavior of the students at all times. Following are some indicators of a potential crisis, factors that should put teachers on "storm watch."

RECOGNIZING ANTECEDENTS OF CRISIS

An "antecedent" is something that happens just before a behavior that may serve to increase or maintain the behavior. Being able to recognize antecedents of problem behavior is the first step toward crisis management. There are verbal, physical, emotional, and environmental cues that indicate that a crisis is brewing. Being able to interpret behavioral signs that indicate students' levels of frustration or aggression is a critical proactive management skill for adults.

Students may act out in an aggressive or violent manner when they are frustrated with a situation that they do not feel competent to manage. Self-esteem is a major problem for most gang members. When they feel as though they might "lose face" in a situation, they will take actions that decrease the risk of failure in front of their peers. Because many gang members do not experience success in school, there will be frequent occasions when they may feel less than competent to manage task requirements or social situations.

In addition, gang members must show allegiance to their gang by following all orders given and attending all required gang meetings. These mandated meetings and various activities may disrupt school attendance and consume after-school and evening hours. Some gang activities may go late into the nighttime hours, resulting in not enough sleep and promoting school tardiness and truancy. When these individuals finally do get to school they are generally unprepared to handle the classwork and social demands of the school environment. They will often react in a physically or verbally aggressive manner towards teachers and peers in an attempt to "save face" and maintain their gang member reputation.

The behavior of the teacher in reaction to students' aggression can help to reduce it to tolerable levels. However, adult responses can also prompt the escalation of student behavior to the crisis point. Adult behavior that is calm, understanding,

---

Speaking Up!

I like history, I like to hear about what all those old guys used to do. But I've been ditchin' class. All we do is read to ourselves then write answers. I had teachers before who made it real interesting, but not this one, man. I can't do all that readin' . . . I don't get it. Last time the teacher in there, man, he put me down. Told me I'd never be nuthin'—just 'cause I didn't do the homework. I couldn't do it. I didn't get it. I need help with the readin'. But I'm never goin' back to that class again, man, never . . . .

– Ramon, 16 years old

and supportive demonstrates respect for students. This does not mean that the adult accepts or condones student behavior, but that the adult respects the student as a human being. This type of adult response will help to prevent aggression and violence from escalating.

On the other hand, when adults do not respect students; do not listen to them, giving them the chance to state their feelings or opinions; and regularly snap commands at them, violence and aggression are guaranteed to escalate. This aversive form of interaction will result in more problems for the teacher and the students. Thus it is important for teachers to be sensitive to students' needs and emotional states.

VERBAL SIGNS OF A POTENTIAL CRISIS

Teachers must be keenly aware of what students say and how they say it in the classroom. Even students who are not particularly expressive in class will often provide oral cues that can warn of impending discord. Some students will make aggressive verbal comments outright. Others will mutter under their breath (usually loud enough for the teacher to hear, but not to understand). There may be a lot of "peer put-down" or other derogatory comments being made. If this sort of verbal aggression is occurring, the teacher should deal with the problem immediately rather than ignoring the situation.

The first step is for the teacher to recognize that this type of inappropriate language is often an intent to communicate. The student is probably looking for a way to make his/her feelings known, but may be a signal that problem behavior is brewing.

The second step is for the teacher to confront the behavior and redirect it in more appropriate channels. Using preventive behavior management, the teacher would talk to the student in an attempt to find out what is bothering him/her. That way, the problem can be defused before it erupts into a crisis situation. This is important because aggressive language can often be a precursor to violent actions. The teacher should then provide the student verbal reinforcement. These four steps are highlighted in Summary Box 4.1.

Summary Box 4.1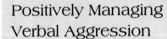

Positively Managing Verbal Aggression

Step 1: Recognize the communicative intent.

Step 2: Confront the problem behavior.

Step 3: Redirect to more appropriate behavior.

Step 4: Provide positive reinforcement.

Examples of aggressive language include swearing, yelling, and talking in a sarcastic or scornful manner to school staff or to other students. A preventive management technique is to "outlaw" the use of aggressive language in the classroom. This practice eliminates verbal comments that would be irritating to staff, and might be provocative or incite aggression or hostility in other students. The best way to communicate this expectation to the students is to make a classroom rule that requires students to speak appropriately in class.

PHYSICAL/EMOTIONAL SIGNS OF A POTENTIAL CRISIS

There are some physical and emotional signs students display that might indicate a potential problem. One of the first signs to note is that students will resist making eye contact. They might be agitated or restless. Their behavior and body language will often convey defiance or anxiety. Their face may looked flushed. Their observable behaviors can be quite varied, as there are two main types of behavior that might be demonstrated when students are showing escalating behavior problems. Their behaviors might appear to be either depressed and withdrawn, or excessively hostile and noncompliant.

Students who are depressed may appear to be sad or discouraged. They may be quite reticent and refuse to talk about their problems. Students who suffer from depression will often resist talking because they are caught in a cycle of learned helplessness; they feel as though no one is going to be able to help them anyway. Hopelessness is a major indicator of depression. Hopelessness for a better way of life is one reason many youth join gangs. They may be looking for a better way of life but often have limited resources and opportunities, as well as lack of support to achieve their goals. Individuals often join gangs because they think membership is a ticket to lifelong prosperity, although the life span may be short. They recognize the violence inherent in gang activity but accept it as a necessary component. Many live such a violent lifestyle that they expect and accept the certainty of an early and violent death (Bing, 1994).

As officer Eric Davis* of the Chicago, Illinois Police Department explains:

---

*Officer Davis is one of three Chicago police officers who, along with their regular police work, provide educational programs for schools, parents, and other organizations on drug and gang resistance. (The other two members of the group are officer James Martin and officer Randy Holcomb.) Their lively program, which includes an appropriate rap music component which is appealing and motivating to students, emphasizes the importance of education and self-responsibility. The group goes by the intriguing name of "The Slick Boys," which is actually street slang for "undercover police officer." For further information, contact: The Slick Boys, 320 West Illinois, Suite 611, Chicago, IL 60610; Phone (312) 670-3720.

Poverty is increasing. This is one of the main causes of gang activity. Kids in Chicago aren't involved in gangs because they have nothing else to do. They definitely have an intention in mind. The intention is to get involved in an organization, make some money—so it's an economic thing. . . .

And in many cases, they've given up on the educational system. The sad thing is that many kids now in the United States have given up hope on the American Dream. they really feel that the situation that now serves them immediately, because they're told they will not live to be 18, 19, 21 years old, is I better go get . . . in a gang, make me some real money. Since I'm going to die young, I might as well live fast.

Teachers need to reassure students who are depressed or hopeless about their situation that they can talk to them at any time, and that talking might help to solve their problem. It is important to be supportive of students' attempts to convey their feelings even though they might not always be very skilled at putting them into words.

Other students might show behaviors that are excessively hostile and on the verge of being out of control. This type of behavior is overly stimulated, defiant, and disruptive. These students may be difficult to converse with constructively. Gang members will be likely to talk in a boisterous and rowdy manner meant to be intimidating to educational staff and students. Their speech will typically include a great deal of street slang and offensive language. Again, the aim is to intimidate others and dominate the situation. Verbally intimidating behavior is a form of purposeful coercion which empowers the gang member.

These students will often deny that there is a problem or refuse to take responsibility for their part in the problem. Teachers will need to address these students in a calm and unemotional tone of voice. The teacher's manner should be reassuring and supportive, indicating that the teacher has faith in the student's ability to settle down and follow established classroom rules.

One strategy teachers can use to talk with students is called reflective listening. Using this method, the teacher listens to and then restates the feelings expressed by the student in order to understand and help resolve the problem. Reflective listening involves three main steps. First, the teacher listens to the verbal message from the student. The teacher then restates the student's message, and the student either confirms or denies the teacher's statement. The third step is for the teacher to redirect the student's thoughts more appropriately. This helps the student to come up with an alternative solution for inappropriate behavior.

This strategy will help students to identify, communicate, and then clarify their feelings. Many students who have problems with aggression will have difficulty identifying their true feelings (it seems that they are always "mad" about something). If a teacher asks them how they feel, they say "mad," when in reality they might be anxious, sad, frustrated, nervous, or depressed. Once students learn to accurately identify their emotions, they will be able to deal with them more appropriately.

Gang-involved youth usually have immense difficulty showing genuine feelings due to apprehension that others might perceive this as a weakness. To maintain their status or to gain rank in the gang, they must continually demonstrate a tough, intimidating, and macho reputation. It is possible for teachers to work through this problem with students by gaining their trust and respect. But it will take time and effort to build rapport with gang members and wannabes because they typically have had aversive school experiences and generally aren't very willing to trust teachers.

Speaking Up!

Last year when I was a freshman, we were going up and down the rows and saying what we wanted to be when we got out of school. And it got to me and I said I wanted to be a singer, or whatever, and Miss Clark told me that was never going to be . . . and they, she started cuttin' me down . . . made me look bad . . . I just walked out of the room. I was embarrassed—made me feel bad.

– Robert, 15 years old

ENVIRONMENTAL SIGNS OF A POTENTIAL CRISIS

Environmental signs are signals that teachers can pick up from the class as a whole. Examples include: (1) a class that is unusually restless or in constant motion, (2) a lot of whispering or talking going on among class members, and (3) an obvious lack of interest from the class or lack of response to the lesson. When any of these indicators are present, even though there may not be any overt behavior problems occurring, the teacher would be wise to stop instruction and address the matter.

The teacher should confront the class with a specific description of the problem behavior(s) noted. For example: "Some of you are doing a great job of following along and paying attention to the lesson this morning. But, I notice that there is quite a bit of whispering going on among some of you. What is the problem?" At this point the teacher should elicit some responses from the students.

If a teacher has worked at establishing rapport with students by being firm, fair, consistent, and respectful with them, they will respond when he/she asks them to talk about a problem situation that is happening. The students will trust the teacher to help remediate the problem and deal fairly with all. However, teachers who have been remote, inconsistent, and/or uncaring about students' physical and emotional needs will likely have a problem in this area because students will not be trusting enough to describe the problem. In order for teachers to expect students to be honest with them and to be cooperative in the classroom, teachers need to work hard at building student rapport and trust on a daily basis.

It is important to find out exactly what is going on and then deal with the problem, if possible. Ignoring this type of classroom behavior will almost always result in an escalation of the behavior. As behavior escalates, a crisis situation will often develop. For example, the gang code of conduct (reputation, respect, and retaliation) may serve to escalate a relatively simple gang-related behavior problem from minor status to a major crisis situation. Teachers need to remember this code in order to avoid this inadvertent escalation. When teachers deal with gang-related problems in a calm, unemotional, supportive manner that is at the same time firm, fair, and consistent, potential crisis situations will be minimized.

Summary Box 4.2 summarizes the signs of a potential crisis in the classroom, and Summary Box 4.3 describes methods to proactively deal with the potential crisis.

Speaking Up!

I had this one teacher when I was in fifth grade in St. Louis. He was, like, he always knew I could be something better than what I was aiming for. He used to always take time to help me, it was with reading. He'd even take his own lunch time, and that meant a lot to me.

— Marshall, 15 years old

Summary Box 4.2

Signs of a Potential Crisis in the Classroom

Verbal	Physical/Emotional	Environmental
• Aggressive comments	• Lack of eye contact	• Unusual amount of physical movement
• Under the breath comments	• Agitation or restlessness	• Lots of whispering/ talking
• Peer put-downs	• Defiant/anxious body language	• Lack of interest in the lesson
• Other derogatory comments	• Flushed faces	

Summary Box 4.3

Addressing a Potential Crisis in the Classroom

Verbal	Physical/Emotional	Environmental
• Confront the inappropriate behavior.	• Encourage communication.	• Stop instruction.
• Redirect the behavior in a more positive channel.	• Use reflective listening.	• Address the student behavior.
• Determine the source of the problem.	• Identify feelings.	• Determine the source of the problem.

Crisis Management Techniques

What types of behaviors constitute a crisis situation? Students in crisis are those who are unable to control their behavior or respond to teacher cues voluntarily. Their behavior is so out of control that they may be a danger to themselves or others. Examples include aggressive acts such as hitting, kicking, or other fighting behaviors; throwing objects; threatening to hurt themselves; or putting themselves or others in a dangerous or compromising position. Putting others in a dangerous situation might include taking a hostage, threatening others with a weapon, or threatening to push another student from a window or upper floor of a stairwell.

One excellent method of preventive management for crisis situations is to provide instruction to students on stress management. Teaching students these techniques will help them to deal with elevated stressors more appropriately. Next, a specific crisis management plan that all staff know how to follow should be implemented school-wide. Finally, the students should be taught their role in the crisis management plan, and the steps they can take on their own to guard their own safety.

STRESS MANAGEMENT

The origin of a crisis is usually a series of smaller events that build up or combine to cause stress for students in the classroom or at home. Children are especially susceptible to stress, but are less well-equipped than adults to handle it in a constructive manner. High levels of stress can be debilitating, or it can result in student behavior that is inappropriate for a given situation.

Sources of stress for children and adolescents include school demands; peer pressure; violence at school, at home, and on the street; family expectations; problems in the home or family situation; drug and alcohol abuse; and societal pressures that force many children to grow up faster than they may be comfortable with. Youth who become involved in gang activity are often exposed to criminal activities involving violence, the use of alcohol and other drugs, and physical and verbal abuse from higher ranking gang members. In addition, because rival gang challenges are so dangerous, gang members always have to "watch their backs." They must be constantly aware of danger and potential threats in their environment. Exposure to this type of turmoil, although fairly commonplace for gang members, increases the stress in their personal lives.

It's Hard Growing Up

It's hard growing up knowing that going around each corner might lead to danger.

It's hard growing up knowing that one day your little brother or sister might get shot.

It's hard growing up knowing that your friend might get into a gang without thinking twice.

It's hard to know that all the knowledge in the world can't make up for a human life.

It's hard growing up never knowing what will happen.

*– Lakeisha Williams, 13 years old
Edison Junior High School
Rock Island, IL*

Teaching children about stress may be one method of defusing it, and thus minimizing the potential for crisis. There are physiological symptoms of extreme stress; these are based on the "fight or flight" reaction instinctual in human beings and other mammals. The physiological symptoms of stress, according to Kaplan (1995), are described in Summary Box 4.4.

Summary Box 4.4

Physiological Symptoms of Stress

Pupils Dilate

Lets in more light so the individual can see better

Heart Beats Faster

Pumps more blood and oxygen to muscles

Muscles Tense

Serves as protective "armor" to protect vital organs, or to spring into action if necessary

Blood Chemistry Changes

Increases clotting time as a protection device in case bleeding should occur

Throat and Nasal Passages Dry Up

Allows more oxygen to be taken in

Once children begin to recognize the physiological symptoms of stress, they can be taught to better manage the symptoms so their behavior does not intensify to the crisis point. When students are feeling high levels of stress, having a trusted adult at school or in the community to talk with will be very beneficial. Specific stress management methods children can learn include: (1) taking deep breaths; (2) doing aerobic exercise; (3) learning a self-instructional strategy to solve problems; or (4) learning new behavioral skills, such as assertiveness skills which help with peer pressure, appropriate decision making, etc.

Self-instructional strategies may be taught to students by educational staff in order for students to better manage their specific problems. This strategy is composed of several steps that the adult teaches and practices with an individual student. To begin, the adult must recognize the problem the student is experiencing. Second, the adult would establish a series of steps for the student to learn and follow in order to successfully and appropriately deal with the problem. Third, the adult models the steps, saying each one aloud while the student observes. Next, the student imitates the steps, saying each one aloud as he/she does so. The adult provides feedback to the student about how well the steps were followed. Then, the student practices the steps, whispering or silently thinking each step to himself/herself. The goal is to provide many safe, structured practice situations for the student to best prepare him/her for the transfer of the new skill in the real world. Commercially available social skill programs (as described in Section 3) can assist teachers in preparing individualized self-instructional strategies for their students.

This and other positive methods for students to deal with their stress are stated in Summary Box 4.5.

Summary Box 4.5

Effective Methods of Managing Stress

Physiological

Breathing exercises, muscle relaxation exercises, and aerobic exercise are methods that children can use to reduce their feelings of stress.

Psychological

Psychological methods of dealing with stress include learning problem-solving strategies or self-instructional strategies. Self-instructional training is simply a series of three to four specific steps that a child learns as a problem-solving strategy that can be used to deal with stress. In both cases, the student learns to think about and choose alternative solutions to a stressful problem.

Simply talking about a problem with a trusted adult may also be very helpful.

Behavioral

Assertiveness training will teach students how and when to appropriately make their wants and needs known to others, and how to stand up for their own rights/values.

At times, it will be more difficult for teachers to confront and redirect students' problem behavior. This will often be true when working with students who are involved in gangs. While many young wannabes may still be receptive to teacher influence, hard core or older gang members will be less willing to share their feelings, explore self-instructional strategies, or engage in problem solving with adult authority figures.

Speaking Up!

I would rebel against whatever teachers told me to do. There was this one teacher in typing class, I completely intimidated her and she was scared of me and you know . . . just having the thought of a teacher scared of me made me feel like I was strong. But now I think—where you gonna get at since your teacher is scared of you. You can't get no education doin' that. Before, it was all me. The teachers weren't the problem, it was me. I didn't want the help.

— Dennis, 17 years old (now attending school at a residential treatment center)

However, it is vitally important that teachers not give up on these students. These may be the very types of activities that will help give students a more positive outlook on school. Gang members typically have not had many positive experiences there. A teacher who is able to motivate and involve these students at school might be the one who can turn the tide in these students' lives.

Yet if one or more students are not responding to a teacher's preventive methods of behavior management, these students' behavior may soon escalate into a crisis situation. When this is the case, there is no other alternative but to activate a crisis management plan, described following.

FORMULATING A CRISIS MANAGEMENT PLAN

Ideally, a school-wide crisis management plan will be formulated through a team effort, including teaching staff and administrators. The fundamental objective of a crisis management plan is to provide behavioral intervention to either avert a crisis or to diminish its impact. The most effective crisis management plan is a practical and constructive school-wide behavior management plan that is implemented consistently and reduces the potential for the development of out of control situations.

Gilliam (1993) developed a general crisis management strategy that can be used in both elementary and secondary schools. (Parents can also use these techniques to deal with out of control behaviors at home.) The main objective of the crisis management plan is to regain control of the student's or students' behavior. This is usually not an easy task, as the behavior may often be so aggressive and hostile that it is intimidating even to adults. But preplanning and practicing/drilling these steps prior to an actual crisis will help to make adults more competent in dealing with verbally and/or physically aggressive behaviors. Being prepared and feeling confident to deal with such severe behaviors makes them seem less intimidating.

The following nine steps, adapted with permission from Gilliam (1993), can guide educational staff in formulating a crisis management plan for their school:

1. **Design the Plan**

   First, use a team effort to develop the crisis management plan. Involve all relevant individuals at the planning stage. Base the plan on the available resources of the school.

   A critical component of the plan is deciding when and how to call for professional assistance. One of the biggest obstacles school administrators must overcome is the fear that calling the police gives the appearance that they cannot "handle" their schools. No educator would hesitate to call the fire department to put out a school fire, yet many wait far too long, or fail altogether, to summon the police when faced with a school crisis involving violent behavior. Police officers are trained to handle crisis situations. While they cannot be expected to handle all the problem behaviors demonstrated by students, they are vital to ensure the safety of all concerned when the crisis has escalated to dangerous proportions.

As police departments across the country restructure their training to address gangs and youth violence, most have also undertaken the responsibility to educate school personnel on these problems. Invite local police officers to participate in establishing crisis management plans at school.

Educational staff should evaluate their own individual school environment when creating their crisis management plan, focusing on the potential for various types of crisis situations. The best predictor of future behavior is past incidents. A student population who have demonstrated severely aggressive behaviors are likely to do so again. Summary Box 4.6 provides an outline that can be used to plan for a variety of crisis situations and formulate a school-wide plan to address gang-related behaviors.

Summary Box 4.6

Components of a Crisis Management Plan

1. Determine which student behaviors connote a crisis situation:

    ■ Describe specific student behaviors.

    ■ Describe possible "outsider" behaviors.

2. Determine a communication plan to use in crisis situations.

3. Assess which personnel in the school are particularly competent to manage which types of crisis situations:

    ■ Provide training for all other staff members.

    ■ Teach nonconfrontational crisis management strategies.

4. Collaborate with community agencies (police, fire, medical, social service, psychological/psychiatric) in the development of the crisis management plan.

5. Inform the students of the crisis management procedures developed:

    ■ Students must know how to follow their teachers' instructions in a crisis.

    ■ Students must know what to do when unsupervised, for whatever reason, during a crisis.

6. Drill crisis management procedures with the staff and students.

7. Decide how to address postcrisis problem solving with the staff, students, parents, and community members involved:

    ■ Assign specific duties to staff members.

    ■ Involve parent volunteers.

    ■ Involve appropriate community agencies.

8. Meet periodically (perhaps annually) to review, evaluate, and revise the plan, if necessary.

All crisis behaviors should be logged on a "Critical Incident Report" form (or similar recording form). This is a protective procedure for the school. It documents all actions of the school personnel during a crisis in case there is a legal challenge later. In addition, if a crisis is gang-related, this form can be used to document a gang problem in the school. Summary Box 4.7 provides an example of a "Critical Incident Report" form also adapted from Gilliam.

Summary Box 4.7

Critical Incident Report

Date/time of crisis incident: _____

Student(s) demonstrating crisis behaviors: _____

_____

1. In objective terms, describe the behavioral sequence of the incident, location, student behavior, and staff reactions. _____

   _____

2. Who was present and witnessed the incident? _____

   _____

3. Describe any known antecedents to the incident. _____

   _____

4. What behavioral signals/cues did the student(s) show immediately prior to the crisis behavior? _____

   _____

5. What action was taken to prevent the crisis? Describe in sequence the intervention(s) used. _____

   _____

6. What professional assistance was required? _____

   _____

7. List the names of persons who were injured, the nature of each injury, and the follow-up service provided for each injury. _____

   _____

(CONTINUED)

---

8. Were the steps of our **Crisis Management Plan** followed? If no, why not?

    _____

9. Was a postcrisis problem-solving session implemented with the problem
    student(s)?_____

    - If not, why not? _____

    - If so, describe the alternative behavior(s) that the student(s) will practice in
      the future. _____

2. **Devise Systems for
    Communication**

A school policy should be established for maintaining the communication among staff during
crisis situations. Since each school
building is different, there is no one
plan that is the most correct to follow. Generally the school intercom
system is the most viable and widely
available method. With an intercom
system, teachers will have immediate contact with the office and the
office staff can contact individual
teachers or all the classrooms simultaneously. It is critical that all teachers be able to contact the office at
any given time from their classrooms or from the playground. Any
teacher whose classroom is not connected to the office via the intercom system should be provided
with some other means of communication, such as a cellular
phone, a pager, or two-way radio

system. Ideally, there will also be an
emergency phone located on the
playground with which staff can
contact the office.

There should also be a plan for
quickly and efficiently accounting
for and identifying every student in
the school. A procedure should be
in place for certain teachers, such as
homeroom teachers, to be responsible for the accurate confirmation of
the whereabouts of a specific set of
students. On a daily basis, these
teachers would report the absence
or tardiness of "their" students. The
crisis intervention plan would specify where all students are to report
in the event of a crisis situation.
Ideally, this would be to the homeroom teacher's classroom. These
teachers could then compare the
morning attendance report to the
presence of the students reporting.
Using this method, it will be much

easier to account for the safety of all the students during a crisis.

When a crisis occurs, school officials must be able to contact the appropriate professionals (e.g., police, fire, medical, social service, psychological/psychiatric) for assistance quickly and efficiently. Decide which staff member(s) will make the decision about who to call and when to call during a crisis.

Lastly, each school should define a policy for interacting with the media, if necessary. School administrators should designate which school staff should address media questions. The other staff members should then be instructed as to how to deflect media questions to those designated. The school should have a written policy to effectively manage the dissemination of information during crisis events. This procedure would also cover notification to parents and the surrounding community about the status of any crisis situation at school. Assigning a "Public Information Officer" can be of great assistance in working with the media. This way, only one person is providing information, and the flow of information is factually accurate.

3. **Rehearse the Plan**

Once the crisis management plan is established, rehearse it just as the school would rehearse fire or tornado drills. All educational staff and students should know what to do when the crisis management plan is activated. Some teachers may not think it is important to rehearse crisis management plans because they believe in the fallacy of "It won't happen to me." They think violence is something that only happens to other teachers, maybe in big city schools. These teachers are simply setting themselves and their students up for a tragedy.

The media has documented violent attacks on teachers, administrators, and students in school districts of all sizes. In grief and shock, after an incidence of violence, many onlookers say, "I can't believe it happened here." Case in point: A national poll conducted by a research team from Xavier University in Ohio (Boothe et al., 1993) indicated that most administrators agree that school violence is increasing all across the country. But ironically, there is a wide discrepancy between the violence administrators perceive in their own districts compared to what they believe is happening in neighboring school districts.

Approximately 39% of the principals polled said that violence is escalating at their school, while 65% said that violence is increasing at **other** schools.

All educators, regardless of what part of the country they live in, must be prepared to deal with violence at school, and to protect their students' welfare in the classroom. Remember: It might happen to you!

4. **Remain Calm During the Crisis**

When a crisis actually occurs, it is crucial to attempt to control your responses. The main objective is to remain calm. Suppressing feelings of fear, anger, or other emotional responses will help to pacify or appease a student who is out of control. Maintaining a calm demeanor will also help in keeping the steps of the preplanned crisis management plan in mind.

Everyone will have to overcome feelings of panic during a crisis situation. But teachers must be a model of calm behavior. If the teacher becomes upset, the students in the class are likely to follow suit. Under these circumstances, the entire class might panic.

Besides endangering the safety of the students in any type of crisis situation, one of the greatest detriments of panicky behavior is

that it usually causes the behavior of the aggressive student to deteriorate. The student in crisis could easily be "pushed over the edge" if the entire situation around him/her deteriorates.

Maintaining calm behavior is of critical importance when weapons are involved. In these situations, panicky or impulsive behavior might easily provoke a student into firing a gun or attacking with a knife. One way to keep feelings of panic under control is to actively control your breathing. Focus on taking slow, deep breaths. Breathing in a fast, shallow manner could cause hyperventilation.

When a crisis occurs, teachers must remember to follow the crisis management plan. That preplanned interven- tion system should be activated at the first sign of out of control behavior. This effort would include sending for professional assistance from the police, fire department, or medical or counseling personnel as soon as it is warranted.

5. **Stay Out of Striking Range**

When a crisis situation occurs, it is important that teachers competently deal with the problem in addition to keeping themselves as well as their other students safe. A component of the crisis management plan should involve teaching the students a classroom evacuation procedure. Based on their teacher's signal, the students in the classroom would know whether to clear the room during a crisis or whether they should remain quietly in their seats.

Evacuating the classroom will remove all of the other students from the danger of the crisis situation. This procedure would allow the teacher to concentrate solely on the problem situation, without having to worry about their safety, until the preplanned crisis intervention back-up assistance arrived. The classroom evacuation signal would indicate that the students should leave the classroom calmly and quietly and go to a prearranged, safe spot (such as a neighboring classroom or the school auditorium). One or more of the students should also be designated as "message carriers." It would be their responsibility to inform the office staff about the problem in the classroom. The students should be guided in practicing this evacuation procedure so

they would be able to carry it out smoothly when necessary.

With this in mind, teachers should arrange their classroom environment with easily navigable exit pathways in case there is a need for a room clear. If all the exit pathways are kept clear and uncongested with furniture, equipment, and materials then an evacuation can take place in a smooth and efficient manner. Place the teacher's desk close to the exit for observation and management purposes. Furniture for main teaching areas should also be near the exit of the classroom if possible. This way, if other teachers, support staff, or administrators are walking the hallways, they can easily observe that the class is functioning normally.

Teachers must, if possible, stay out of striking range of a student who is demonstrating out of control behavior. The teacher must respect the student's personal space. "Moving in" on the student might be perceived as returned aggression, serving to escalate the student's behavior. Maintaining distance will also help to show the all-important respect to a gang member, so that he/she does not feel forced to react aggressively in order to maintain his/her reputation (to avoid "losing face").

As long as the student is not physically attacking anyone, stand a safe distance away. About eight to ten feet is usually prudent, but is still close enough to see and prepare for sudden physical attacks. This distance also makes it possible for the teacher to make requests or give commands in a quiet but firm voice.

6. **Tell the Student Why the Behavior Must Be Stopped**

The next step of crisis management is for the teacher to tell the aggressive student why he/she needs to stop the problem behavior. To convince the student to stop the behavior, the teacher should provide a relevant reason for why the behavior is unacceptable. This should be a clear, concise explanation possibly referring to school rules, social expectations, or the loss of certain privileges.

A reason that may be effective in a problem related to gang aggression is to appeal to the student's values of respect and reputation. Or, a teacher might point out that in the school environment, many friends, or possibly younger siblings of their own or fellow gang members might be injured in the crisis. Most gang members are very aware of and concerned about the safety of their fellow gang members and family members.

Another method that can be used to help stop the behavior is to relate to the student personally, based on the rapport between the adult and the student. Use the student's first name when making the statement (e.g., "Jason, I would really appreciate it if you would give me the gun and then we can talk about this problem."). Another example would be to appeal to the student's values: "Susan, if you do this, you might hurt someone— maybe one of the younger children here. Do you think it is okay to hurt others like that?" A third technique is to relate to the student's sense of self and intelligence: "Leon, you are too smart to let this fight with Tyrone get out of control. Why don't you give me the knife so we can talk about it?"

Regardless of the method used, simply hearing a clear, concise, and common sense reason for stopping the behavior might help the student to deescalate. Students are conditioned to respond to authoritative (not to be confused with authoritarian) teacher commands. Authoritative means decisive, definitive, reliable, and trustworthy, while authoritarian implies dictatorial, tyrannical, harsh, and inflexible.

A command given by the teacher in a no nonsense tone of voice such as, "Stop that right now," or "Sit down!" is a verbal cue to the student to immediately terminate the behavior. However, it is important to note that this technique will not be effective for a teacher who frequently uses yelling as a means to manage or control inappropriate behavior. In other words, past treatment of the student is going to affect how he/she will react in this situation. This is where consistency and fairness pay off. Teachers who have reputations of being strict but fair and consistent will find handling crisis situations much easier.

7. Use Verbal Problem-Solving Skills

Teachers and parents should always attempt to intervene **verbally** in a crisis situation. Practice in verbal mediation will do more good than all of the training one could receive in the use of force. For that reason, physical restraint techniques as a method for dealing with problem behaviors of children and adolescents are not recommended. (Summary Box 4.8 provides an information source for readers who would like to learn more about safe methods of physical restraint.)

Summary Box 4.8
National Crisis Prevention Institute (CPI)

The National Crisis Prevention Institute, Inc. (CPI) trains educators in the techniques of nonviolent crisis intervention. Program literature states that the techniques have been effective in resolving potentially violent crises. The techniques, which are provided in a variety of individualized seminars, are developed and taught by certified CPI instructors. Emphasis is placed on the deescalation of problem behaviors. More detailed information can be obtained from:

National Crisis Prevention Institute, Inc.
3315-K North 124th Street
Brookfield, WI 53005
Phone: (800) 558-8976
FAX: (414) 783-5906

Physically restraining a child, if absolutely necessary, should be a team effort in order to be completed safely and effectively. This is true even for very young or small students. But especially when students are older or of a larger size, physical restraint is not a safe alternative. The average teacher will not have access to adequate training, practice, or back-up support necessary to safely carry out physical restraint. Adults who try to use force usually just end up in a physical power struggle in which both opponents lose—both are likely to get hurt as this situation quickly deteriorates into a fight or a wrestling match.

Verbal mediation and problem-solving methods are advocated as the most effective means for teachers to deal with crisis behaviors. Many police departments across the country are providing training for their officers in the art of verbal intervention as opposed to hands-on control methods. It has been proven over and over again that hostile and aggressive individuals can be more effectively controlled through appropriate language than by resorting to force.

After the teacher has told the student why the behavior must be stopped, it is important to give the student time to think, process, and actually stop the behavior. When the student begins to demonstrate signs of deescalating behavior, use verbal positive reinforcement to reward the student's intent to stop the undesired behavior. Continue to make encouraging remarks that show faith in the student's ability to stop the behavior.

It is important to remember that what the teacher initially says when confronted with a crisis, and how it is said, will usually set the tone for his/her effectiveness in handling the situation. If one counters the aggressive student with hostile and aggressive actions or speech, the situation is likely to deteriorate and take an immediate turn for the worse.

8. **Maintain a Positive Attitude**

A student in crisis will often be aggressive and verbally abusive in a personal manner. Even though this is a frustrating situation, the teacher must not "take the bait" by responding with counter-aggression. This response will usually cause the student's out of control feelings of anger, anxiety, or distress to escalate. Thus, the student would become more dangerous.

While engaging in verbal mediation, if the student begins to deescalate the teacher should continue to remain calm, unemotional, and supportive. For example, if a student relinquished a weapon and began to calm down, it would be very easy for the teacher to get the weapon from the student and then resort to harsh, sarcastic, or negative speech. However, it is important to maintain the trust of the student in order to bring the crisis to a close and to possibly avert another crisis situation of this type in the future.

9. **Engage in Postcrisis Problem Solving**

The final step of a crisis management plan should involve postcrisis problem solving, both with the aggressive student, and with the staff as a whole. When the crisis is over, the school staff will need to evaluate the effectiveness of the crisis intervention techniques employed, and also determine what consequences (if any) should be applied to the student or students involved. Depending upon the school district policy and/or the nature and severity of the crisis, police involvement, school suspension, or even school expulsion may be required.

However, simply punishing the crisis behavior through school suspension is likely to ensure that it will happen again, because the student will not learn a socially appropriate replacement for the problem behavior. (This cycle can be compared to prison time, during which social rehabilitation is not usually achieved by discharge time. Recidivism rates are spiraling, as can be seen by the increasing number of repeat offenders.) A more effective strategy, if appropriate, is to employ a problem-solving technique with the student in order to discuss what has occurred and to devise behavioral alternatives to use in the future. This technique will be addressed in greater detail elsewhere in this section.

Another critical element of this last step is to use the problem behavior of the student as a learning situation for the staff and the students. A complete debriefing by the entire staff is essential in determining refinements to or alternate plans that will bring a crisis to an end more quickly and effectively in the future.

Summary Box 4.9 relates the nine main steps of crisis management.

Summary Box 4.9

Crisis Management Techniques

Step 1 **Design the Plan**

Use a team-based approach to outline the procedures that should be followed during a crisis to manage aggressive student behavior.

Step 2 **Devise Systems for Communication**

Preplan the method that will be used to summon assistance from other educational staff, the police, and/or medical or psychological personnel. Also determine how the school should interact with the media in the event of a crisis.

(CONTINUED)

Summary Box 4.9 (CONTINUED)

Step 3   **Rehearse the Plan**

All staff and students must know and be able to carry out their responsibilities when a crisis situation occurs.

Step 4   **Remain Calm During the Crisis**

The teacher must be a model of calm behavior so that the students do not panic and so that the crisis management plan can be carried out efficiently.

Step 5   **Stay Out of Striking Range**

The preplanned and practiced evacuation procedure should be activated to move students to safety, if necessary. The teacher should be alert for either stealthy or quick, agitated movements that are behavioral indicators of a physical attack. Ideally, the teacher should be positioned about eight to ten feet from the aggressive student. This distance will keep the teacher out of striking range but will allow for communication in a calm, quiet voice.

Step 6   **Tell the Student Why the Behavior Must Be Stopped**

The teacher should tell the student, in a no nonsense but calm manner, why the behavior should be stopped. Suggestions for reasons include relating to the student on a personal level or appealing to the student's sense of moral values or intelligence.

Step 7   **Use Verbal Problem-Solving Skills**

During the crisis situation the teacher should calmly employ verbal mediation strategies, while avoiding threats/ultimatums and the use of force.

Step 8   **Maintain a Positive Attitude**

The teacher should not allow himself/herself to be drawn into the aggression, but should instead continue to demonstrate an attitude of respect and concern for the student who is having the problem.

Step 9   **Engage in Postcrisis Problem Solving**

Following the crisis situation, it is important to both debrief the crisis with the staff, and to plan to teach the student a more appropriate way to handle problems in the future.

PREPARING STUDENTS FOR INDEPENDENT ACTION

Once a crisis management plan has been developed for a school, the students should be taught their role in the plan. Students must know how best to react in a variety of crisis situations. An important component of rehearsing the crisis management plan is to prepare students to carry out the plan when the teacher is not able to provide leadership. During a crisis, the classroom teacher might be absent, might be individually dealing with the aggressive student, or might be incapacitated due to a violent act. Students should know the objective of the plan and how to react in a somewhat composed and orderly manner when a crisis occurs. Rehearsal of the plan ahead of time will help the students to avoid hysteria in a crisis situation.

The main objective of the crisis management plan is to maintain the safety of the students and staff. To remove students from harm's way when a crisis is occurring in the classroom, staff should be familiar with room clear procedures. The students must be able, without assistance, to evacuate the classroom in an organized and systematic fashion. Two or three students per class should be designated as room clear leaders. These individuals would be taught to take leadership responsibility if their teacher was incapacitated. They would dismiss the students by groups, such as rows or

tables, to get up and walk from the classroom to a preplanned meeting spot in the school building or schoolyard. Essentially, the students need to know how, when, and where to go. Teachers should designate a signal word or phrase that would indicate to the students that they are to leave the classroom.

Based on the actual crisis situation occurring in the classroom, the teacher would need to make a decision as to whether the students would be better off evacuating the classroom, staying in their seats, or even using their desks for protection. What sort of movement the students should make is dependent on where they would be most safe. If the crisis situation is contained to one classroom and the students can safely clear the room, they should by all means do so. If they are apt to become "targets" by getting up and moving through the classroom, they should remain in their seats, possibly with their heads down and covered. Or if they can move without too much commotion, hiding underneath their desks for cover may be advocated.

Another objective is to teach students to summon help from another teacher or administrator, from the police, or for medical assistance. If the students have access to a telephone, they should know how and when to dial 911 (or "0," if the school is located in a rural area not covered by the "911" emergency response service). They should role play talking to a 911 dispatcher to give pertinent information. More importantly in school, all the students should know how to use the intercom system to contact the office. Every classroom in every school building should have direct and immediate access to assistance from the main office through a school-wide intercom system. If an intercom system is not available, designated student messengers must know where to go and who to contact for help.

One school in Stockton, California faced dire consequences for their insufficient intercom system. Cleveland Elementary School principal Patricia Busher described a horrifying and tragic incident in which a gunman, armed with an AK 47 assault rifle, hid in one of the school's four portable classrooms (it was empty at the time) adjacent to the playground and opened fire on more than 500 first, second, and third grade students in January 1989 (Smith, 1989). After the shooting stopped, 29 students and one teacher were injured and five students were killed. The students and teachers in the main building received instructions via the intercom system. However, the teachers in the other three portable classrooms, which were closest to where the shooting was taking place, could not communicate directly via the intercom system. To make matters worse, there were substitute teachers in two of these portable units.

In the aftermath of the crisis, Busher stated:

> *I think every principal should have an intercom connection with every classroom in the school. Any school district that does not prioritize funds to allow intercom hook-ups for every classroom is behaving irresponsibly and opening them-selves to possible liability and lawsuits* (p. 9).

When gunfire attack occurs, teachers and students must learn how to and practice "hitting the deck." A signal should be given to cue the students to drop to the floor and use their desks or other available furniture for cover. If gunfire is coming from outside the building in through the windows, everyone should drop to the floor and roll to the wall closest to the source of the gunfire. This procedure will help to protect students and staff from flying glass and ricocheting bullets. Students who stand up or try to run for the door are likely to become targets. Students must be able to carry out these procedures in a calm manner and remain in the protected position until a teacher gives them an "all clear" signal to move about.

Students should also be taught what to do if there is gunfire while they are out on the playground. There have been instances of drive-by shootings directed at rival gang members while students were congregating outside the school building (such as during lunch, recess, or after school). While the aggression may be directed at a certain student or group of students, others on the school grounds are cast in the sometimes fatal "innocent bystander" role. Students must learn to fall to the ground when a teacher signals, or when they hear shots, in order to be less of a target. If there is any sort of cover around, they should roll to it immediately.

In these instances, the students must avoid running in a group or "herd" to the school doors at all costs. All this does is slow down their retreat and create a bigger target for the shooter. Most shooting incidents occur quickly and are over in seconds. Students need to learn to react instantly when shots are fired, and must remain low and in their protected positions until an "all clear" signal is given from a teacher or playground attendant. Drilling students on these behaviors will reduce panic attacks if and when they're actually necessary.

If there is a fight or other type of playground disturbance involving students from the school, the playground staff should attempt to remove all the student bystanders from the area and begin implementing the preplanned crisis management plan. The staff member should approach the area swiftly but calmly, after calling for or sending a reliable student for back-up assistance. The adult should use a loud, authoritative voice commanding everyone to stop and to clear the area. It is best for the staff to not get involved physically but to try to keep the situation under control until back-up arrives. Any students with weapons should be dealt with according to established school policy (see Section 3).

Every school should have a clearly written policy regarding school visitors both on the playground and in the school building. All visitors should be expected to sign in at the front office, stating the time of entrance and exit, purpose of the visit, and whom they are visiting. Many schools now keep their outlying doors locked during school hours so that the main door can be patrolled by staff, parent volunteers, or a police liaison officer during school hours. (Note, however, that fire codes require that all school doors open freely from the inside.) This is a good method of enforcing the school's visitor code.

Self-Defense Strategies for Staff

Prior to the onset of a crisis situation, school staff should learn basic methods of self-protection from students who pose a threat of violence. As identified in the crisis management steps, simply staying out of striking range is one strategy to use. However, if the student has a weapon or is actively aggressive, the adult might need a more cautious plan in order to remain safe. Following are some simple yet effective self-defense strategies that staff can employ in a crisis.

THREE PRIMARY CONSIDERATIONS

Considering the three factors of **time**, **distance**, and **cover** will help to prepare staff to deal more safely with an aggressive student. These three elements will assist school staff in separating themselves from the threatening student, and thus preserve their personal safety.

Time

In an extremely dangerous situation, a student may be threatening to use a weapon of some type or to attack physically. Under these circumstances, the adult must be constantly aware of the student's demeanor and actions. The time it would take for the student to reach the adult would vary from situation to situation. So the teacher will need to make split second decisions concerning what to say, when to stand and talk, and when to run for cover.

Time can be gained by using nonconfrontational behavior management strategies with the student. In an attempt to get the student's behavior back under control, the adult should remain calm, keep his/her voice low, and speak slowly. The adult's position should be at least eight to ten feet from the student and at an angle rather than face to face, as standing at an angle is less confrontive than being face to face with the student. This method of communicating with the student may be effective in gaining time to negotiate a peaceful resolution.

Distance

Distance refers to the physical space between the adult and the aggressive student. The adult should always watch the student's hands for a cue that the student might have and use a weapon. If the student has a weapon, it is critical that the adult stay out of striking range and not make any quick or threatening movements.

The composition of the space between the adult and the student should also be considered: Is the space covered with carpet, an area rug, linoleum, tile, cement, grass, blacktop, or concrete? The composition of that surface will determine how quickly the distance could be covered if the student were to charge the adult or if the adult would need to run to safety. School staff should always wear comfortable shoes that will provide traction and agility if there is a need to move quickly. Female staff members, in particular, should wear clothing that they can move in easily and run in if forced to do so.

(**Note**: Overall, staff members would be advised to dress in a manner that will minimize the risk of injury. Some items of clothing can be used as a "weapon" against the adult. For example, neckties, scarves around the neck, long necklaces, or dangling pierced earrings could be grabbed by an aggressive student and used to injure.)

Cover

Cover refers to objects in the environment, such as furniture or equipment, that could provide protection from an aggressive student. School staff should preplan specific pieces of furniture or equipment in their working environment that could be used as protective cover for either the students or for themselves if the need arose.

School staff must also learn and practice the "hit the deck" procedure of dropping and taking cover in case of gunfire. Safe procedures would be to crawl underneath a desk or, if the gunfire is coming through the windows, to drop and roll to the wall closest to the windows where there will be a reduced chance that they will be hit by bullets or flying glass.

AVOIDING VICTIM MENTALITY

In a crisis, school staff must take care not to think of themselves as victims. That sort of thinking usually results in the person **acting** like a victim. Once the victim mentality sets in, the likelihood that rational crisis management procedures will be carried out decreases significantly. An individual who is overcome with feelings of incompetence and defeat will be powerless to act in a competent manner. This purposeless behavior will not be beneficial to others who are depending on the staff to carry out their part of the crisis management plan. Conversely, those who think like survivors, act like survivors. This mentality will keep the school staff strong and focused on the specific steps of the crisis management plan.

KNOWING THE WORST THAT COULD HAPPEN

Police officers are taught to expect the worst in situations involving violent behaviors. This pattern of thinking prepares them to react in the most appropriate manner. School staff in many instances may be able to deescalate violent situations, but it will be more difficult to react in a competent manner if they are not prepared for a range of problem behaviors. While maintaining an "I will survive" attitude, educators should realistically think ahead to the worst that could happen in various crisis situations.

The most severe type of behavior that school staff will likely need to be prepared for is a student who is brandishing a weapon such as a knife or gun. The adult who mentally accepts the fact that this situation might occur will more competently handle the problem according to the crisis management plan.

LEARNING TO WATCH THE HANDS

Police officers are trained to keep a suspect's hands in sight. A student will not be able to pull a gun or knife or attempt a physical attack without using his/her hands. Thus learning to keep the student's hands in sight will help protect the adult from a surprise assault. It is important to watch for either sudden or stealthy movements towards pockets or other places where a student might conceal a weapon.

When school staff confront a student who may be armed, ask the student to keep his/her hands in sight. If the student asks why, simply say, for example, "It is for safety reasons. If you have a weapon both of us might get hurt. I don't want to be injured and I don't want you to get hurt because I care about you. If your hands are in plain sight, I do not think you will use the weapon."

Gaining Nonconfrontational Control of a Crisis

To gain control of a crisis situation in a nonconfrontational manner, school staff should approach the aggressive student using the following procedures. First, the adult needs to maintain a calm and quiet tone of voice while talking to the student. Voice tone, verbal language, and body language all must convey respect for the student as a human being. Reassure the student that the problem can be managed. Express a willingness to help solve the problem.

Second, do not attempt to touch a potentially violent student. A distance of at least eight to ten feet from the student is recommended. If possible, stand at an angle rather than face to face with the student. This position is less challenging in potentially volatile situations.

> Speaking Up!
>
> *If it's all you got [gang member status/reputation], it's worth dyin' for.*
>
> — Gang member talking with newspaper reporter

Third, try to establish and maintain eye contact with the student. Eye contact facilitates meaningful communication. If the student is not making eye contact, the staff member might say, "Please look at me. I need to tell you something." When the student does look, a simple praise statement should be provided followed by an opening comment related to the desire to remedy the problem. For example, "Thanks for looking. I am sorry about this problem. What can I do to help?" A statement of this type lets the student know that the staff member respects the student's feelings, understands that there is a problem, and is willing to help resolve the situation. In addition, the adult should also provide a specific reason why the student should stop any aggressive behavior.

Finally, the staff member should attempt to guide the student through verbal problem solving. During the conversation, the student needs to be allowed to express his/her feelings, and should be encouraged to determine alternative solutions to the problem. However, the adult should be prepared to guide the student toward a solution that is safe and constructive for all parties involved. If the student expresses a desire to hurt another individual, the adult must state that hurting others in not an acceptable solution and that it will only complicate the existing problem.

School staff will have to provide structured guidance to students who seem unable to problem solve effectively. Giving a structured choice is a method that can be employed. Rather than having the student devise his/her own solution independently, he/she is given two choices, both of which would have a

positive outcome. If the student has a weapon or is suspected of having a weapon, an example might be to either talk to the school staff and cooperate, or to talk to the police. A structured choice promotes rule-following behavior. Plus by taking a nonconfrontational position, the adult does not become the aggressor. This strategy helps set the stage for effective problem solving and a peaceful resolution to the crisis.

Engaging the student in this problem-solving conversation is a method of buying time. This time is necessary in order to carry out the crisis management plan, and to negotiate the most optimal strategy for dealing with the student. The conversation can also help build confidence between the adult and the aggressive student. By keeping the student busy with this conversation, it will be possible to keep his/her mind off of possibly escalating the situation. It also buys the time necessary for help to be summoned.

Summary Box 4.10 summarizes a nonconfrontational procedure for approaching potentially violent students.

Nonconfrontational Approach to Violent Students

- **Voice tone**—Use a calm, quiet voice that demonstrates respect and understanding for the student.

- **Provide personal space**—Do not attempt to touch the student; remain about eight to ten feet away; stand at an angle rather than face to face.

- **Establish and maintain eye contact**—Eye contact facilitates communication.

- **Assist in problem solving**—Guide the student to resolve the situation peacefully.

Verbal Mediation Strategies

Verbal mediation is a problem-solving strategy effective in calming down individuals who are angry, agitated, and potentially violent. Language can be used either as a weapon or as a means of peaceful negotiation. The substance and content of a staff member's verbal interactions with a potentially violent student could mean the difference between life and death.

A mediator assists an individual, or two disputing parties, to reach an agreeable solution to a conflict. Verbal mediation teaches and models communication skills and conflict resolution strategies. Verbal mediation allows each party the opportunity to tell his/her side of the story (conflict). With this process, each of the disputing parties is encouraged to suggest a solution to the problem. Then, the mediator assists them in agreeing upon a mutually beneficial solution to the problem.

Using verbal mediation strategies to respond to gang-related conflicts has been found to have positive consequences. Some schools have utilized verbal mediation successfully with gang members due to the respectful and fair nature of the process. The gang members are allowed to help make decisions on dress, activities, discipline, etc. Making them part of the process helps to get them on "your side." Verbal mediation has been effective in reducing violence and preventing student suspensions from school. The long-term outcome is that less students become clients of the juvenile justice system.

Verbal mediation strategies teach constructive and nonviolent forms of conflict resolution. This process also allows underlying issues such as safety, the need for protection, and the need many gang members have for respect and recognition to be explicitly and conclusively discussed. Verbal mediation can both increase school safety and teach new, socially appropriate behaviors to school-age students influenced by gangs.

The basic steps of verbal mediation are shown in Summary Box 4.11.

Summary Box 4.11

Verbal Mediation Steps
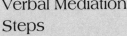

Step 1—Each of the disputing parties tells his/her own side of the conflict.

Step 2—The feelings of the disputing parties are clarified by the mediator.

Step 3—Each of the disputing parties suggests a solution to the conflict.

Step 4—A mutually agreeable solution is negotiated by the mediator.

Specific Crisis Situations

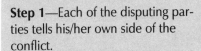

In any type of crisis situation it is important for the teacher to take control by following the predetermined crisis management plan. The steps outlined in this plan will help the teacher to remain calm and to use nonconfrontational techniques to help the aggressive student to regain self-control while maintaining his/her dignity and self-respect. In addition to this general plan, following are tips on four specific crises a teacher may encounter at school: (1) a verbal conflict between students; (2) assaults or fights; (3) strangers in the school; and (4) weapons at school.

VERBAL CONFLICT BETWEEN STUDENTS

There may be cases in which a teacher will have to mediate differences between students rather than between the teacher and a student. The steps of the crisis management plan are still used, but the teacher acts as a mediator between the students. An example is a dispute between two students who are threatening violence against each other. Following the crisis management plan, the teacher would remain calm and unemotional while staying out of striking range of both the students. The teacher could immediately send for back-up assistance according to the crisis management plan.

The next step is to confront the problem behavior and tell the students why it must be stopped. (Any of the verbal methods presented in Step 6 of the crisis management plan could be used.) In gang-related situations, the best reason for immediately stopping the behavior is that aggressive behavior is dangerous. Someone is going to get hurt if it continues. Calling upon the personal rapport between the teacher and student would be appropriate at this time. For example, "It would really help me out if you two would both take a seat so we can talk about this problem. I will help you get it figured out."

A second method to prevent dangerous or violent behavior is to appeal to the students' values. For example, in a situation in which a group may be attempting to intimidate either one student or another group of students, the teacher might make a comment such as, "If you all decide to fight about this problem, someone, and possibly all of you, is going to get hurt. Do you think that will solve the problem?"

A third method to encourage students to stop a problem behavior requires the teacher to make a statement that appeals to the students' sense of self or intelligence. An example for two groups of students who are threatening to fight each other would be, "You all are too

smart to get involved in a fight of this type. Not only will you get hurt, but you will probably end up missing school and you will get behind in your work. You have been doing so well at keeping up this semester. I know that we can come up with a better solution than fighting to solve this problem. Let's talk about it."

The purpose of using a verbal statement of this type is to give the students a logical reason for stopping the behavior. This simple procedure is one that could be used to begin the process of verbal mediation, which will help the students learn to solve their problems in a non-violent manner. Once verbal mediation is begun, it is essential that the teacher continue to act in a supportive manner and to follow through on the remaining steps of the crisis management plan as necessary.

ASSAULTS AND FIGHTS

More teachers and administrators are injured in the attempt to break up fights than any other type of school disturbance. This is usually the result of school staff making one or more of several mistakes.

The first error that teachers commonly make is to run up to a fight and "jump right in." While trying to pull the combatants apart the teacher may be struck or otherwise injured by the students. The students' defense will be that in the confusion of the fight they never knew they hit a teacher. This may or may not be true. However, the result would be the same. A teacher might very well end up with an injury caused by instinctively reacting to the fight without first thinking through the situation.

A reason that teachers often jump between students who are fighting is concern for student safety. However, teachers must remember that they could be incapacitated by an injury, and then would be unable to provide any type of assistance to anyone. When adrenaline starts flowing, even smaller or very young students can cause serious injury.

Teachers need to take the time to analyze the situation. The fight may be a challenge or retaliation between rival gangs. Or the students may be looking for attention or peer approval. If the fight is serious, all teachers need to clearly understand and follow school policy on intervening in fights. Physical intervention on the part of school staff is **not** recommended. It is critically important to call for appropriate back-up, as detailed in the crisis management plan. Let the experts intervene.

Blauvelt (1991) offers these rules for breaking up a fight at school, adapted as follows:

1. Make sure someone is sent to the office to summon back-up assistance (trained staff members, administrators,

a school liaison officer, or police officers). **Walk**, do not run to the fight. This keeps the teacher from being the one who attracts additional bystanders to the fight. If other students see a teacher running, they will assume there is an emergency and will also run to "catch the action." All this does is create a bigger crowd to deal with.

2. If possible, while walking quickly to the fight, stop at other classrooms and obtain help from other teachers. Remember, there is safety in numbers.

3. The minute staff members come within sight of the altercation, they should state in a loud, authoritative voice that authorities are approaching and the fighting must be stopped immediately.

4. Call out to any familiar students and begin giving orders. Tell the students things like, "Mary, go to Mr. Frank's room"; "Calvin, take James, Stephan, and Robert and go to the commons area"; etc. It doesn't matter what they are told to do. The idea is to get them away from the fight. Remember that kids are conditioned to respond to directions, so give them directions. Just get them away from the altercation.

5. If the staff member knows the fighters by name, call out to them and

let them know that the authorities know who they are. Give orders for them to stop the fight at once. Verbal commands are more effective than physical restraints because the teacher keeps his/her distance and refrains from becoming a participant.

6. Teachers must let the experts designated in the crisis management plan intervene, physically if that becomes necessary. Teachers who impulsively jump into fights are likely to get hurt and/or hurt the students involved.

The steps for handling a student fight are summarized in Summary Box 4.12.

STRANGERS IN THE SCHOOL

Some schools have experienced tragedies caused by "visitors" to the building. For example, gang members have been known to infiltrate a school looking for rival gang members, resulting in violence. Part of the school's crisis management plan should include a method of identifying and monitoring visitors. Ideally, all exits of the school should be either monitored or locked (while still allowing for emergency exit from inside the building). Some schools have recording cameras and/or staff or police liaison officers positioned at the main entrance doors to observe all visitors who enter the school building.

Summary Box 4.12

Steps for Addressing a Student Fight

1. Walk, do not run to the fight. Survey the situation on the way. Try not to draw additional student attention to the fighters.

2. Obtain back-up assistance from other educational staff, school security, or the police, as necessary.

3. Use an authoritative voice to demand that the fighters: "Stop!"; "Break it up!"; "Everyone clear the area, **now**!"; etc.

4. Clear bystanders from the area. Call students by name and tell them to leave.

5. Call the fighters by name, but do not try to step between them.

6. Wait for the designated back-up assistance to arrive. Do not try to be a hero/heroine.

Visitors should be required to register at the office before conducting any business in the building. After classes begin for the day, the school staff might lock all the exterior doors except the main entrance (while still allowing for emergency exit from inside the building). This leaves fewer entrances to monitor. Periodically throughout the day, custodial or security staff might check these doors to make sure that a student has not left one ajar for fellow gang members or strangers to enter.

In the event that a stranger did enter the school building without following the established visitor's policy, and was able to bypass the checkpoints just discussed, then additional steps would need to be taken. Appropriate security measures include first notifying appropriate personnel, those who would be responsible for locating the stranger. Second, this staff member would use a reasonable approach to determine the stranger's business in the school. It might be that the individual was simply unaware of the school's visitor policy. If that were the case, the staff member would escort the individual to the main office to sign in and then direct him/her to the desired destination in the school.

In the event that the stranger resisted following the school's visitor policy, he/she should be escorted from the building by designated school staff, security officers, or a school liaison police officer. If the individual was uncooperative in leaving

the building, the police should be immediately called to supply professional back-up assistance.

If the uncooperative stranger was at large somewhere in the school building, but his/her exact whereabouts were not known, the teachers should be notified via the intercom using a code word/phrase so as not to frighten the students. (This might be a component of the written crisis management plan.) The teachers should then account for the whereabouts of their students at that specific time. If any of the students have passes out of the room, for example to the restroom, the library, or the computer lab, those students should be instructed by the staff in those locations to remain where they are until an "all clear" code is given. Staff should keep all the other students in their classrooms until further directions or the "all clear" code is announced.

If there was an indication of further danger or violence toward staff or students, another code phrase should be broadcast over the intercom. The appropriate response might involve having the staff and students take cover or evacuate to a more safe location. As stated previously, these responses should be rehearsed to reduce feelings of panic and victimization if a crisis of this nature were to take place at school.

WEAPONS AT SCHOOL

There may be no words more frightening than "There's a gun in the school!" Violence in schools has been on the rise for the past decade, as has the number of cases in which teachers and students have been injured or killed. Weapons, especially guns, play a critical role in the gang culture. Whether being used to intimidate or protect, weapons in the hands of kids has become one of America's most serious problems. Gang activity in a school results in an increase of weapons available to students: They are bound to show up. Teachers and school administrators who think otherwise might find themselves making a deadly miscalculation.

Officer Randy Holcomb, of the Chicago, Illinois Police Department explains:

> Teachers have to be prepared for the possibility of guns in school. Society tells [youth] now that in order to do anything in society [they] need money. Kids who don't have it will try to get money by whatever means are necessary. . . . Many of them want jobs—but there are no jobs for them. The drug dealer stands on the corner and says, "You can come work for me. I'll give you $400-500 per night to deliver or sell." . . . The eight- or nine-year old kids with $1,000 or $1,500 in their pockets are very intelligent, [they] know [they] need a gun to protect what [they have]. . . .

Teacher training programs lack preparation in dealing with students who carry weapons in school. Law enforcement personnel and educators must collaborate to prepare teachers to cope with the ever increasing problem of weapons in the classroom. The following guidelines are presented to stimulate thought when creating a crisis management plan. Educators must remember that each student and situation is different, and they must be flexible in their response. Being able to "think on your feet" is a critical skill for teachers today.

Real-Life Teacher Tale
Weapon as Self-Defense

I was teaching English at a junior high school in a suburb of a large midwestern city. It was my second year, and most of my students were from middle income, white families.

I walked into my class one day after lunch and found four boys standing up in the back of the room. Three of the boys were taunting the other in a half-circle formation. The boy in the middle was holding out his hand and was clenching something as he tried to keep an eye on the other three. The few other students who had arrived early were watching in silence, all looking really scared.

As I approached the group, I noticed that the boy was holding a razor blade box opener. He was not swinging it or poking it, but I could tell by the look on his face that he was terrified. He was breathing heavily, sweating, and speechless. My first thought was that he was defending himself from the three other boys who were surrounding him. I found out later that I was right.

I started yelling at everyone to sit down. I was screaming. That did nothing to calm the situation. After screaming my instructions to sit down a couple of times, the three surrounding boys found their seats. All that was left was the boy with the box cutter. Even after the other three sat down, he continued to hold the weapon at arm's length in a defensive stance.

I was now confronted with something I had never been taught to handle; a terrified student clutching a weapon. In a panic, all I could think of doing was to yell at him to put the knife down. Suddenly, I realized that he was just as afraid of me in this state as he was of the aggressors. I was not his teacher, just another person scaring him.

I then toned down my voice and tried to be his friend. It took an eternity, at least it seemed like it, but he finally put the knife down on his desktop. I picked it up and he and I walked to the principal's office.

There I learned that for weeks the three other boys had been picking on this kid, stealing his lunch money, and pushing him around. The box cutter was his means of protection.

(CONTINUED)

■ *Gangs—Straight Talk, Straight Up* ■

Real-Life Teacher Tale (CONTINUED)

What I came to realize was that in addition to being unprepared to deal with violence in the classroom, I made the situation worse by overreacting and becoming nervous and excited. Hopefully, I will never be faced with this type of situation again because I am still not sure what made the boy put the knife down. I was lucky, I guess.

– T.J., 7th grade English teacher

Any time there is a weapon, or even the rumor of a weapon, being brought into the school, the entire school staff should be notified. It is also a good practice to notify the local police department once it has been determined that there is indeed a weapon. Until their arrival, teachers and administrators must do all that they can to protect themselves and the students and reduce the element of danger.

Two separate situations involving weapons are presented following: (1) when a weapon is actually seen by a staff member, and (2) when there is a rumor of a weapon in the school. These examples will help school staff in addressing the most intimidating school crisis situation—the presence of a weapon—if the need arises.

Observed Weapons at School

If a weapon has been displayed, the adult must realize that the student with the weapon is in control. Heroic tactics are not called for here! At this point, the teacher needs to try to remain calm and follow the crisis management plan. The first step would be to notify the central office of the problem either by using the intercom system or by sending a student messenger. This procedure should have been preplanned and rehearsed. The police department must be called at once so that their intervention tactics can commence.

Depending upon the severity of the situation, a calm demeanor and persuasive voice may be all it takes to convince the student to give the weapon to the adult. Using the nonconfrontational control tactics presented previously, the teacher should try to keep the student talking and calm. The teacher should maintain a distance of eight to ten feet, so as not to appear challenging to the student.

If the student is highly agitated, the teacher must remain as calm as possible to help in preventing the situation from becoming violent. The main attempt is to "talk the student down." This process will be more readily accomplished by a teacher who projects a calm, quiet, and reassuring manner with the student. Remember, gang members or other violent students will attempt to take advantage of individuals who they perceive as being weak or easy to intimidate.

The armed student may be giving orders to the adult. No matter how unreasonable the demands seem, the teacher must attempt to comply in order to avoid further agitation. A continued dialogue must be attempted. The longer the student talks, the better the likelihood for a peaceful settlement. This conversation buys time, which is the most essential element as the situation unfolds. This time allows for the police to arrive and for deescalation of the student's out of control behavior.

In this situation, the teacher becomes a negotiator first and foremost. The manner in which the teacher reacts to the situation and what he/she says will go a long way in determining what type of outcome is experienced. The teacher must control the situation to the best of his/her ability until the weapon is confiscated and/or the police arrive and take over the dangerous situation.

Rumor of Weapons at School

If there is a rumor of a weapon in the building the school staff need to take the rumor seriously in order to prevent a possibly fatal outcome. As the best source of information in this situation is the student body, the staff should try to get the students talking to them. Once the kids see or hear about a weapon in the building, word will spread through the grapevine like wildfire. If possible, determine which students are the key links in the rumor chain. Teachers and administrators must ask these individuals questions as soon as possible in order to determine who might be in possession of the weapon.

However, it will be critically important to protect the confidentiality of these students and their responses. One strategy is to call more students in that would actually be needed for information. Question them individually. Assure each one that complete and total confidentiality will be guaranteed to them. This way, no one will know exactly which students supplied the relevant information.

Another suggestion is to implement a type of hotline or information box to which students could call in/write in anonymous tips pertaining to violence, weapons, or gang activity at school. A number could be assigned to each student who calls in and reports a tip. Then, a liaison police officer is assigned to the school to investigate the tip(s). If any tip is substantiated (meaning it leads to the solution of a crime or the confiscation of a weapon), the reporting student receives a financial reward.

Once the student who might have the weapon is identified, he/she must be separated from the rest of the student population and taken to the office. The main concern is to determine if the student actually has a weapon. If so, the goal is for the school staff to gain possession of the weapon. In the office, it should be explained to the student that it is believed he/she has a weapon. The student should be given the opportunity to turn over the weapon to the school staff. State clear expectations for the student's behavior.

Give structured choices (e.g., "You need to turn the weapon over to me now or tell the police where it is.") At this point it is not a good idea to negotiate with the student about "deals" for turning over the weapon. It is not likely that school staff will be able to follow through on a bargain of that type. Most schools have severe penalties for carrying weapons, such as expulsion from the school.

If the student will offer no information, school staff may "pat down" the student if there is good cause to believe that he/she is concealing a weapon. This is accomplished by using the hands to externally feel the student's clothing, and inspect his/her purse or book bag. Make every attempt to have a male teacher pat down a male student and a female teacher pat down a female student.

Never attempt to strip search any student. This will likely result in legal problems for the school. If there is reason to

believe that the student has a concealed weapon, but these attempts to find it have failed, summon the police. Keep the student under constant surveillance until they arrive. It is also good practice to notify the student's parent(s), and have them meet with the school and police authorities at the school.

If it cannot be determined exactly who has the weapon, give the students the impression that the school staff is supervising everywhere. Make the students aware that the staff are watching every move they make every minute of the school day. High staff visibility must be present during the periods between classes, during lunch, recess, and at any other times when the students are mingling in less structured areas which might typically have less staff supervision. Teachers and administrators should be out in the hallways while the students are moving about.

The entire student population needs to know that the staff has heard about and is on the lookout for a weapon. Maintain this level of visible staff presence until the weapon is located or classes have been dismissed for the day and the building is empty. Being on the alert is essential when there is a rumor of a weapon. This demonstrates to the students that their safety is of utmost importance, and that the staff is alert for the presence of weapons and/or associated violence. These observation tactics should be continued daily until the rumor is either cleared or substantiated.

Weapon Removal Tactics

Weapon removal tactics by teachers are not advocated. Besides being unsafe, trying to do so can easily make the crisis situation much worse. It is not possible to provide in this book a plan of action for weapon removal that can be described "cookbook" style. Instead, school staff must let law enforcement personnel remove weapons from students. This is an exceedingly dangerous and sensitive situation that must be handled by experts. Even police officers, who are highly trained, explain that there is no sure-fire method of taking a weapon away from another individual. In fact, many people have been hurt or killed trying.

What school staff must do is to try to remain calm when faced with a student who displays a weapon and/or threatens to use the weapon. This is a situation in which verbal mediation methods should be used. Get the student talking and keep him/her talking. Use a consistently calm voice and project a composed manner. This behavior will help to keep the student from becoming more agitated. Remember, the student is probably very scared, confused, and distressed about the situation. Reassure the student that his/her safety, as well as that of the rest of the class, is of prime concern.

Ask, but do not demand, that the student turn over the weapon. Summon assistance if possible, and keep the "time, distance, cover" theory in mind so that the safety of staff and the other students is foremost. The adult should be positioned between the threatening student and any other students, if possible. This will help to protect the others from physical or weapon attack.

Adults must convey to the armed student that they are just as concerned for his/her welfare as they are for those around him/her. This will help the staff members to gain the student's confidence. (**Note:** If the teacher's past demeanor has been one of little compassion or respect for the student, he/she could be in big trouble at this point. Teachers must treat students respectfully at all times so that if a crisis is encountered, it is possible to build upon a past positive relationship.)

It is essential to remember that time is on the side of the staff member. Do not try to rush the student or hurry the situation. Be the concerned, caring negotiator. The time bought may save or protect the teacher's life as well as the lives of students. Leave the weapon removal up to police officers, who are trained to deal with this type of situation, if the student will not willingly relinquish the weapon.

School staff are primarily teachers. They do need to be skilled in dealing with many student behaviors. However, they cannot be expected to be crisis intervention experts. When implementing crisis management procedures, professional back-up assistance should be identified for each type of crisis situation. For example, if the crisis was a suicide attempt, the assistance of a counselor/therapist would be appropriate. If the crisis was a drive-by shooting, the police should be called.

Postcrisis Intervention

Following a crisis situation, educators will need to be prepared to help the student rejoin the classroom environment as smoothly as possible. Some behaviors demonstrated by students are so violent and dangerous that they need to be referred to more specialized personnel or agencies for remediation. Residential treatment centers, psychiatric hospitals, detention centers, and correction institutes have specially trained professionals to work with youth who show behaviors that are so violent, dangerous, and antisocial that they cannot be managed effectively in a regular school situation.

Yet as stated in Step 9 of the crisis management plan presented previously, postcrisis problem solving is the final, and a very important, step to crisis

management for most behaviors exhibited by students in the school setting. Students must learn that their aggressive and violent behaviors are not an acceptable means for solving their problems. However, it is critically important that they learn a **socially acceptable replacement behavior** for the problem behaviors they have demonstrated.

The problem-solving component of crisis management should encompass seven main steps. The goal of implementing this procedure is to teach the student socially appropriate behavior instead of those that resulted in the crisis situation. This process will also provide the student with a model for effective problem solving, in direct contrast to simply reacting in an impulsive, hostile, and aggressive manner as he/she did previously.

The first step of the problem-solving procedure is to define the problem behavior for the student. This means that the behavior must be stated in observable, measurable terms. In order to change the behavior, the student must understand exactly what actions or conduct compose the problem behavior (observable), and how often it happens (measurable).

Second, the student needs to take ownership for his/her actions related to the problem behavior. Advancing through the rest of the problem-solving steps will not be possible until the student can admit responsibility for the problem. This is a critical hurdle to leap.

Some students may initially resist this process. In a nonthreatening and respectful manner, the staff member should encourage the student to participate. An ultimatum of " . . . do it or you can't come back in my classroom" will probably result in escalation of the problem behavior. The teacher should try to create a positive rapport with the student, letting the student know that the teacher cares and has his/her best interest in mind. Using this type of approach is likely to result in successful problem solving for staff and students.

Third, the teacher should assist the student in identifying new behavior chains that can replace the problem behavior and that will help to prevent it from reoccurring. A behavior chain is simply all of the components that comprise the total behavior. For example, when a crisis erupts between two gang members in the classroom, a series of lesser behaviors led up to the crisis. These behaviors probably involved verbal skirmishes, threats, boasts, and challenges. Intervention early in this behavioral chain may have been effective in averting the crisis situation.

Identifying alternatives to the problem behavior allows the student to learn a new, more socially appropriate pattern of behavior. This is a form of preventive behavior management. Rather than simply punishing a problem behavior, a

replacement behavior is taught. Have the student brainstorm a list of possible alternative behaviors that he/she might use to replace the problem behavior that escalated into a crisis situation (assisting the student if necessary). (**Note:** Some crises may include more problem behaviors than educational staff will effectively be able to address. These situations will require assistance from specially trained personnel, such as mental health personnel.)

The fourth step requires the student to identify the consequences of the various alternatives. For each alternative, the student should think ahead to what possible consequences might result from taking that action. This procedure will help the student to become more aware of his/her own behavior, rather than simply reacting impulsively to various problem situations.

The fifth step involves choosing one alternative solution to try. Use role play and various other activities in a guided and safe situation to have the student practice the new replacement behavior. Structure the role plays to reflect real-life classroom situations in which the student might use the skill. After the student successfully demonstrates the skill in this role play situation, rehearse the skill in other situations outside the classroom. This process will help the student to transfer the training and skill to other real-life situations in which he/she might also need some assistance.

The sixth step involves trying out the chosen alternative behavior in a real-life, rather than a practice, situation. The student will need to plan where, when, and how to perform the new behavior. Again, this will help the student to plan ahead and to be less impulsive when confronted with another similar problem.

The seventh and final step of the problem-solving process is for the student to report back the results of using the new behavior in a real-life situation when it was necessary. At this time the alternative behavior should be evaluated and revised, if required.

Summary Box 4.13 provides an outline of the problem-solving process that can be used with students after a crisis.

Summary Box 4.13

Problem-Solving Procedure

1. Say the problem in your own words. Describe the problem carefully. Explain how it affected you. How did it affect other people?

   _____

   _____

2. List all the different things you could have done to try to solve the problem appropriately.

   _____

   _____

3. Write down what would happen if you did each solution. (Use extra paper if necessary.)

   _____

   _____

4. Which solution would work best? How did you decide on this one?

   _____

   _____

(CONTINUED)

---

5. Look at the solution you chose and write out a step-by-step plan for carrying
    it out. Write exactly what you will do and say. Write what you will do first,
    second, third, and so on. (Use extra paper if necessary.)

    _____

    _____

    _____

I pledge to carry out this plan next time this problem occurs. I understand that the
plan will help me to solve my problems in an appropriate way.

_____   _____
Student Signature   Date   Staff Signature   Date

Summary

The crisis management plan presented in this section can be adapted for any elementary or secondary school. The main goal of the crisis management plan is to prepare school staff and parents to deal with out of control student behavior in an effective and competent manner. Two main outcomes are important: (1) the safety of the adult and the other students is a foremost concern, and (2) the adult must cope with the aggressive student in a manner that is calm and unemotional, and which will allow the student to salvage his/her dignity and self-respect following the crisis. The importance of respect for youth gang members especially, is paramount, and the teacher's outward demonstration of respect in both voice and actions could make or break the crisis situation.

Like fire and tornado drills, the crisis management plan must be rehearsed and periodically drilled so that the school staff and the students all know their roles. The students should be able to carry out the plan without the assistance of their teacher, if necessary.

In a crisis, verbal mediation strategies, as opposed to any type of physical restraint, should always be a first choice method. Unless used by specially trained personnel, physical restraint is too dangerous to both the student and the teacher to use in school settings. The average teacher does not have the necessary experience to use physical restraint safely or effectively. However, verbal mediation and negotiation allows the teacher or parent to model appropriate problem-solving strategies for the student.

References/Resources

Bing, L. (1994). *Do or die*. New York: Harper Collins.

This book is based on direct interviews the author conducted with juveniles incarcerated with the California Youth Authority. The juveniles tell the story of their experiences in gang life.

Do or Die (ISBN #0-06-016326-7) may be ordered from Harper Collins, 10 East 53rd Street, New York, NY 10022; Phone (800) 387-0117; FAX (800) 668-5788; Email: hcorder@harpercollins.com.

Blauvelt, P.D. (1991). *Effective strategies for school security*. Reston, VA: National Association of School Principals.

The purpose of this book is to provide school administrators with strategies to promote school security. School vandalism and violence are addressed.

Effective Strategies for School Security (ISBN #0-88210-129-3) may be ordered from the National Association of School Principals, 1904 Association Drive, Reston, VA 22091; Phone (703) 860-0200; FAX (703) 476-5432.

Boothe, J., Bradley, L., Flick, T.M., Keough, K., & Kirk, S. (1993). The violence at your door. *The Executive Educator, 15*(1), 16-22.

This national survey was conducted for *The Executive Educator* by a team from Xavier University in Cincinnati, Ohio. The study analyzed responses from 1,216 school executives regarding their perceptions of school violence.

Colvin, G. (1992). *Managing acting-out behavior: A staff development program to prevent and manage acting-out behavior*. Eugene, OR: Behavior Associates.

This program, which includes a manual and two videotape presentations, teaches school staff and parents effective ways to identify and intervene with the seven main phases of escalating the acting-out behavior chain, including teaching alternative behaviors, teaching problem-solving skills, using precorrection, and disengaging techniques.

Managing Acting-Out Behavior: A Staff Development Program to Prevent and Manage Acting-Out Behavior (ISBN #0-9631777-0-2) may be ordered from the program distributor, Sopris West, 1140 Boston Avenue, Longmont, CO 80501; Phone (800) 547-6747; FAX (303) 776-5934; http://www.sopriswest.com.

Gilliam, J.E. (1993). Crisis management for students with emotional/behavioral problems. *Intervention in School and Clinic, 28*(4), 224-230.

This article describes a step-by-step procedure that teachers and parents can use to effectively manage student behavior in crisis situations. A positive approach is emphasized. Precrisis goals, predicting the crisis situation, and postcrisis follow-up are addressed.

Kaplan, J.S. (1995). *Beyond behavior modification*. Austin, TX: Pro-Ed.

This is a college text designed to teach behavior modification techniques. The author uses many pertinent examples and provides a variety of charts for teachers to use in the classroom. A number of humorous cartoon-type illustrations are sprinkled throughout.

Beyond Behavior Modification (ISBN #0-89079-663-7) may be ordered from Pro-Ed, 8700 Shoal Creek Boulevard, Austin, TX 78757-6897; Phone (512) 451-3246; FAX (512) 451-8542.

Prothrow-Stith, D. (1995). *Hidden casualties: The relationship between violence and learning*. Washington, D.C.: National Health & Education Consortium.

In this manual Deborah Prothrow-Stith and Sher Quaday of the Harvard School of Public Health take a developmental approach to explore the impact of violence on a child's receptivity to education and ability to learn.

Hidden Casualties: The Relationship Between Violence and Learning (ISBN #0-937846-38-4) may be ordered from the National Health & Education Consortium, c/o the Institute for Educational Leadership, 1001 Connecticut Avenue NW, Suite 310, Washington, D.C. 20036; Phone (202) 822-8405; FAX (202) 872-4050.

Prothrow-Stith, D. (1987). *Violence prevention curriculum for adolescents*. Newton, MA: Education Development Center.

This program is a ten-session course that addresses the growing problem of violence and homicide among young people. Part of the Teenage Health Teaching Modules (THTM) program, this comprehensive school health curriculum for adolescents is designed to help youth deal with their anger in productive, nonviolent ways. The program includes print and videotape materials.

The *Violence Prevention Curriculum for Adolescents* (ISBN # not necessary for ordering) may be ordered from EDC Publishing Center, Education Development Center, 55 Chapel Street, Suite 24, Newton, MA 02160; Phone (800) 225-4276; FAX (617) 630-8402.

Slaby, R.G., Wilson-Brewer, R., & Dash, K. (1995). *Aggressors, victims, and bystanders: Thinking and acting to prevent violence*. Newton, MA: Education Development Center.

This manual has been extensively field-tested with nearly 700 students (grades 6-9) in urban, suburban, and small-city school districts at high risk for violence. The curriculum helps to change students' thoughts and actions away from support of violence to beliefs that aggression is not a desirable response, and the intention to avoid or resolve conflict peacefully.

Aggressors, Victims, and Bystanders: Thinking and Acting to Prevent Violence (ISBN # not necessary for ordering) may be ordered fro EDC Publishing

Center, Education Development Center, 55 Chapel Street, Suite 25, Newton, MA 02158-1060; Phone (800) 255-4276; FAX (617) 630-8402.

Smith, D. (1989). The Cleveland Elementary School shooting. *THRUST for Educational Leadership, 18*(7), 8-11.

This article describes the tragic shooting spree that left 30 individuals wounded and five dead after a gunman used an automatic weapon to spray bullets randomly across the Cleveland Elementary School playground. The events are reconstructed and suggestions are provided for dealing with other tragedies of this type in a proactive manner. Principal Busher makes recommendations to other administrators based on her experience with this firearm assault at school.

CHAPTER 5

Case Studies

This section consists of seven case studies. Each depicts a situation involving teachers and youth gang members demonstrating aggressive behavior. The case studies are meant to be interesting to read. Following each is a set of cooperative learning exercises, ranging in complexity from straightforward questions to answer to more involved tasks for problem-solving groups within schools. These cooperative learning exercises can be used by school staff in a group situation to discuss different methods of planning for and managing gang-related aggression and violence. A role play situation for each case study is also provided. After staff have a chance to read and discuss the various aspects of each case study, they might want to assign themselves roles and actually practice saying and doing some of the strategies that were discussed.

Case Study 1:
Mrs. Jackson's Fatal Lapse

The nightmare vision seemed to be playing out in slow motion. Unfortunately, it was not nighttime, it was not a dream, and the performers acting out this drama were not really moving in slow motion. The volatile group of five students was composed of four students against one. The lone student was waving a pistol, using it to keep the other four at bay. However the presence of the firearm did not seem to faze the other four students.

Linda Jackson, high school history teacher for the past 18 years, stood in frozen silence as the four students in her classroom continued to circle the lone student, spitting verbal threats at him. The remaining 22 students in the classroom sat in breathless silence, their eyes darting between the group and their teacher. Some of the students who had been sitting in close proximity to the group were now gathered in a corner at the back of the classroom.

Mrs. Jackson knew she needed to take control of the situation, but a sensation of icy fear and panic traveling up her spine was making her feel weak and dizzy. Her desk was situated in a corner of the classroom next to the windows. The only exit from the room was diagonal from her desk, meaning she would have to pass by the out of control group of students in order to go for help.

Mrs. Jackson had read the warning in the school bulletin about potential youth gang activity in the school. Since the school district was very large, a wide range of socioeconomic neighborhoods were represented in the student population. Rival gang members were brought together during school hours. Mrs. Jackson's thought after reading the warning was that youth gang violence certainly would not take place in her classroom—that was only a concern in big cities.

Some literature about gangs from the local police department had been routed to all the teachers at the school. Mrs. Jackson had noticed that the pamphlet contained examples of gang graffiti similar to some doodling she had seen in the margins of some of her students' papers. Mrs. Jackson's opinion was that she had enough to worry about without trying to decipher a bunch of "chicken scratch" on the edges of her students' papers or on the covers of their notebooks. Consequently, Mrs. Jackson threw away her copy of the police department pamphlet without reading it thoroughly. The day she entered her classroom and found some graffiti scrawled on the blackboard, she erased it without a second thought.

As Mrs. Jackson stared at the five students, she wondered if this could possibly be some sort of gang-related problem. The four students were wearing red and black clothing in addition to Chicago Bulls hats tilted over to the left side. She knew from past observation that these four hung around together most of the time. The single student with the gun was wearing khaki trousers with a plaid flannel shirt, unbuttoned except for the top button, hanging out over a white T-shirt. He was wearing a Pittsburgh Pirates baseball cap, also tilted to the left.

The aggressive tones of the students and the potential for serious violence appeared to be escalating. Mrs. Jackson knew that she had to make a move before someone got hurt. She thought she might be able to slip out of the classroom in order to summon assistance. As Mrs. Jackson made a hesitant move towards the door of the classroom, the student with the gun swung towards her and snarled a warning to stay away. Simultaneously, pandemonium erupted as the other four students leapt towards him. A gunshot exploded, and screams of terror echoed through the classroom. One of the onlooking students had been shot.

COOPERATIVE LEARNING ACTIVITIES

1. Outline the steps that led to the crisis situation and eventual tragedy in Mrs. Jackson's classroom.

2. For each of the steps, identify a proactive intervention that could have been implemented.

3. What steps could Mrs. Jackson have taken to be more informed about the youth gang problem at her school?

4. Review the typical examples of graffiti and the colors of the major youth gangs (see Section 2). Have one person draw an example of graffiti or state the main colors and representation of a gang. Then have the other staff members in the group identify the gang. Continue this process for all of the major gangs covered.

5. What visual gang identifiers that were described in this case study should Mrs. Jackson have recognized?

6. What student behavior(s) should Mrs. Jackson have observed in order to intervene with the problem early and avert the crisis that occurred?

ROLE PLAY

Create a role play situation to demonstrate appropriate teacher behaviors that could be used to deescalate and safely manage the gang-related crisis outlined in this case study. Also incorporate the proactive intervention strategies identified in Cooperative Learning Activity #2 ("Miss Harrison's Dilemma") as role play components.

Case Study 2: Miss Harrison's Dilemma

Samantha Harrison had just begun her third year of teaching art at LaFollette High School. She greatly enjoyed the variety of artistic subject matter she presented, as well as working with the students themselves. Samantha was also the director and coordinator of a regional art show for high school students that took place once each year. Winners at the art show were awarded scholarships at an arts college in the area. Many of her students went on to that college to further their artistic talents.

The students in Miss Harrison's art class were continually inspired and encouraged to set and consequently master their personal artistic goals. Due to Samantha's enthusiastic, motivating personality, her youth, and her "cool" reputation, her art classes were always filled to capacity and contained a variety of students ranging from the "brains," the "jocks," to the "nerds," and gang members. While most of the teachers at the high school feared and disliked the gang members, Samantha had taken it upon herself to learn as much as she possibly could about the rival gangs in the city. The location of LaFollette High School resulted in the enrollment of two gang

factions: the Vice Lords and the Black Gangster Disciples.

During her years of teaching, Samantha had found that several gang members had an extremely high degree of artistic ability. She had encouraged them to develop their talents and to enter their projects in the annual art show. A few of the gang members had won art scholarships as a result. Because Samantha treated the gang members with the same respect demonstrated to all of her students, she had had only minor problems with them in her classroom.

Samantha prided herself on her ability to relate to the gang members (even using their own lingo), and didn't expect to have any major conflict with them in the future. However, gang-related problems were beginning to reverberate through the school.

The turf war at the school was escalating. Many gang members were rumored to have guns at school. Graffiti scrawled on school property was increasing. The frequency of drug sales was reported to be increasing. The school board members and administrators were in a quandary. They recognized that there was a problem, but were not sure how to solve it.

This year, Samantha had become aware that several of the gang members' projects in her classroom depicted gang-related colors, slogans, and symbols. But she wasn't quite sure how to confront the gang members about their projects. She decided just to ignore the problem, but it kept cropping up in the back of her mind. A police officer who had given a short talk at the last faculty meeting had told the staff in no uncertain terms that the school must adopt a zero tolerance policy to combat its gang activities. Yet, Samantha could not decide how she could, or even whether she should, limit the gang members' artistic creativity. To make matters worse, she was reluctant to discuss this problem with her colleagues.

Then an incident happened one morning in Miss Harrison's classroom that brought her concerns to a head. A known Vice Lord gang member, named Reggie, had requested a very large canvas on which to complete a painting project. He was using spray paint with various shaped nozzles to create what Samantha had understood to be a representation of several Disney cartoon characters. As she more closely scrutinized his work during the class period, Samantha noted that the cartoon characters were not represented in the usual sense. Reggie had painted Mickey and Minnie Mouse and the Tasmanian Devil, but not in their traditional cute form.

Mickey and Minnie both had long, sharp teeth and Mickey was smoking a cigar. Both mice wore red baseball caps embellished with the letters VL below a Playboy Bunny logo. Mickey and Minnie were brandishing AK 47s and viciously shooting several Tasmanian Devils who were bound, gagged, and kneeling executioner style in the foreground of the picture. The Tasmanian Devil characters were wearing Black Gangster Disciple colors. Their black and blue shirts had a five-pointed star drawn with broken lines. The T-shirts were similar to those worn by many Black Gangster Disciple members at school, only theirs did not have broken lines on the star. A cartoon caption bubble was above Mickey's head which read, "That's All FOLKS!"

As Samantha considered the painting, she knew that it was composed entirely of gang-related symbolism designed to show gang rivalry. She also realized that there would be a violent explosion of tempers if any of the Black Gangster Disciples caught wind of the picture. As she stood in thought, the Vice Lord member turned and said, "What do you think of my picture, Miss Harrison?" Samantha decided to seize the moment and address the graffiti that the gang members were creating in their art projects in order to put a stop to it once and for all.

Miss Harrison felt very nervous about what she was about to say. While she felt she needed to be honest with Reggie, she was worried about the repercussions. Nevertheless, she gathered her courage and said that he " . . . would not be able to continue a painting that portrayed gang violence." Impulsively, she reach out and began to remove the picture from the easel as she spoke. In a flash, the Vice Lord member grabbed Samantha's arm and shoved her backwards shouting, "Don't touch that or I'll kill you, you b!?@!"

COOPERATIVE LEARNING ACTIVITIES

1. Categorize Samantha Harrison's actions into those that were appropriate or beneficial and those that were not. Discuss the reasons for your responses.

2. In this case study, Samantha tried to handle a problem with a student on her own. When is that a good idea? How do teachers know when to ask for intervention assistance from colleagues or administrators? What advice would be appropriate for a teacher having this problem?

3. Describe specific strategies that teachers can use to effectively address aggressive student behavior.

4. What steps, if any, had the administration taken to address the gang problem at the high school?

5. What were the primary indicators of gang activity that should have been recognized and dealt with at an early stage?

6. Make a list of several types of support services that the school could provide to its staff to help them intervene with current gang activity and prevent further escalation. Address both the students in the gangs and those who do not belong to a gang.

7. How might school personnel collaborate with community agencies in order to provide gang intervention/prevention services for the students?

ROLE PLAY

Create role plays to explore some alternative solutions to the following situations. Assign more than one role play situation to each group to achieve some variance in the possible actions that Samantha Harrison might have taken. Discuss the advantages and disadvantages of employing the assorted solutions addressed in the role plays:

■ Samantha asks colleagues/ administrators for advice on the gang-related art project.

■ Samantha confronts the Vice Lord gang member about his picture of gang violence.

Case Study 3:
Sirens in the Evening

Late one afternoon, Mr. Wilson was sitting at his desk contemplating the events that had been occurring at his school for the past few months. Some of the circumstances he was mulling over were quite positive. The baseball team, which he coached, was doing well, and most of the students in his math classes seemed to be catching on without much trouble. However, the increasing rate of violent outbursts between students in the school concerned Mr. Wilson.

North High School, where Mr. Wilson taught, was in a mid-sized, previously quiet town. He had lived in the area all of his life and knew many of the parents of his students. Mr. Wilson had even attended high school with some of them. However, in recent years he had encountered a new population of students he was not familiar with.

Several years ago a maximum security prison had been built on the outskirts of town. The city administrators had been elated thinking about the revenue and employment opportunities that the prison would bring to the somewhat economically depressed area. However the prison had also brought one other addition to the area that had not been considered during its planning stages.

Once the inmates filled the cellblocks, the families of many prisoners moved into town. (**Note:** This is a common occurrence that many small towns do not consider when they bid for prisons. City officials consider the benefits without planning for the criminal element that takes root around prisons.)

The children of these families who had relocated to be near the prison were now in the local school system, and two main problems had developed. The first was an increase in criminal activity, mainly drug sales. The second was an explosion of brutal youth gang activity. Additionally, other local students were being lured into the gangs by the promise of protection from the rivaling gangs and by the parties and excitement associated with gang life.

Gang violence was now raging on the streets in certain parts of the town and consequently erupted frequently in the school building. School officials had tried to develop policies to deal with this problem. But so far, they had been only minimally successful. The school's policy of suspending students for gang-related behavior seemed to be causing even more problems on the street. As the students were banned from attending school they consequently had more unsupervised time than ever before. Thus, a joint faculty/law enforcement meeting was scheduled for the next week to begin formulating revisions to the insufficient gang policy that was currently in effect at the school.

As Mr. Wilson sat thinking, noise from some type of commotion in the student parking lot drifted up to his open window. Looking out the window, Mr. Wilson saw two groups of students facing off in a space between some parked cars. One group was composed mainly of black students as well as a few white kids, and the other group appeared to be mainly Hispanic. There were two or three students standing in front of each group who seemed to be acting as spokespersons. Mr. Wilson sprinted out the door of his classroom, down the stairs, and out into the parking lot.

He ran over to the area where the students were congregating and tried to squeeze through the students to reach the "leaders," but the kids had closed ranks and he had to force his way through, stepping on toes and thrusting students aside. Mr. Wilson was a big, strong man, and he had every confidence in his abilities to intervene physically with these students. Mr. Wilson was used to using his size and his voice to deal with problem behaviors in his classroom, and saw no reason why this wouldn't work in this situation as well.

As he pushed through the students, he recognized some from his classes. He shouted at them to "Break it up!"; "Leave the area!"; etc. But no one

appeared to be paying any attention to him. In fact, at that moment, as if on some command or signal, the students rushed towards each other. Mr. Wilson was caught in the middle, and he had a panicky feeling that he was no longer among other human beings but that he was surrounded by frenzied animals. It was madness.

In trying to stop a gang war, Mr. Wilson was now trapped within it. The level of noise and chaotic movement all around him was confusing his sense of direction. Every way he turned seemed to be obstructed by another human roadblock.

Suddenly he felt a searing pain in his gut. As he collapsed, Mr. Wilson realized that he had been stabbed. Through a fog of pain and disorientation, Mr. Wilson watched tiny pinpoints of light dance in front of his eyes in the encroaching darkness. As the hysteria escalated, sirens wailed in the distance.

COOPERATIVE LEARNING ACTIVITIES

1. Mr. Wilson dashed headlong into a dangerous situation without thinking about the possible consequences. What should Mr. Wilson have done instead of placing himself in danger?

2. When a prison is to be located in a town, how can city and school officials prepare for the associated criminal influence that has

historically been shown to follow? In particular:

- What specific preparation and training should be provided to teachers?

- How, when, and where would that training be delivered?

3. Brainstorm a list of consequences that educators may use as alternatives to suspension for gang-related behavior. Focus on consequences that are aimed at teaching students positive and socially appropriate replacement behaviors:

- List consequences appropriate for elementary students.

- List consequences appropriate for secondary students.

- Determine methods of collaboration between schools, the police, recreation centers, and social service agencies that might provide community-based consequences.

4. Develop (or review, if one already exists) a written policy to address the management of student fights at school.

5. What services might have been requested from the gang unit of the local police department to help establish a zero tolerance policy in the school?

6. What strategies could teachers like Mr. Wilson, who is a well-liked and successful teacher and coach, use to motivate students at school? How can teachers influence students who are at-risk for gang membership to take more of an interest in academics or to join extracurricular activities and/or school sports teams?

ROLE PLAY

Create role plays to practice addressing fights between students. Many different situations can be explored, such as a fight:

- Between two students in the school hallway.

- In which the students turn on the teacher who is attempting to intervene.

- Between two groups of students surrounded by spectators outside, but still on school grounds.

- Between rival gang members, in which weapons are displayed.

- Between one student and an opposing group of students.

Case Study 4: Harry Howard, the Coward

"Harry Howard the coward . . . Harry Howard the coward . . . Harry Howard the coward . . . ." The sing song chant rang through Harry Howard's mind as he tried in vain to get to sleep. As he lay awake in bed, little Harry Howard began to formulate a plan.

Harry was a fourth grader this year. He had always been rather small for his age. When he was in kindergarten, he had suffered a case of rheumatic fever which had left him with a weak heart. Throughout elementary school, Harry was the target of various types of bullying behavior from other students. Even the girls picked on Harry Howard.

Harry did not have any allies who were willing to intervene on his behalf with the bullies who tormented him. And Harry never told any adult about this problem because he figured that they couldn't help him anyway. So Harry became quite adept at hiding his emotions from others. He continually tried to ignore the bullying behavior of his schoolmates, although inside he raged about the treatment he received at their hands.

Never one to be particularly social, athletic, or outgoing, Harry felt that his

delicate heart condition did have some advantages. No one expected or asked Harry to play on sports teams which he didn't care for anyway. He was not involved in any extracurricular activities, and didn't have any real friends. Harry did have one interest, and that was reading. After school hours, when Harry wasn't reading in the safety of his own room, he was engrossed in the stacks at the public library. Action adventure books were his favorite. He liked to read about how the heroes overcame the evil forces that confronted them.

Harry had heard about gangs and knew a little about the symbols, colors, and types of clothing that gang members wore. He had heard adults say, "We don't have to worry about gang problems in the elementary school. That's only a problem for the high school teachers." Harry knew differently. Many other students in the elementary school also knew which kids were involved with the gangs. Those kids bragged about how much money they earned delivering drugs for older gang members. They wore the colors and the clothing of their gang, but the school staff simply thought the kids were playing a game. They called those kids "harmless wannabes." Unfortunately, they weren't harmless and they were playing a dangerous game.

On the day of his sleepless night, Harry Howard had been wandering around the playground during recess, alone as usual, wishing the teacher would just let him stay inside and read his book. Three older students started following him around, teasing him and calling him names. Harry thought of the latest book he was reading, in which the superhero could handle a whole crowd of bad guys singlehandedly using expert martial arts techniques. Right then and there Harry vowed to begin taking karate classes. He was pretty sure his mom and dad would let him. However that would not help in the present situation.

The three bullies on the playground had cornered Harry. He noticed that all three wore blue bandannas. They were demanding that Harry give them all the money he had in his pockets. Harry did not bring money to school because he always ate a sack lunch that his mother fixed for him. Harry was a rather finicky eater and didn't like the hot lunches at school. The three boys threatened to beat Harry up the next day—badly—if Harry did not bring $20.00 to school for them.

Harry was really scared. He wished the playground supervisor would help him. But what Harry didn't know was that many teachers have no training in the area of behavior management, or recognizing and dealing with the problems he was experiencing. Teachers learn how to teach their content areas—but usually not how to deal with social problems unrelated to the academic areas.

Harry Howard felt totally alone. He didn't tell his parents about the threats and the demand for money because he figured they wouldn't believe how serious the danger was. Instead he told his mother he was too sick to go to school the next day. While at home that day, Harry put his plan in action. He knew that the superheroes he read about would not tolerate all the humiliating taunts or the extortion demands of the gang members.

The next day, Harry brought a knife to school. It was a simple matter to take the knife—it was a sharp knife from the block in his family's kitchen. That morning when Harry went into the boys' restroom, the three gang members followed him in. They immediately began demanding the money from him. One shoved Harry into the wall of the restroom. But Harry felt as though he had the power of the superheroes on his side. He quickly pulled the knife out of his jacket pocket, brandished it in front of him in both hands, and warned them that he would "use it if they didn't leave him alone."

The gang members stared at him appraisingly for a moment. One of the boys, Benjamin, then grinned and swaggered up a little closer to Harry. He said he "didn't believe Harry had the guts to use the knife." Another of the gang members, Demetrius, agreed. Both were demanding to see Harry actually use the knife. Benjamin lunged forward and attempted to grab it from Harry's hands. The other two closed in as well, shouting their encouragement to Benjamin in his struggle for the knife.

In desperation, Harry began jabbing indiscriminately with the knife. He had to keep Benjamin away from him! He had to get out of there! He was screaming, and the three gang members were pushing and shouting. Just then a faculty member threw open the door to the restroom and yelled, "All right you guys, what's going on in here?"

COOPERATIVE LEARNING ACTIVITIES

This case study depicts two main problems. First, many students are continually victimized without any adult intervention. Young victims of gang intimidation generally do not have adequate coping strategies to help themselves. Second, students who lack social skills often do not have a means for asking for help, from either peers or adults, when they need assistance. Students who experience these two problems often feel hopelessly negative. They will often use extreme, and inappropriate, measures to solve the problems they perceive to be overwhelming.

1. What types of behaviors should teachers be able to recognize that could be considered intimidating at the elementary level? at the secondary level?

2. What types of consequences could teachers use when they observe intimidating behaviors:

    - On the playground?

    - In the hallways?

    - In the cafeteria?

    - In restrooms?

3. Develop a simple strategy that teachers can use to intervene with intimidating behaviors between students at school.

4. How can educators teach students who are victimized to be assertive and to stand up for their rights? What coping strategies do these students need to learn?

5. Devise a set of role plays that teachers could use in the classroom to have their students practice being assertive and requesting assistance when confronted by the intimidating behavior of other students. Examples of situations to rehearse include:

    - One student attempts to extort money from another student.

    - A gang member uses threats and fear to recruit new gang members at school.

    - A gang member threatens a student with a weapon.

- A student is carrying a weapon to protect himself/herself from gang intimidation.

6. Make a list of general classroom management procedures that are important for all teachers to utilize. Suggest ways teachers might now gain crucial behavior management skills they probably weren't taught in college.

7. Discuss specific and effective methods of behavior management teachers can use with the most common forms of student intimidation towards other students or staff, including intense staring (mad dogging), personal ridicule, cursing, and other inappropriate language.

8. What steps might teachers take to establish classroom climate that is positive and projects realistically high expectations for all students' achievement?

ROLE PLAY

Create role play situations to practice dealing with aggressive and intimidating students. Try videotaping these role plays so the participants can view their behaviors and reactions. That way, they can readily participate in the follow-up discussions about the effectiveness of the solutions portrayed. Following are some suggested situations to role play:

- One student, obviously dressed in full gang apparel, is extorting lunch money from several students.

- Two girls are attempting to coerce a third to steal from a locker. They promise her membership in their gang if she will steal the item and bring it back to them.

- A teacher discovers that two male students have been beating up another student every day after school in order to intimidate him to give them his math assignments.

- A female student confides to a teacher that several male students who wear gang colors have told her they will kill her brother if she doesn't agree to have sex with them.

- A teacher has a group of gang wannabes in the classroom. As a group, the students are noncompliant to the teacher's requests and verbally belligerent.

- A female gang member attempts to intimidate her teacher by invading her personal space. The student may or may not be verbally intimidating as well.

- A first year teacher attempts to establish rules and expectations in a classroom of students who have a reputation of being hard to handle.

- A student threatens to hit a teacher who is attempting to implement established school discipline procedures.

Case Study 5: Fallen Angel

Angela Ramirez appeared to have everything any teenager could want in life. She was from an upper middle class family and lived in a nice neighborhood. As a senior at Apollo High School, Angela had plenty of friends, earned good grades, and was president of the Student Council. Angela had scored well on her college placement exams and was still contemplating her choices of colleges to attend.

Up until this year, Angela had been very involved in a number of school activities. She was a particularly accomplished writer and served as assistant editor of the school newspaper and worked on the yearbook staff. Angela had a goal of pursuing a career in photojournalism. She had completed an internship with the local newspaper during her junior year and had liked the experience.

Angela had also enjoyed spending time with her parents. She and her mother used to do a variety of activities together such as visiting art galleries, going to lunch downtown, or visiting the big public library. Mr. Ramirez and Angela used to have fun together, too. One of their favorite things to do was to go skeet shooting at the gun club. Angela's father was an avid hunter, and had taught all of his children to handle guns safely. But among her siblings, Angela was the one who had really liked to go shooting with her father. However, her relationship with her parents was very different now.

Things had changed a couple of months ago when Angela met Rafael Santos. The first time Angela saw Rafael was at The Pizza Place. This was the favored spot among the city's teens for hanging out on Friday and Saturday nights. It had the best pizza in town as well as a big game room and a dance floor with a deejay. Angela and her friends were watching the boys play pool while they waited for their pizza order. Rafael was sitting with a few older guys, and some guys that she recognized from her high school who were part of the "rough crowd." When she saw Rafael, she asked her friends if anyone knew him. Someone said she thought he was from Los Angeles. They all thought he was gorgeous!

Angela couldn't stop watching Rafael. He was so sophisticated! Rafael had a lot of charisma. He was older, and the guys from her school seemed to idolize him. She knew he was the type of boy her parents would disapprove of. He wore saggy, baggy jeans with a long T-shirt, British Knights shoes, and a blue L.A. Dodgers jacket. His shoulder length, jet black hair was tied back with a blue rubber band. Angela could see that he had a tattoo that read "Crips" on his forearm.

Angela was intrigued with Rafael. She had learned a little about the Crips and Bloods through her newspaper internship. She thought Rafael was probably a gang member, and that he made gang members look pretty exciting. Angela thought Rafael was so handsome, and couldn't believe it when Rafael came up and asked her to dance with him. Out of all the girls there, he was interested in her!

From that night forward Angela was in love. Rafael often came to pick her up after school. He asked her to come down to the huge city park where he and his friends hung out in the evenings, but her parents wouldn't let her go out on school nights. Angela discovered that if she told her parents that she was going to the library, she could meet Rafael. But that only worked twice. The third time, her father came by the library to pick her up and she wasn't there.

When Angela admitted that she had gone to the park, her parents asked her to invite Rafael for dinner so they could meet him. Angela brought him over, but she was exactly right when she thought they wouldn't like him. Rafael didn't like her parents, either. There seemed to be nothing that they could all talk about. After he left, Angela's parents told her that they didn't want her to see him again.

Angela became more creative about sneaking out to see Rafael. She had been sleeping with him since the third night she sneaked away to see him. He seemed to expect this from her. Angela didn't think what she was doing was right, but she was afraid she would lose Rafael if she didn't do what he wanted her to do. Anyhow, it meant that he loved her too, didn't it?

During the next few weeks Angela learned that Rafael had organized his friends into a group that called themselves the Main Street Crips. Almost every night, out in the park, there was some type of fight going on. Rafael told Angela that if other guys wanted to be in his gang, they had to get " jumped in." That was how his brothers had initiated him into their neighborhood gang when he was eight-years old.

One night at the park, Angela saw Rafael selling a bag of marijuana to a strange man. The next day he brought some to her school and told Angela to keep it in her locker until he needed it. She also kept two guns in her locker for him that he said he needed because he lived in such a bad part of town.

As the weeks went by, Angela began to spend more and more time with Rafael. She was skipping classes and her grades had deteriorated drastically. She quarreled with her parents constantly and didn't want to participate in any of the usual family activities. She also quit wearing all of the fashionable clothes she used to like, and started to wear only khaki slacks, skimpy sweaters, and the blue L.A. Dodgers jacket that Rafael suggested she buy when they were at the mall.

Ms. Peterson, the Student Council advisor, had been Angela's favorite teacher. They had previously spent a lot of time talking about journalism and Angela's career plans. Angela's abrupt change in behavior concerned Ms. Peterson. Angela had even been skipping Student Council meetings. Ms. Peterson knew that Angela was dating Rafael Santos, because she had seen them together on the school grounds; she also knew, from his appearance and behavior, that he was a gang member.

Ms. Peterson wanted to have a talk with Angela, but Angela kept avoiding her. Ms. Peterson called Angela at home to try to set up a meeting time. But Angela was very rude and told Ms. Peterson to "mind her own business." When Ms. Peterson tried to reason with her, Angela slammed the phone down.

Ms. Peterson was not sure what to do. In the past, Apollo High School had not experienced any significant gang problems. The faculty had been having discussions about the recent emergence of youth gang activity in the school, but they were not yet prepared to deal with the aggressive actions and the problems that the youth gangs were creating. They were all a bit intimidated.

One night Rafael said that if Angela was really serious about being his girlfriend, she would have to prove it. Other girls had started hanging around the park as well, and Angela knew that Rafael could have his pick of the girls. She realized she would have to do what he said if she wanted to hold onto him. Rafael told her that the leader of the Bloods from across town had disrespected him earlier in the week. Tonight he planned a drive-by shooting to retaliate against the Bloods.

Rafael demanded that Angela go along with him to be a "shooter." She had told him about skeet shooting with her father, and how she was very accurate. Angela didn't want to go, and told Rafael. She said she couldn't shoot at another human being. Then Rafael savagely turned on Angela, slapping her across the face. As Angela lay on the ground sobbing, Rafael told her she had better do what he said, or he would shoot her himself.

As Angela sat in Rafael's car with some of the other Crips, she desperately tried to figure out how she had gotten herself into such a mess. All she knew at this point was that she wanted out. Suddenly, Rafael's car leapt forward and roared off down the street. There were two other Crip cars as well, one in front of them and one in back. Rafael was driving, and began shouting at everyone to get ready. Angela was holding a loaded rifle. Rafael pointed a loaded nine-millimeter hand gun at Angela and told her if she didn't do her part, he'd "blow her head off."

As the cars pulled into the parking lot of the club where the rival gang hung out, they could see the Bloods on the other side of the lot. Rafael gave the signal, and the three Crip cars roared into action. Angela had her rifle positioned out the front window, but she was frozen with horror and fright. Gunfire seemed to be blazing from everywhere in the lot. Rafael was screaming at Angela to fire as they careened in a tight circle around the group of Bloods. Suddenly, Angela's arms felt useless; they were like a dead weight, and a torrent of pain washed through her chest. At that moment Angela knew she had been shot.

Rafael saw Angela slump over in her seat. Rather than helping Angela, he leaned over, opened the front car door, and brutally shoved her out onto the parking lot. Then he and the Crips tore away.

As Angela lay on the ground, she was aware of people screaming, sirens screaming, she thought she was screaming, but she couldn't really tell, and she couldn't move her arms or her legs. In Angela's mind the terrifying scene played over and over again, then slowly faded to black.

COOPERATIVE LEARNING ACTIVITIES

1. How do educators determine if there is a gang problem at their school?

2. Apollo High School is experiencing an emerging gang problem that the teachers are not prepared to handle. What community resources are available to provide information about gangs to educators?

3. How might the teachers at Apollo High School form a community-wide gang intervention team to suppress the emerging gang problem in the community?

4. How can teachers and parents work together to combat youth gang problems and violence in the community?

5. Angela Ramirez got caught up in the excitement of having a gang leader as a boyfriend. What can teachers do to educate students about the disastrous and sometimes fatal effects of gang membership/involvement?

6. Plan an after-school program that will provide structure and supervision for students between 3:30 and

6:00 PM. Think of a funding source as well as an activity program.

7. Design a discussion group or seminar for your school's students to discuss age appropriate problems. Examples include: dealing with peer pressure, assertiveness skills, how students can recognize gang identifiers, what activities students would like schools to provide to reduce gang membership, and how teachers can help students at risk for gang activity. What topics would be included? How would the information be presented to the students? Where and when would the students meet?

ROLE PLAY

Role play the part of Ms. Peterson, the Student Council advisor. She is very worried about the deterioration of Angela's grades and her poor attitude. How can a teacher approach and reach a student who is bent on being part of a negative peer group?

Case Study 6:
Nowhere to Turn

Alicia was afraid. It was a little after 8:00 PM. It was dark outside and she and her younger brother were alone in the apartment, watching TV in the living room. Someone was knocking at the door. She looked through the peephole and saw that some of the other kids from the neighborhood were standing in the hallway. A few of them were older than Alicia, but several were her age and a couple were even younger. For weeks these kids in her neighborhood had been asking her repeatedly to join them in their "games." Alicia had a feeling the games would not be very fun. The kids bragged about skipping school, stealing, making money by selling drugs for some older guys, and belonging to a gang that roamed the neighborhood.

Alicia was nine years old and lived with her brother Thomas, who was six, and her mother. Their home was one of the top floor apartments of an older house. Alicia's single mother worked hard to take good care of her children and to make their home nice and cozy. However, they lived on a street in a neighborhood that often echoed with gun fire and police sirens.

Because Alicia's mother worked the afternoon shift at a nearby factory, Alicia and Thomas were alone after school until at least midnight every weekday. There was not enough money for after-school care or supervision on a regular basis. So it was Alicia's job to take care of Thomas after school, get her homework done, make she and her brother supper, and see that Thomas got to bed on time each night.

Alicia's mother had a rule: No other kids in the house while she was at work. Thomas asked Alicia if he should answer the door. Alicia didn't want Thomas to see that she was scared. She reminded him that Mamma had said not to, and that no one else could be in the house while she was gone. After several more minutes the pounding on the door stopped and the kids went away. Alicia was relieved. She told Thomas that if he would go get his pajamas on, she would read him three books before he went to sleep.

The next morning Alicia got she and Thomas ready to go to school. They had to be very quiet because their mother slept on the couch in the living room. Their apartment only had one bedroom which Alicia and Thomas shared. As they left, Alicia was worrying that those kids would bother them on the walk to school. But she didn't want to wake her mother to tell her about the kids, thinking "Mamma has enough to worry about as it is."

That day at recess, the kids were pestering Alicia about doing a job for them. Alicia tried to walk away from them like Mamma told her to do, but they kept following. Then one of the kids, Darrell, told her he would pay her $20.00 if she would deliver a package to his friend's house that night at 9:00. The friend lived just two blocks from Alicia's apartment. Alicia stopped walking and turned to look at Darrell. "Twenty

dollars . . . " she thought. "If I had twenty dollars, I could buy something nice for Mamma and still have enough left over to take Thomas to McDonald's." Thomas loved to go to McDonald's, but they rarely had enough extra money for a treat like that.

So Alicia agreed to deliver the package for Darrell. The package was not very big and she stuck it in her book bag. Darrell told Alicia that she would get the $20.00 after she delivered the package. Darrell warned her not to talk to any "slobs" about what she was doing, gave her the address, and left her alone for the rest of the recess.

Alicia was worried about what she had agreed to do. That night she made supper for herself and Thomas, but she was so apprehensive about going out after dark to deliver the package that she couldn't eat a bite. Then she told Thomas she had to go run an errand and she would be back in a few minutes. "Lock the door when I leave, Thomas," she instructed. "Do not open it for anyone except me when I get back. Do you understand?" Thomas said he did and was content to stay home and watch TV.

Alicia was just getting ready to leave. She went into their bedroom for her book bag. Just then a loud pounding began on the apartment door. Alicia froze. No one had ever pounded on the door like that before. A man's voice roared,

"Open the door." Alicia and Thomas were terrified. They huddled together in the hallway between their bedroom and the living room. It sounded as though there were several people out in the hallway shouting and banging against the door. Suddenly, the door crashed open, springing the lock.

Five young men piled into the living room. All were wearing red plaid shirts and khaki slacks. Two had red bandannas over their foreheads. Alicia screamed as one grabbed her and another grabbed Thomas. Thomas was sobbing, and one of the guys was laughing and calling him a "crybaby."

Alicia shouted at him to leave Thomas alone. She kicked and bit and scratched at the teenager who was holding her arms behind her back. One of the other teenagers cruelly slapped her across the face, yelling at her to "shut up." Two of the others were going through the apartment, pulling out drawers, looking through the cupboards, and looking under the cushions of the couch. The guy restraining Alicia yelled at her to tell him where the "stuff" was. She knew exactly what he was talking about—the package.

Alicia was so terrified it never occurred to her not to tell. She replied that it was in her book bag laying right there on the floor. The gang member grabbed her bag, dumped everything out onto the floor, scooped up the package, and headed for the door. He made a remark about "the crabs being dumb enough to give the stuff to a little kid to deliver." After giving Alicia and Thomas a final shake and a hard shove to the floor, the other guys followed him out.

None of their neighbors came to investigate the commotion. Alicia was so scared. She was hugging Thomas on the living room floor trying to think about what to do now. She remembered Mamma telling her "if there was ever an emergency to dial 911." The emergency operator told her he would send a police officer to investigate.

When the police officers arrived, Alicia told them about how the group had broken in the door looking for the package she had agreed to deliver. They asked her what was in the package, and Alicia hesitated. She knew that she had agreed to do something her mother would not have liked her to do. She also knew she would be in big trouble if she told the police officers that she thought there were drugs in the package. Plus she knew she was going to be in trouble with Darrell at school tomorrow! She decided she better tell the police everything.

By the time she finished telling the whole story, Thomas had stopped crying and was sitting on one of the police officer's lap as she took notes. It was almost 10:00 PM, and their mother would not be home for another two hours or so. The landlord of their apartment came to fix the door after one of the police officers called him. One of the police officers then called Alicia's mother at work and stayed with them until she got home.

Just as Alicia expected, Mamma was furious with her poor judgment. She told Alicia that presents and treats were meaningless if a person had to break the law to get them. After the horrible experience, Alicia was sure her mother was right. Now she would just have to deal with that boy at school; the one who talked her into delivering the package in the first place.

The next day on the way to school, Alicia decided that she would simply tell Darrell the truth about what had happened. She would tell him about how the group in the red plaid shirts broke into the apartment and took the package from her. As Alicia and Thomas walked the final block to school, a group of guys approached them from across the street. One of the boys in the group was Darrell.

Darrell walked up too close to Alicia and asked her what happened to the package. Alicia tried to tell him about the people breaking into their apartment the night before, but she never got to finish. One of the boys grabbed Thomas. He and several others were hitting and slapping Thomas. Alicia dropped her book bag and flew at the nearest boy, but he easily shoved her

backward. Alicia's head hit the sidewalk hard. Through her pain she could hear Thomas howling. The group was punching and kicking her as she lay on the sidewalk. Alicia tried weakly to get up—she knew she had to help Thomas—but she couldn't move. Thomas was screaming for her and she couldn't see him or reach him.

Finally the beating stopped. When Alicia woke up, a woman with a kind face was bending over Alicia. Alicia turned her head and saw Thomas laying on the ground a few feet away. The woman was a police officer patrolling the area. She called an ambulance which came and took Alicia and Thomas to the hospital. It took a long time for Alicia and Thomas to recover from the beating.

Someone had tipped the police officers about which kids assaulted them. The witnesses remained anonymous. Because this beating occurred so close to the elementary school, the faculty, the P.T.A., and the police decided they needed to begin collaborating to deal with the gang-related violence that was erupting near the school grounds. Over time they established a partnership that helped identify gang members and assisted students like Alicia, who were alone a lot of the time, to learn how to resist negative peer pressure.

COOPERATIVE LEARNING ACTIVITIES

1. Outline the steps that led to Alicia agreeing to deliver the package. What home environment factors might indicate a need for more educator support for a student like Alicia?

2. Which behaviors of Alicia, as well as other students, might teachers have recognized to help Alicia deal with the problems she was facing?

3. What type of school policies might be instituted to reduce the type of problem that Alicia was confronted with?

   - How would the school policies address gang activity?

   - How would the school policies address drug possession/use?

   - How would the school policies address weapons at school?

4. Discuss methods the school could use to educate parents about the dangers of gang involvement during unsupervised after-school hours.

ROLE PLAY

1. Create a role play to depict how teachers might assist a student who is being lured into the fringe of gang activity through delivery/messenger activities. Include methods of teaching students skills to resist the peer pressure to join gangs. Keep in mind that many student will join gangs due to a lack of support and options in other areas of their lives including school, home, and the community.

2. Role play how a teacher might employ home telephone calls to a student who is lacking supervision or support during after-school hours.

3. Role play a strategy that teachers could use during parent/teacher conferences to educate parents about any youth gangs in the area.

Case Study 7:
Keep the Faith

During his first year as a French teacher, Mr. Bryant encountered many surprises that his university education never prepared him for. For some naive reason, he had thought that his students were going to sit in rapt attention as he provided them rules about irregular verbs and anecdotes about the French culture. He was sure his students would be enthralled with his favorite foreign country.

Well Mr. Bryant was wrong. There were a few students who lived up to his expectations, and were a joy to teach. There were many who went through the motions because they knew they needed foreign language credits to graduate. Mr. Bryant got along fine with most of the students, even though he thought many were not working to their potential. Then there were those few students, just a handful, who seemed bent on making his teaching life miserable. They didn't want to be in school at all let alone French class, and they didn't seem to understand or even want to learn that beautiful language.

In short, Mr. Bryant appeared to be constantly at odds with this group of students. One student in particular gave him trouble. He was a constant source of irritation and aggravation.

This student went by the nickname T.J.: his full name was Timothy James. Mr. Bryant had made the mistake of calling him Timothy on the first day of class. How was he supposed to know that the boy hated to be called Timothy? His attendance sheet read "Timothy." During role call that day Mr. Bryant called out Timothy's first name just as he did for all the other students. Timothy did not respond during role call. Mr. Bryant sensed there was something going on in the room as the students gave each other sidelong glances, and there were a few nervous giggles from several sections of the classroom. When he asked if there was a problem, there was no response. So Mr. Bryant repeated the name of Timothy James and then thinking out loud to himself, said, "I guess Timothy is absent." This caused a number of mumbled comments and a few more giggles.

Suddenly a student sitting in the back had lunged out of his desk and strutted up to the podium where Mr. Bryant was standing. The boy challenged Mr. Bryant in a manner that was confrontational and physically threatening. Leaning close to his face, T.J. looked Mr. Bryant in the eye with a cold, calculating glare and said, "My name is T.J. And don't ever call me anything else or you'll be sorry."

Mr. Bryant was stunned, but he had managed to maintain his composure and control of the classroom. In the ensuing days he attempted to repair the rocky start he had experienced with T.J. His first strategy was to try to kid the boy out of his threatening demeanor with joking remarks. This method seemed only to escalate the level of hostility. Then Mr. Bryant decided he needed to be more authoritarian with T.J., and took every opportunity throughout the period to give him commands.

The relationship between teacher and student deteriorated from there. Mr. Bryant knew T.J. hung out with one of the gang-involved crowds. Mr. Bryant hadn't known much about gangs when he had begun teaching in the fall. But since that time the school had provided several seminars on gangs. He now knew T.J. belonged to a Folk Nation gang set calling themselves the Simon City Royals.

Many of the teachers expressed a level of discomfort, some even outright fear, of the gang-involved students. There had been local news reports about the Simon City Royals gang, and how violent they were in the neighborhood they considered their turf. It was rumored that even the young members who attended the middle school were probably carrying weapons to school due to the retaliatory activities occurring between the rival gangs in the city.

T.J. was proud of his gang affiliation and used it to intimidate both staff and students at school. Mr. Bryant had decided that T.J. was not going to intimidate him. While T.J. was in French class, Mr. Bryant was determined that he learn French. So, as the semester wore on, Mr. Bryant had numerous encounters with T.J. due to his constant limit testing and dominating behavior. Mr. Bryant held the line with T.J., trying to reason with him. However, as the weeks went by T.J.'s behavior was not improving.

Although T.J. was not visibly responding to the classroom management technique Mr. Bryant was using, he continued to provide a great deal of positive reinforcement for the efforts and progress of all the students in his classroom. He built upon their small triumphs to help make the students believe they had the skills and abilities to be successful students.

T.J. frequently and audibly scoffed at Mr. Bryant's positive comments to the class, mimicking him in an exaggerated French accent. On the bright side, however, T.J. was attending class almost every day, turning in his required assignments, and earning a grade in the high C range.

One day Mr. Bryant asked T.J. to come in for a few minutes after school. He thought if he could possibly speak with T.J. alone, without an audience, he might be able to communicate how pleased he was with the progress T.J. had made with the difficult language. Mr. Bryant thought this might make a difference in T.J.'s attitude and help to reduce the number of disparaging remarks he made in class.

T.J. did come in that day, with a major attitude problem. He was sarcastic and insolent. Then T.J. suddenly erupted, yelling at Mr. Bryant that he always thought he was "the man" and that the students were "just a bunch of dummies he could hassle." T.J. then turned to walk out the door of the classroom. Mr. Bryant still wanted to try to talk to T.J., but he was losing patience and getting frustrated with his hostile attitude. He leapt after T.J. and grabbed his arm, saying, "Not so fast, buddy, I'm fed up with this." As T.J. whirled around, Mr. Bryant found himself face to face with T.J.'s upraised fists.

COOPERATIVE LEARNING ACTIVITIES

1. What steps can teachers take to promote a positive classroom climate?

2. What are some examples of positive classroom rules a teacher can construct to promote appropriate student behavior in the classroom?

3. Discuss the effects of different types of teacher behaviors that might be used to deal with hostile students:

- Strict disciplinarian/authoritarian

- Understanding/nurturing

- Confrontive

- Fair, but firm

4. Describe typical aggressive student behaviors that might be demonstrated at school.

5. For each hostile student behavior identified, discuss a method educators can use to constructively address the problem.

6. Discuss motivating methods that teachers can use to promote student cooperation and achievement in school.

ROLE PLAY

1. It is often difficult for teachers to give positive reinforcement to students who demonstrate intimidating and hostile behaviors in the classroom. Role play constructively confronting and positively reinforcing students who display the following behaviors:

- Under the breath comments

- Verbal disregard for school achievement

- Expressing an admiration for gang-related behavior/gang members

2. Many students live in environments where they are bombarded by negative feedback that often results in their loss of self-esteem. Role play methods that teachers can use to bolster students' self-esteem in the classroom.

3. When students demonstrate physically or verbally threatening behavior at school, it is usually very difficult for teachers to maintain their composure and objectivity. Role play how teachers should react to students in situations of this type. Keep in mind that the problem behaviors should be confronted and then redirected so that the teachers aren't intimidated and the students maintain their dignity and self-respect.

Conclusion

Most youth are lured into destructive gang activity because their needs are not being met at home, at school, or in the community. Some grow up in environments immersed in gang culture and don't know any other way of life. Concerned adults need to form a collaborative cadre to get these kids back on the right rack; back to educational achievement and appropriate community involvement. Reading this book is a step in the right direction. You are now armed with the basic knowledge necessary to recognize gang characteristics and to deal with aggressive and violent student behaviors in an effective manner. From here it is up to you to collaborate with others in your school and/or community to establish a zero tolerance policy for gang activity, and to provide the structured, consistent direction and support to all the youth you encounter to help make them socially appropriate, successful adult citizens tomorrow.

We would like to take this opportunity to thank all of you who have taken the time to read this book. Working with children and youth who exhibit hostile, aggressive, and antisocial behaviors is not an easy job. Many times the rewards and successes are few and far between. However, every single success and every single child who is motivated to stay in school and stay out of a gang makes all the anguish, the time, and the effort worthwhile. We would be most interested to hear about any of your own "Real-Life Teacher Tales" and/or success stories from professionals and parents. Please send any such correspondence to:

Dr. Mary Jensen
Department of Special Education
25 Horrabin Hall
Western Illinois University
Macomb, IL 61455
Phone (309) 298-1778
FAX (309) 298-2222
Email: mm-jensen-wilber@wiu.edu

Appendix: Gang Prevention/Intervention Resources

Following are programs for gang intervention and/or prevention in various locations across the nation. It is important to note that some are subsidized by grant funds, and may not be permanent programs. Also included are some print materials, as well as Internet sites (current at the time of this printing) which are intended to be a springboard for additional research and readings on gangs.

Internet Sites

- Youth Intervention and Gang Prevention
  http://civic.net2401/lgnet/youth.html

- National Youth Gang Center
  http://www.iir.com/nygc/nygc.htm

- Eliminating Gang Influence in Schools
  http://www.ncrel.org/sdrs/areas/issues/envrnm/drugfree/
  sa2deq04.htm

- Violence Prevention/Reduction
  http://www.teachersworkshop.com/twshop/vioprev.html

Gang-Related Information

- A summary of the 1992 Texas Attorney General's Gang Report is available from the Texas Youth Commission, 4900 North Lamar, P.O. Box 4260, Austin, TX 78765; Phone (512) 483-5000; FAX (512) 483-5089.

- The Center to Prevent Handgun Violence provides written materials for the general public on statistics related to handgun violence. They also have an educational curriculum entitled *Straight Talk About RISKS (STAR): A PreK-Grade 12 Curriculum for Preventing Gun Violence*. The program, intended for school district-wide adoption, includes the curriculum materials, inservice training for school staff, implementation planning, technical assistance, parent and community awareness activities, and program evaluation. The Center to Prevent Handgun Violence may be contacted at 1225 I Street, NW, Suite 1100, Washington, D.C. 20005; Phone (202) 289-7319; FAX (202) 408-1851.

- The National School Safety Center (NSSC), a program of the United States Departments of Justice and Education at Pepperdine University, serves as a clearinghouse for school safety programs and activities related to campus security; school law; community relations; student discipline and attendance; and the prevention of drug abuse, gangs, and bullying. The Center's primary objective is to focus national attention on the importance of providing safe, effective schools. The National School Safety Center may be contacted in care of Pepperdine University, 4165 Thousand Oaks Boulevard, Suite 290, West Lake Village, CA 91362; Phone (805) 373-9977; FAX (805) 373-9277.

- The National Youth Gang Information Center may be contacted with questions about youth gangs and requests for programs (such as the National Youth Gang Suppression and Intervention Program) and literature at P.O. Box 12729, Tallahassee, FL 32317; Phone (904) 385-0600; FAX (904) 386-5356; Email: krosier@iir.com.

- The National Crisis Prevention Institute, Inc. provides information on nonviolent crisis intervention techniques. Contact the Institute at 3315-K North 124th Street, Brookfield, WI 53005; Phone (800) 558-8976; FAX (414) 783-5906.

Gang-Related Programs

- Adopt-a-Student, Office of Job Development, Atlanta Public Schools, Atlanta, GA 30312.

  The Adopt-a-Student program pairs volunteers as mentors, or "big brothers/sisters," with low-achieving high school juniors and seniors. Through monthly job preparation workshops and a relationship with a volunteer, students are encouraged to finish high school and develop post-high school career plans. The program is jointly run by the Atlanta public schools and the Merit Employment Association (MEA).

- Bright Futures Project, Memphis Area Neighborhood Watch, Inc., 1835 Union Avenue, Suite 266, Memphis, TN 38104-3943; Phone (901) 726-6912.

  This juvenile delinquency prevention project provides academic and social support to African-American youth ages 5-15. The Bright Futures Project provides study resources to help youth complete their homework assignments. Reading and comprehension testing and prescribed tutoring are available for a limited number of youth. Supervised opportunities allow youth to contribute to their community by participating in neighborhood improvement projects.

- Delinquency Awareness Program, Project Turnabout, 6456 West Ohio Street, Indianapolis, IN 46214; Phone (317) 248-1818.

  This is an educational presentation designed to teach children to avoid getting involved in crime. It is a speaker and slide presentation designed to get a "say no to crime" message to children before they get into trouble.

- Family Ties Program, Department of Juvenile Justice, 365 Broadway, New York, NY 10013; Phone (212) 925-7779.

  Family Ties is administered by the New York City Department of Juvenile Justice (DJJ), and began serving adolescents and their families in February 1989. The program was designed to avert juvenile placements and reduce recidivism:

  - Family Ties averts from placement 65% of the juvenile cases referred to the program by the Family Court—which falls within the normative range for similar programs.

- Eight out of ten juveniles who participate in the program remain crime-free and out of placement 12 months later.

- The program is highly cost-beneficial. It saves the state and city governments an estimated total of $2.7 million per year. The program also delivers in a cost-efficient manner.

- Youth and parents who enter the program like the home-based services. They feel, however, that it should be longer for some youth.

■ Anger Management Program, Police Youth Bureau, Bismarck Police Department, 700 South Ninth Street, Bismarck, ND 58504-5899; Phone (701) 221-7224.

The Anger Management Program is a multi-agency approach teaching anger control skills to youth and parents through an eight-session group process. The target groups for this program are fifth and sixth grade elementary, junior high age, and senior high age youth that are experiencing ongoing problems with aggressive behavior at school, home, and in the community. This is a community-based program, meaning the vast majority of youth involved in this program are not in placement. Most of the target youth would be considered high risk for placement, or have experienced short-term placement in psychiatric or attendant care/time out programs already.

A key component is mandatory parental involvement in the parent groups. Parents receive needed support from other parents, learn anger management skills for themselves, and become familiar with the skills being taught to their children.

The program is sponsored by the following agencies: Police Youth Bureau, YouthWorks, Bismarck Public Schools, Burleigh/Morton Social Services, Southeast Juvenile Court, ND Division of Juvenile Services, and Adult Abused Resource Center.

■ Choices: Alternatives to Violence, CONTACT 214, P.O. Box 800742, Dallas, TX 75380-0742; Phone (214) 233-2427.

CHOICES: Alternatives to Violence is a multi-strategic approach designed to reach a large number of the general population of youth (ages 6-18) in Dallas County with violence prevention skills based upon crisis management, self-understanding, self-management, relationship building, and building positive community relations. The program design is flexible and can be utilized in a variety of settings. Schools, youth organizations and clubs, and community and recreational centers can all participate.

- Community Youth Gang Services (CYGS) Project, 144 South Fetterly Avenue, Los Angeles, CA 90022; Phone (213) 266-4264.

The central idea of the Community Youth Gang Services (CYGS) Project is to coordinate the activities of the police, schools, and other community organizations to prevent young people from joining gangs, to intervene in the lives of gang members, and to mobilize citizens to reclaim their neighbor- hoods from predatory gangs. CYGS is the largest non-law enforcement anti-gang program in the country.

- Violence Prevention Curriculum for Adolescents, Education Development Center, Inc., 55 Chapel Street, Newton, MA 02160.

The Violence Prevention Curriculum for Adolescents was developed by Dr. Deborah Prothrow-Stith, and attempts to address the issues of violence and homicide among young people by helping students to become more aware of:

- Homicide and the factors associated with it

- Positive ways to deal with anger and arguments, the leading precipitants of homicide

- How fights begin and how they escalate

- The choices, other than fighting, that are available to young people in conflict situations

Other Sopris West Publications of Interest

The Tough Kid Book:
Practical Classroom Management Strategies

by Ginger Rhode, William R. Jenson, and H. Kenton Reavis

If you are preparing to teach—and thus work with "Tough Kids"—*The Tough Kid Book* will be a survival manual for your first years of teaching. If you are a practicing teacher, this is a resource they should have used when you were in college. With more than 100,000 copies in print, the wildly popular *The Tough Kid Book* has become an indispensable resource for both regular and special education teachers. The research-validated solutions included in this book help to reduce the disruptive behavior of Tough Kids without big investments on the teacher's part in terms of time, money, and emotion. This book contains a wealth of ready to use strategies and identifies other commercially available, practical resources for teachers who want even more in-depth assistance. 120 PAGES

A Study of Heroes: A Program That Inspires and Educates Through the Example of Heroes

by the Raoul Wallenberg Committee of the United States

Polls indicate that most young Americans cannot differentiate between true heroes and popular sports/entertainment celebrities. *A Study of Heroes* is a comprehensive interdisciplinary program that helps to revitalize the tradition of heroes by studying the lives of true heroes—positive role models from many different periods of history, ethnicities, nationalities, and areas of accomplishment.

A Study of Heroes is a classroom-tested, multicultural program that readily complements any curriculum. The program includes an *Instructor's Guide*; 22 Hero Profile Units (approximately 60 pages each) containing an array of student activities and worksheets integrating skill areas such as history, reading, creative writing, political/ social topics, and conflict resolution; and eight Auxiliary Units, such as a "blank" unit for students' own choice of heroes. Instructional materials for three readability levels— recommended for ages 5-9, 9-11, and 11 and older—are included in each unit, and can be easily adapted for use with varying skill levels or to help remediate content skills or concepts as needed. Educators or other youth leaders can elect to use any or all of the *Heroes* units, in any order.

Through the *Heroes* program, students learn about character development and discover that heroes can be figures they encounter daily—parents, public officials, teachers, neighbors, fellow classmates, and most importantly, themselves!

1,000+ REPRODUCIBLE PAGES

Bully-Proofing Your School:
A Comprehensive Approach for Elementary Schools

by Carla Garrity, Kathryn Jens, William Porter, Nancy Sager, and Cam Short-Camilli

Bully-Proofing Your School meets an important target objective—making the school environment safe for all students both physically and psychologically. This book presents a comprehensive process which assists elementary school staff in recognizing and intervening in bullying situations. The *Bully-Proofing* techniques also empower the "caring majority" of students to assist victims of bullying and to deny bullies the peer reinforcement which perpetuates their behavior.

Bully-Proofing Your School provides educators with the tools—including scripted lessons and handout, transparency, poster, and button reproducibles—to create a secure environment in which children can focus on learning. 384 PAGES

To order or receive more information on these
and other Sopris West products:

Phone **800.547.6747**   FAX **303.776.5934**
Internet http://www.sopriswest.com
Mail Sopris West ▪ 1140 Boston Avenue ▪ Longmont, CO 80501